Advance Praise for
Expanding Horizons: Short Readings and Images from Unusual Topics

"The readings in *Expanding Horizons* are of high interest and accessible to the developmental student. The topics are challenging and require that students think critically about them. The topics also introduce students to subjects that they will encounter in college-level courses. I like that this reader integrates multicultural themes into the topics. My students would definitely say that this book is more interesting than our current text."

Susan Smith
West Valley College

"*Expanding Horizons* has cross-curricular appeal, meaning that it can be used to teach Reading or Composition both at the college preparatory or college level. The chapter subjects deal with issues that can stimulate discussion in the classroom because they are of particular interest to college-age students, but they also appeal to teachers. (Who, in the modern world, has not received a "friend of a friend of a friend" urban legend e-mail?)"

Edward Glenn
Miami Dade College

"Words I would use to describe this text would be—relevant; thought-provoking; easy to respond to; and helpful in expanding students' knowledge."

Roberta Orona-Cordova
California State University, Northridge

"I like the philosophy behind *Expanding Horizons*. It feels like the author has a sense that students should be reading and grappling with the everyday texts, issues, and ideas around us, and I definitely have the sense that most students will be better informed about their lives and the world around them after having grappled with these readings. The tone, for a developmental text like this, is very positive—things students might need assistance with (vocabulary, for instance) are presented matter-of-factly, so that there is nothing 'developmental' in how helpful tools are presented."

Andrea Reid
Spokane Community College

"The need for such a text as *Expanding Horizons* is greater now than ever before. It encourages students to think critically and philosophically through various written and oral methods, so that students can get their own powerful stories out, their experiences felt, their insights shared, and their views heard."

Hubert C. Pulley
Georgia Southern University

About the Author

Susan Thurman has taught reading, writing, and other English skills from the junior high to the college level. For 11 years, she was the editor and publisher of *Class Act*, a national magazine that featured grammar, writing, and other ideas for English teachers. Her works include two books on English grammar and writing (*The Only Grammar Book You'll Ever Need* and *The Everything Grammar and Style Book; All the Rules You Need to Know to Master Great Writing*) and 18 film study handbooks, including guides for *Rear Window; Vertigo; My Fair Lady; Decoration Day; Caroline?; Death on the Nile; Murder on the Orient Express; One Against the Wind; The Mirror Crack'd; The Man Who Knew Too Much; Casablanca; North by Northwest; Skylark; Sarah, Plain and Tall;The Shell Seekers; The Dollmaker; Midnight Lace;* and *Dial M for Murder.* In addition, she has written more than 60 English-related articles, as well as a number of other educational materials, including *On the Spur of the Moment, Kernels for Journals, The Sherlock Holmes Study Guide, Second Harvest, Dear Miz Jones,* and *In the Beginning* (co-authored with husband, Mike Thurman). With Gail King, she co-authored *Currents: Henderson's River Book,* a local history. Her online study guides for ExxonMobil *Masterpiece Theatre* and other PBS productions include "*A Death in the Family* Study Guide," "Viewing Guide for *Song of the Lark,*" "Viewing Guide for *The American,*" "Eudora Welty: Daughter of the South," "Edna Earle Ponder: Belle of the South," "Viewing Guide for *The Ponder Heart,*" "Literary Kentucky from A to Z," "Beyond the Core: *Highland Laddie Gone,*" "Viewing Guide for *Almost a Woman,*" and "Study Guide for *Cane River.*" She currently lives with her husband in Henderson, Kentucky, and teaches developmental reading and writing at Henderson Community College.

For my parents, Charles and Catherine Sommers, who fostered my love of reading and gave me the freedom to choose what I read.
And, as always, for my husband Mike Thurman, who understands my personal reading-writing connection.

Expanding Horizons

Short Readings and Images from Unusual Topics

Susan Thurman
Henderson Community College

PENGUIN ACADEMICS

New York   San Francisco   Boston
London   Toronto   Sydney   Tokyo   Singapore   Madrid
Mexico City   Munich   Paris   Cape Town   Hong Kong   Montreal

Acquisitions Editor: Melanie Craig
Associate Editor: Frederick Speers
Production Manager: Eric Jorgensen
Marketing Manager: Thomas DeMarco
Senior Supplements Editor: Donna Campion
Project Coordination, Text Design, and Electronic Page Makeup: Electronic
    Publishing Services Inc., NYC
Senior Cover Design Manager/Designer: Nancy Danahy
Cover Image: ©The Image Bank/Getty Images, Inc.
Photo Researcher: Anita Dickhuth
Manufacturing Buyer: Lucy Hebard
Printer and Binder: R. R. Donnelley & Sons
Cover Printer: Phoenix Color Corporation

For permission to use copyrighted material, grateful acknowledgment is made to the
copyright holders on pp. 293–294, which are hereby made part of this copyright page.

Library of Congress Cataloging-in-Publication Data

Thurman, Susan (Susan Sommers)
    Expanding horizons : short readings and images from unusual topics / Susan Thurman.
        p. cm.
    Includes index.
    ISBN 0-321-27669-8

    1. College readers. 2. English language—Rhetoric—Problems, exercises, etc. 3.
Academic writing—Problems, exercises, etc. 4. Critical thinking—Problems, exercises,
etc. I. Title.
    PE1417.T53 2006
    808'.0427—dc22   2006007201

Please visit our website at http://www.ablongman.com

ISBN 0-321-27669-8

1 2 3 4 5 6 7 8 9 10–DOC–09 08 07 06

Table of Contents

Rhetorical Modes

Description

Narration

Definition

Illustration and Example

Process

Analysis

Evaluation

Compare and Contrast

Cause and Effect

Argument

Preface for the Instructor

Welcome to *Expanding Horizons* and thank you for choosing this text.

Over the years that I have taught developmental reading and writing classes, I have seen many students are who apprehensive about their college classes—an apprehension that often translates into reticence about participating in class. Other students feel somewhat uncomfortable being in a developmental class, and they worry that their abilities will never be adequate to allow them to succeed in college.

With these problems in mind, I designed *Expanding Horizons* to help students gain more confidence in their abilities, to more actively engage them in classroom topics, to move them into a deeper level of thinking and understanding, and to increase their reading skills—in other words, to expand their horizons. When looking at ways for students to focus on issues and study them from a variety of angles, one of my goals was to create a text that challenged students to read and think critically; at the same time, I wanted a text that was easy to understand but did not talk down to students.

The result, *Expanding Horizons*, contains 11 chapters—probably more material than you will be able to cover in your class (certainly more than I can deal with in a traditional semester). Your option, of course, is to choose which topics work best for your students, for your own interests or expertise, or even for what is happening in current events. While I arranged the chapters in the sequence in which I would typically use them, there is nothing sacred about the order; in fact, you may find that a different arrangement works better for your class or for connections in your area of the world. In looking through the chapters, please note that several selections could fit into more than one category. "About Identity Theft," for instance, could easily have been included in the chapter on ethics, urban lengends, or even employment; the same is true of other selections that have relevance in multiple areas. I did this intentionally to help students understand the link between different disciplines.

I chose the chapter topics in *Expanding Horizons* with student relevance in mind; I did not want to include those stodgy, overused topics that instructors—and, sometimes, students—have seen many times before. My feeling is that if students focus on themes and issues that are contemporary, realistic, and enjoyable, they can feel more at ease in class and enjoy greater success in college. For this book, I first looked for topics that students can easily talk about on a surface or introductory level; in fact, in many cases the topics are everyday ones that students already discuss, such as food, money, and relationships. In addition, I purposefully chose reading selections that would elicit a variety of responses, from "I didn't know that" to "That's just what I thought" to "I don't agree with that at all." After students' initial reading of the selections, their critical reading and critical thinking can come into play as they delve into the topics more deeply.

All of the chapters are organized in essentially the same way. They begin with a graphic image or piece of art pertinent to the chapter topic, followed by a list of quotations to whet the readers' appetite for and begin their association with the topic. The quotes range from inspirational to philosophical to amusing to controversial, but I chose each to stimulate interesting written or oral responses.

In each chapter, I have included an introduction about the topics before the reading selections. You can use this short piece to launch students into the topic and give them a sense of what to expect in the individual selections.

In addition to the readings, each chapter has an "extra added attraction"— a pertinent cartoon, poem, graph, or other material that you will find before the final reading selection. Chapters end with a "Read On!" section, which lists additional books, articles, or online sites that students may use to further explore what they have learned in the chapter.

The reading selections have identical formats, beginning with a prologue about the reading or the author. "Starting Out" offers questions and activities that expand on students' background knowledge and experience; these serve as a springboard to help students begin to discuss the topic. These prompts can lead initial classroom discussion to a more insightful level, one that helps the students read more critically and think more deeply or write more reflectively. You may also want to use these questions to generate discussion after students have read the selection.

"Words to Watch" lists vocabulary terms that may be new to or difficult for students. Not every challenging word or phrase is included in the vocabulary list (see the instructor's manual for other demanding vocabulary), but I thought it was especially important to define coined and idiomatic words or phrases, as they seem to be stumbling blocks for many developmental students— especially students for whom English is not their first language.

The reading selections in each chapter are purposefully varied in their interest and reading level. In the instructor's manual, light bulbs (from one to four) designate the level of reading ease for particular selections; this designation is determined by the vocabulary, sentence structure, and length of the sentences and selections. If your students are like mine, however, sometimes they overcome a challenging reading level when their interest in the topic is high.

Immediately following each reading is "From Where I Stand," suggestions for journal responses from which you or your students may choose. In responding to these prompts, students extend the ideas in the reading selection to their own experiences, or they express their views and find ways to validate and substantiate their opinions.

"Just the Facts" is a set of five comprehension questions that you can use as homework or for in-class review for individuals or groups. These questions are designed for you and your students to check for comprehension and retention of material. Discussion of these questions can be a catalyst leading to more in-depth analysis of the selections.

The suggested activities in "Expanding Horizons" explain or broaden parts of the reading selection, thus helping students chart their own course in probing further into the selection. Many reviewers and other instructors of developmental reading have stressed that their schools require more student knowledge of technology and research. To that end, a number of these activities promote the development of research as an extension of critical reading, analysis, and thinking. Suggested Internet sites help students find places where they can initiate their research. Because of the diversity of student and instructor interests, I have intentionally included more material than time will allow; this lets you and your students choose which options in this section fit particular needs or interests.

The final section, "Write On!," gives suggestions of more in-depth writing prompts. Like the journal responses, these ideas are intended to help students develop a deeper and clearer connection with and appreciation of the ideas presented in the selections they read.

The last part of the final chapter, "Hurricanes 2005: An Online Odyssey," contains another feature unique to *Expanding Horizons*. Because students have an increasing need to learn from material on the Internet, I have included the URLs for three Katrina-related articles that students must find online. The pedagogical elements for each of the online readings (vocabulary, journal responses, comprehension questions, writing prompts, and "Expanding Horizons" sections) are in the text, but as a challenge, this last reading requires students to go online.

After the final chapter are two appendices. Appendix A deals with explanations and examples of various writing genres and definitions of writing-related vocabulary. Appendix B is a reference for research skills, with sections about how to research in the library, definitions of library terms with which students may be unfamiliar, suggestions for how to research on the Internet, and various hints about conducting interviews.

In the instructor's manual, you will find a feature that saves time and minimizes frustration. Because so many typing mistakes arise when students key in long URLs, I converted all of the long ones in the text to much shorter "tinyurl" versions. For instance, the text lists the URL www.globalsecurity.org/military/agency/army/82abn.htm; the instructor's manual references it followed by its "tinyurl" version (in this case, tinyurl.com/nxpmc). When the shorter version is typed in, the same site comes on the screen, but students have far fewer problems—and waste far less time—using the "tinyurl."

I look forward to any questions or comments that you have about how you use this book to help students expand their personal horizons. If you have suggestions about how to improve future editions, I welcome those as well. Please e-mail me at susie.thurman@kctcs.edu.

A number of people have been extremely helpful in helping me shape *Expanding Horizons*. Editor nonpareil Fred Speers has continually guided me through the revisions—the *many* revisions—of the original manuscript, and his insight and foresight have molded the manuscript into what it is today. I thank Fred for expanding my own horizons in the editing and publishing world.

Members of the library staff at Henderson Community College, particularly Lynda Sinnett, Mike Knecht, Kevin Reid, and Barb Claspell, have been kind enough to field many questions and provide many answers—all the while smiling and proclaiming that they actually enjoy my persistent pestering.

Other HCC colleagues—Doris Cherry, David Fritts, and Bill Gary—have been sounding boards for many months and have provided invaluable ideas and suggestions as the book has developed.

Thanks also to novelist Joey Goebel. I'm lucky that this former student is now my friend. I am also grateful to two communities of friends I have never met: the members of CE-L, (an online discussion list for copy editors) and those of Project Wombat (formerly Stumpers, an online discussion list dealing with difficult reference questions). The accommodating people on both of these lists have often provided their time and their intelligence when I asked for help—a suggestion for print or online material, a particular wording, a hard-to-find address, an international perspective of topics in the book. You name it, these people can help. And help me they did—any number of times.

A tip of my hat also goes in thanks for the assistance and suggestions given by production editor Jim Hill of Electronic Publishing Services and copy editor Kay Mallett.

My longtime friend Paula Fowler continues to be a frequent source of encouragement, intelligence, and insight. Without her keen eye, many typos and mistaken turns of phrase would have found their way to the publisher.

I would also like to thank the many reviewers who, through their helpful comments, helped make *Expanding Horizons* the best book it could be.

Karen Batchelor, City College of San Francisco
Patricia B. Geehr, Fairleigh Dickson University
Edward Glenn, Miami Dade Community College
Jennifer Jett, Bakersfield College
Barbara Kaiser, San Jose State University
David Merves, Miami Dade College
Roberta Orona-Cordova, California State University–Northridge
Hubert C. Pulley, Georgia Southern University
Tina Ramsey, Imperial Valley College
Andrea Reid, Spokane Community College
Stephanie Satie, California State University–Northridge
Susan Smith, West Valley College
Monica C. Zewe, Mercyhurst College Northeast

And I especially thank my husband Mike, whose unquestioning and unending support helped me through many rough spots in completing this book. He reads me well.

SUSAN THURMAN

Introduction: An Invitation to the Reader

Welcome to *Expanding Horizons*. If this is your first semester or quarter in college, welcome to collegiate life. Maybe you've just graduated from high school, or perhaps your high school years are long behind you. You may be living at home, or you may have moved far away. Maybe the class is filled with friends of yours, or you may not know anyone yet (you soon will).

Academically, you may have been a rousing success in your earlier schooling, or you may have an educational record that you're not very proud of. No matter what your experiences were, your scholastic slate is now clean, and the record of your future begins today. This is a time of transition and change, and your spheres of self-discovery are about to increase with just this one class. In short, you're about to expand your personal and educational horizons.

Your college experiences will help you learn discipline and how to be a better manager of your time. You'll meet and learn from people—maybe some who are sitting in class with you now—who will become lifelong friends. And, no matter what your age, you'll gain more personal independence. You'll study subjects you never knew that you had an interest in, maybe some you've never heard of; you may also discover and explore talents you didn't know you had. A college education will set you apart from other candidates for future jobs, and your employability will mean potential for a far greater earning power, translating into a higher standard of living. Also, as studies show, college graduates have longer life spans than high-school graduates, along with better health practices and greater access to health care.

Before class gets started full-speed, I hope that you'll read this short introduction to *Expanding Horizons*. In general terms, this book is designed to increase a number of skills that will help you in both your collegiate life and your personal life, to engage you in more classroom topics, to increase your confidence in your academic abilities, and to guide you to a deeper level of comprehension and learning.

More specifically, the purpose of *Expanding Horizons* is to enhance your reading and writing abilities, skills that often go hand-in-hand.

But, you say, I can already read and write. I'm reading this and doing just fine, and I can write whatever I need to—been doing it for years.

My reply to you is that reading is more than just going over words. For example, take a look at this paragraph:

> Technical commission people free community students luggage will never pamphlet if type code a little 25 thinks idea doesn't get among drive work back might rid sell minute.

Yes, you can read it; you know the words. But they don't make any sense, do they? Unless you can learn from what you read and retain that knowledge, you might as well be reading something like the paragraph above.

Just as you learn from college reading, you also learn from college writing. Because college writing is often different from the types of everyday writing that you're used to, your skills in the writing area probably need some fine-tuning. For instance, have you ever had to write an essay that centers on a thesis statement (do you know what a thesis statement is?) and provides areas of support for an argument that you assert? As you progress in college, you'll probably have to read and write material that's more focused, reasoned, and complex than what you've read and written in the past. The material in *Expanding Horizons* will help you to read and write with more critical and analytical methods, and in doing so will help you develop both those skills and your learning proficiency.

In looking through *Expanding Horizons*, you'll notice that it contains 11 chapters. You won't cover all of the material in the book (your instructor will tell you which chapters or selections he or she has decided will work best for your class), but, of course, if something that isn't assigned piques your interest, you can read it on your own.

In order to set *Expanding Horizons* apart from other readers, I purposefully chose individual topics and reading selections that students would find relevant and important. My own students have found that they're far more motivated to read if they already have a connection to a subject, and it's with this in mind that I selected the particular topics in *Expanding Horizons*.

In order to stimulate your interest in reading—which will add to your growth in writing—I looked for articles that showcased unusual aspects about topics that you already discuss or are involved in. For instance, if you've recently

- been on the Internet (who hasn't?)
- donned a favorite pair of jeans (who hasn't?)
- listened to music (who hasn't?)
- watched television (who hasn't?)

you already have a connection to the reading selections in Chapter 2, "Popular Culture—What's Hip, What's Hopped, and Who Cares?"

Or if you've ever

- had a terrible meal at someone else's home (who hasn't?)
- eaten at a fast food restaurant (who hasn't?)

you can quickly identify with some of the reading selections in Chapter 4, "Food, Glorious Food."

You'll bond with the topics that you'll read about in Chapter 9, "Ethics, or 'Do the Right Thing,'" if you've ever

- told a white lie (who hasn't?)
- seen students cheat (who hasn't?)
- read about questionable ethics in the medical and business fields (who hasn't?).

You get the picture. Because you already have a connection with the topics in *Expanding Horizons*, you can progress to a more insightful collegiate study of the material. As a result, you'll read and think on a deeper level and you'll write more reflectively.

The Structure and Features of *Expanding Horizons*

Each chapter in *Expanding Horizons* begins with an image or piece of artwork that highlights part of the chapter topic; included with this are some thought-provoking questions to start your mind working about the topic.

This is followed by a section with quotations relevant to the chapter, another feature that's found only in *Expanding Horizons*.

Quotations serve many purposes; they can

- encapsulate something you've been struggling to express.
- help you connect with people who've been in similar situations.
- motivate you to some action.
- help you understand history or other cultures.
- stir your hearts.
- enlighten you about something completely foreign to your life.
- make you laugh at some absurdity or comedy.
- even make you roar in disagreement.

In *Expanding Horizons*, you'll find almost 200 quotations. Each day, pick one that you identify with or that enlightens or inspires you in some way—or with which you completely disagree. Ponder it and then share it with class members, family, or friends. In doing this, you'll find that expanding your horizons into the lives and opinions of others will help to solidify your own beliefs.

Following the series of quotations is a short introduction to each chapter, including general statements about the topic and specific features about the chapter's longer reading selections. This opening material helps you get an overview of what you can find as you study the chapter in more depth. In looking at the various selections, you'll note that I've included several different types of readings so that you can be exposed to multiple slants on various subjects.

Each chapter contains several reading selections. At the beginning of each selection you'll find an introductory activity titled "Starting Out," a section that helps you begin to think about the topic covered in the reading. Studies show that activating any connection to or background knowledge that students have about a topic helps to improve their reading comprehension. In this section, questions and activities take what you already know and then expand on that knowledge and experience. These statements, which serve as springboards for later discussion, reflection, or writing, survey information about the topic and incorporate activities that encompass interdisciplinary skills, such as creating graphs and tabulating percentages. They also help build a platform for more in-depth study of the reading selections. The purpose of this section is to ignite your connection to the topic; it isn't a test. You aren't supposed to know everything here; in fact, you may come back later and change your mind after you read, discuss, or write about the selection.

Next you'll see "Words to Watch," a list of terms that may be unfamiliar to you; these are included to help you develop your reading and writing vocabulary. Preview this list before you begin reading the selection so that you learn any unfamiliar words or phrases. When you're reading the selection and are stumped by a word or phrase that's not included in "Words to Watch," first try to determine its meaning through context (how it's used in the sentence) or through clues such as its prefix (letters added to the beginning of a base word to create a new meaning, like *re-* in *reset* or *un-* in *unhappy*), suffix (letters added to the end of a base word to create a new meaning, like *-less* in *helpless* or *-ful* in *hopeful*), or root word (the fundamental part of a word). If you're still stumped, look up the word in a standard dictionary.

You'll notice that in the "Words to Watch" list I included not only vocabulary words but also any idioms or coined words in the reading selection. These words or phrases can be confusing if English isn't your first language or if they aren't widely used in your part of the country. Idioms (also called "sayings") are those figures of speech that aren't supposed to be taken literally. For example, the idiom "in the doghouse" doesn't really mean that someone is in a dog's house; it means he or she is in trouble. Coined words are the creation of the author. An example is the word "cellannoyer." You won't find this word in the dictionary; it's a made-up word that the author uses to mean someone who's speaking on a cell phone and annoying you.

Like the quotations, some of the reading selections, will have you nodding your head in agreement, some will have you laughing out loud (I guarantee you'll chuckle when you read the mock funeral in the "Food, Glorious Food" chapter), some will give you an "I-didn't-know-that" reaction, and some may even have you shouting in protest. In looking for material to include in *Expanding Horizons,* I intentionally chose the readings for their reading level, interest, relevance, and whether or not they would generate good discussion, reflection, and writing.

The last selections in the book, included in "Hurricane 2005: An Online Odyssey," give you the URLs for three Katrina-related articles. You may choose to read these online and do the homework that your instructor assigns, or you may feel more comfortable printing them and reading them from the hard copy.

One characteristic you'll notice about a number of the reading selections that the topics often overlap. For example, "About Identity Theft" is in the chapter about money, but it could have easily been included with the chapter on urban legends, hoaxes, and scams, or the one on ethics or employment; in fact, your instructor may choose to have you study it in conjunction with either of those chapters. Similarly, "Food Icons: Immortal in the Eyes of the Television Beholder" is in the chapter about (surprise!) food, and "Foul Language Enters Pop Culture Lexicon" is in the chapter about censorship—but either also lends itself to a discussion of pop culture and could be studied in that chapter. Material in any reading selection extends beyond a single pigeonholed subject; indeed, I suppose you could say that topics themselves expand their horizons beyond a single category. As you read the various selections, take a little time to look for other connections or expansions to see how areas of study often share characteristics with one another.

When you read the selections, you'll find that an important strategy is annotating—that is, making notes by marking material to which you need to return. You might use underlining, highlighting, or circling—whatever works for you. A good tip for additional annotation is to develop your own shorthand so that you can easily return to the material and study it later. For instance, you might use an asterisk or check mark for material that seems very important, a question mark to the side of a vocabulary term or reading passage that is unclear, "MI" for the main idea, or "ex" for examples that are important.

At the end of each reading selection are several journal response options in "From Where I Stand." Depending on your former teachers, you may or may not be familiar with journal responses, but they're simply your written reaction to what you read, and they create another link with your reading, thinking, and writing. Response journal entries highlight your thoughts by expressing your reaction, opinion, or experience in relation to something in the reading selection. In your journal responses, you create a sort of dialogue with what you read, and in doing so, your reading becomes more personal. Your opinions, your feelings, and your experiences are just as valid as those of any other student, so there are no right or wrong answers in a journal response if you've carefully read the selection.

The five questions in "Just the Facts" allow you to think and reason more critically, find meaning in context, and expand your reading comprehension skills. This is important in order to make sure that you distinguish facts as presented in the selection from opinion that you may formulate as you read; they also help to verify that you read the selection carefully. After you've read the material and answered the questions in "Just the Facts," reread the selection and check to see whether your answers are correct (as you have already read the selection, you'll have a good idea of where to look in the text to find the answers). If you've made any mistakes, take a little time to read the paragraph more carefully so that you can determine why you made a mistake and you can understand what the correct answer is.

After checking your comprehension, you'll move to "Expanding Horizons," another distinctive feature of this book. In this post-reading section, you'll explore more deeply the topics introduced in the readings. Here, critical thinking—that is, clear, precise, and purposeful thinking—comes into play. You'll move beyond a basic level of comprehension (for instance, being able to distinguish fact from opinion or recalling facts, terms, basic concepts, and answers) to more advanced studies involving researching and writing about multifaceted, real-world problems or issues. Using various library or Internet resources, you may

- explore a number of answers or explanations to topics related to the reading selection.
- synthesize information from a variety of sources.
- write about a more complex part of the selection.

The types of assignments in "Expanding Horizons" most closely reflect what you will be asked to read, research, analyze, or write about in higher-level college classes. They aim to give you more depth of learning and more personal enlightenment, helping you to evaluate your own reading, thinking, and writing, and preparing you for future collegiate work.

The final section for each reading selection, "Write On!," gives you different writing ideas addressing the topic of the selection. These are longer writing assignments than those suggested in "From Where I Stand" or "Expanding Horizons" and they develop some of the ideas presented in the reading selections. For instance, a few of the writing ideas in the first chapter, "Urban Legends," include writing

- an outrageous story of your own.
- a letter of advice to someone younger than yourself.
- about sessions with a psychic.
- a letter to the editor.
- about unusual superstitions practiced by friends.
- about your personal feelings of safety.

As with the other sections in *Expanding Horizons*, these writing activities use the interdependence of reading, thinking, and writing, and they help you clarify your opinions and reactions to what you read in the selections.

You can expand your personal and educational horizons in many different ways. To illustrate this, I've also selected an "extra added attraction" for each chapter, something unique that conveys its point in a nonprose format—a poem, a photo, a cartoon, a song, or a graphic aid. by showing a relationship among the reading selections and the material presented in a nontraditional (nonprose) manner, these varied formats demonstrate that learning can be conveyed in many ways. As you study these, think about how the different formats interact. We don't read a poem the same way we read an essay, nor do we look at a cartoon the same way we look at a piece of fine art, so why would an author purposefully choose a particular format? Also, think about your expectations of the various formats. For example, is a cartoon always funny? Does a poem have to have a somber tone? See if the examples in *Expanding Horizons* break those molds.

At the end of each chapter, you'll find "Read On!," which suggests additional resources—both printed and online—so that you can further investigate the topics in each chapter. This list of resources is by no means complete, and you and your class may find it instructive to add to the list. Use your library's resources or online searches to find additional books or articles that are germane to the topic, and then compare and contrast the information you find in these new sources to some that are listed in "Read On!" Questions that you might address include these:

- Which source did you find easier to read? Why?

- From which source did you learn more?

- What specific information did you find particularly informative, interesting, inspiring, or controversial?

- What do you know about the author of the new source? For instance, do you know any of his or her credentials or additional writings?

- Could you detect any bias in the writing? If so, where did it occur, and did it add to or detract from the article? Why?

- What additional material would you like to have seen included in the selections?

- What methods did you use to find your additional resource?

Alternately, you can compare and contrast online and print sources listed in "Read On!" and answer the first four questions above. Or you might choose one of the sources in "Read On!" and address some of the following issues:

- Which aspects of the work did you find the most interesting? Why?

- Which aspects of the work did you find the least interesting? Why?

- What makes the work particularly effective or ineffective?

- From what you read, what new impressions do you have of the people or situations in the work?

- If you could ask the main person or people in the work two questions, what would they be? Why would you ask these particular questions?
- What is or will be a major problem mentioned or alluded to in the work?
- The person or situation you liked the best/least in this work was _____

  _____

  because _____.
- The part of this article that you liked the best/least in this work was _____

  _____

  because _____.
- You felt _____ when you read

  _____ (specify which

  part of the work) because _____

  _____.
- After reading the information in this work, you predict _____

  _____.
- If you were to write a sequel to this work, _____

  _____.
- To improve this work, the author would have to _____

  _____.
- You would/would not recommend this work because _____

  _____.
- After reading this work, you wonder _____

  _____.
- After reading this work, you think that the author's message is _____;

  _____; quotes from the

  article that support your reason include these: _____

  _____.
- An interesting quote in this work was _____

  _____ because

  _____.
- One feature of the work that you'd like to learn more about is _____

  _____.
- If you were writing a follow-up to this work, you'd concentrate on _____

  _____ because

  _____.
- You found this work to be/not to be inspiring because _____

  _____.

You'll quickly become familiar with this format of the main parts of the book. First, read the introduction to each chapter and study the quotations that are pertinent to the subject. Then, before you read individual selections, take a look at "Starting Out" to ignite any background connections or prior knowledge that you have with the topic, and study the vocabulary that comes in the selection. As you read the selection, annotate to return to important or unclear material. Continue your connection to the reading by writing your reaction, opinion, or experience as you respond to selections in "From Where I Stand." Answer "Just the Facts" questions and then check the reading to make sure you responded correctly. Use your research and writing skills as you develop more critical analysis through the various activities in "Expanding Horizons." Then continue the reading-writing connection by focusing on the topics in "Write On!"

Adding On—Appendix A and Appendix B

At the end of the book are two appendices that will be helpful both in this class and in your future college classes. The first, Appendix A, deals with different types of writing. Do you recall that at the beginning of this introduction I asked if you know what a thesis statement is? Here you'll find the answer to that question. Appendix A explains various writing models, defines writing terms you may not be familiar with, and gives you examples of types of writing you may encounter as you wend your way through college. For instance, if your assignment is to write

- a paragraph
- a descriptive paragraph
- a compare-and-contrast paper
- a newspaper article
- a company newsletter article
- a movie review
- a synopsis

- a summary
- a summary-and-response
- a personal narrative
- a letter to the editor
- a response journal entry
- an essay

read the information in Appendix A to get a clear picture of how you should approach this form of writing. Pay attention to details about what is expected with the assignment; then study the examples of the particular writing and read some of the other sources cited for additional information.

Turn to Appendix B when you need a handy reference for research skills. Throughout your college career—in fact, in your home and work careers as well—you'll often need to research certain topics in order to determine backgrounds, conditions, causes, effects, reasons, and motivations. Learning how to research quickly and accurately is another part of expanding your personal and educational horizons. You'll find this section helpful when doing any research, and especially when you're pursuing some of the issues listed in the "Expanding Horizons" sections of the reading selections. Appendix B includes sections on

- how to research in the library.
- researching for college papers.
- library terms that will aid your research.
- researching on the Internet.
- conducting an interview.

Expanding Horizons: Reading, Writing, and Beyond

Reading instructors have long known about the reciprocal effects between reading and writing. For instance, students can improve their reading comprehension by engaging in basic writing activities (such as summarizing, note taking, and outlining), in addition to more advanced types of writing (such as essays, critical analyses, and compare-and-contrast papers). Plus, writing contributes to advanced critical thinking. Studies show that even elementary-school writers mirror the content and structure of what they read and then reflect this in their own writing; in your advanced stage of schooling, reading well-written material helps you to write more well-written material. Also, when you're writing, usually you must reread (sometimes more than once) material to make sure that you have interpreted certain pieces correctly or to obtain additional information. Plus, you must revise (which, of course, means you must reread) your own material to make certain its content and mechanics are correct. Reading therefore becomes an integral part of the writing process.

But once you're ready to start writing, how do you begin? The first step is called prewriting, which means getting ideas for your future finished product. And just how do you get these ideas? To quote the poet Elizabeth Barrett Browning, "Let me count the ways." Probably the most frequently used method is one you're already familiar with: brainstorming. In this, you simply think about your topic and write a list of random ideas as they occur to you. You don't worry about complete sentences, spelling, punctuation, or grammar. You might allow yourself five minutes for a brainstorming session, and then later make time for other short sessions. On the spur of the moment, you'll probably think of some additional ideas to add, so keep your list close by.

When you are ready to write your assignment, take a look at your list and see which items are broad categories and which are details of these broad categories (don't worry if you have some items that don't seem to fit; you don't have to use everything on your list). For instance, if you're writing about recent odd weather in your area, your list might include "thunderstorm in January," "70 degrees in the middle of February," "10 inches of snow after real warm weather," and "strange winter weather." The first three items would be details of a paragraph that could be devoted to "strange winter weather."

Another effective method for cultivating ideas is called freewriting, a sort of cousin to brainstorming. To get ideas through freewriting, put your topic at the top of the page, take note of the current time, and allow yourself about ten minutes. Then just start writing about your topic. Write anything that comes into your mind, and, as with brainstorming, don't worry about the fine points of spelling, punctuation, or grammar. Keep your pen or pencil (or your fingers at the keyboard) moving for that entire time, but know that you'll probably come up with some thoughts that are irrelevant. Use anything that occurs to you—words, phrases, whatever bits of thought that pop into your mind. If you find yourself stuck for an exact word, just write "???" or "XXX" and come back to it later. If, during your allotted ten minutes, you can't think of anything else to write, keep writing— even if it's something like "I can't think of anything else about our weather"; chances are another idea will spring into your head. At the end of your time, go back over what you've written and decide which ideas are good and which can be tossed. Return to the ones that you think are good and underline the key parts to them. Now you have a strong start to your writing assignment.

Still another way to generate ideas is to ask a reporter's fundamental "5 Ws and an H" questions: *who? what? when? where? why?* and *how?* If you approach the general topic "our area's recent weather," you could ask yourself questions such as these:

> *Who* was affected by the weather?
> *What* weather pattern was the strangest?
> *What* happened to the streets during and after the thunderstorm?
> *What* accounted for the sudden snowstorm?
> *When* did this strange weather occur?
> *Where* did this strange weather occur?
> *Why* did this strange weather occur?
> *How* did citizens react to the unexpected warm weather?
> *How* did citizens react to the snowstorm?
> *How* did the road department handle the situations?
> *What* types of accidents occurred during the snow?
> *What* warning signals were given for the thunderstorm and snowstorm?
> *Who* benefited from the weather pattern?
> *How* could citizens have been better prepared?

Alternately, you may find that your brain works better with drawings rather just words. In that case, try clustering (also known as mapping), a prewriting strategy that uses use circles and lines to connect your thoughts.

Begin by drawing a circle in the middle of your paper and writing your topic (in this case, recent odd weather) inside it.

Next, think of words or phrases associated with your topic and write them in circles and connect them to the main idea.

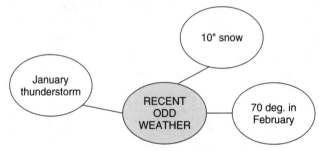

As you think of details about the new circles, draw more circles, write the new information in them, and then connect them to the circle they are describing.

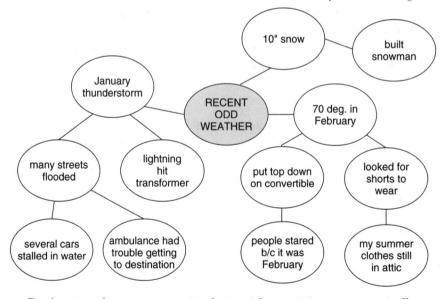

Don't worry about your mapping being either artistic or grammatically correct. And if you run out of ideas, try asking yourself one of the *who? what? when? where? why?* and *how?* questions.

Another way to generate ideas is to create an informal outline. To try this, first write your topic and one clear, concise sentence that covers what your writing will include (this is called your thesis statement). Put your major points closest to the left-hand margin, skipping a number of lines between them; then go back, indent a little, and write details about these points (again skipping lines). If you have further details (points about the details), write these under the appropriate details (again, make sure you indent a little with each new subcategory). Your outline might look like this:

Identity Theft

Identity theft has become an increasingly dangerous problem in the United States.

More people being "robbed" of their identity

Elderly especially vulnerable

Teenagers at high risk

Thefts up almost 100 percent in last five years

Expected to rise more in coming years

Rate may be even higher

Some victims don't report crime to police

Thieves getting bolder

Go through trash cans

Get information through phone scams

Set up phone requests online

Let's Get Going

Expanding Horizons was written to help enhance your reading and writing skills you as you begin expanding both personal and educational horizons while you're pursuing a college education and securing a better future. You'll use the various reading selections in this book and the activities that accompany them as cornerstones to building more critical thinking and more in-depth writing skills that you're sure to use throughout your college career and in your personal life.

Exciting times lie ahead for you in your college life. You'll have new experiences and make new friends in your fellow students and your instructors, of course, but more importantly you'll grow as a learner and as person. Your expanding horizons can begin as you start your study of this text. When you read the selections, pretend that you can speak with their authors or the people highlighted in them. What interested you the most about what you read? What irritated you, astonished you, or called you to action? What would you like to know more about?

As the author of *Expanding Horizons*, I look forward to reading any comments you have (I would be very interested to know which selections you felt were most interesting, entertaining, or educational, and I'd also like to know how you responded to the questions in the preceding paragraph), answering any inquiries you have, or reading any suggestions you might have for future editions of this book. Feel free to e-mail me at susie.thurman@kctcs.edu.

SUSAN THURMAN

Expanding Horizons

Take a look at the Loch Ness monster, said to lurk deep in the waters of the long and narrow loch (lake) in the Scottish Highlands. Sightings of Nessie (as the monster is affectionately called) have been reported since the 6th century; in 1933 the first photograph was taken of what was reported to be the monster.

Is the monster real or a hoax? At least one photograph of her has been proven to be a hoax, but study of—and fascination about—Nessie's existence continues. Write about your opinion of Nessie, or her counterparts around the world, like Bigfoot, the Abominable Snowman (Yeti), Sasquatch, Storsie, or Mokele-Mbembe; or write about an unbelievable experience that you have had. Alternately, you may create a story of your own that features a monster or another incredible creature.

CHAPTER ONE

URBAN LEGENDS, HOAXES, SUPERSTITIONS, AND OTHER FICTIONS

You Won't Believe What I Just Heard

A lie can travel halfway around the world while the truth is putting on its shoes. —*Mark Twain*

A lie told often enough becomes the truth. —*Vladimir Lenin*

Dreaming of a white cat means good luck. —*American superstition*

Fear is the main source of superstition, and one of the main sources of cruelty. To conquer fear is the beginning of wisdom. —*Bertrand Russell*

I have only one superstition. I touch all the bases when I hit a home run. —*Babe Ruth*

If you see a one-eyed cat, spit on your thumb, stamp it in the palm of your hand, and make a wish. The wish will come true. —*American superstition*

In superstition, wise men follow fools. —*Francis Bacon*

It is bad luck for an actor to receive flowers before the play begins, though flowers given after the play has ended is considered good luck. —*Superstition from the theater*

Superstition is the religion of feeble minds. —*Edmund Burke*

Superstition is the weakness of the human mind; it is inherent in that mind; it has always been, and always will be. —*Frederick the Great*

Superstitions are habits rather than beliefs. —*Marlene Dietrich*

The religious superstitions of women perpetuate their bondage more than all other adverse influences. —*Elizabeth Cady Stanton*

The truth is rarely pure and never simple. —*Oscar Wilde*

Truth is beautiful, without doubt; but so are lies. —*Ralph Waldo Emerson*

When in doubt, tell the truth. It will confound your enemies and astound your friends. —*Mark Twain*

Urban Legends, Hoaxes, Superstitions, and Other Fictions

Did you hear about what happened to my sister's friend's cousin? It's so weird you won't believe it—but I swear it's true.

*

Beware! "As the Wind Blows," the latest computer virus, is spreading all over the Internet. If you get an e-mail with the subject line "Wind Blows," don't even think about opening it. If you do, your computer will crash instantly and you'll lose all your data. Pass this along to all of your friends so that they will be aware of this horrible virus!

*

If you send this e-mail to five friends within an hour, you'll have three months of good luck; send it to ten friends and your luck will last a year. If you don't send it, then you'll have one year of bad luck. THIS IS NOT JUST A HOAX!

The above are just three examples of hoaxes, viruses, scams, superstitions, or urban legends. Someone hears or reads an incredible story. This narrative often comes from a reliable source (who could doubt a sister's friend's cousin?), and the story usually includes a great deal of information that could indeed be true. The end of the story, however, often contains a shock of some kind—a dire warning or details of a horrifying incident.

While most of these fantastic stories turn out to be false, some of them turn out to be in the "strange but true" category. For instance, did you hear about . . .

- the little girl who had been bitten by spiders while on vacation. When she came home, the bites had grown to look like boils, so the girl's parents decided to take her for medical treatment. Before they could get to the doctor, however, the boils burst. To the amazement and horror of everyone, the girl soon had hundreds of baby spiders crawling over her face.

- students at a certain college have been warned that, whatever they do, they must not enter their college library; it is in danger of collapse at any minute. This is because when it was built, the architect and engineer forgot to include the weight of the books in the design. As a result, ever since the building was completed and the books were brought in, the library has been sinking.

- the fact that, almost a year before Hurricane Katrina hit in 2005, the tragedy was forecast in a *National Geographic* article that said, in part, "It was the worst natural disaster in the history of the United States."

Two of these urban legends are not true, but they have enough elements of truth that many people passed them on as fact. What's your guess about which are the true stories?

In this chapter, you'll look start by looking at Neal Gabler's "How Urban Myths Reveal Society's Fears," which relates a number of popular urban myths that continue to circulate, even though they're obviously fictitious. The selection then delves into the question of why people in a modern age so captivated by urban legends and willing to accept them as being true.

Two e-mail hoaxes that may have come your way are highlighted in "If It Sounds Too Good To Be True…." The get-rich-quick claims in these e-mails are outlandish, but that hasn't stopped some people from being duped by them.

If you've ever refused to open an umbrella inside, or thrown a pinch of salt over your shoulder, or changed your course so a black cat wouldn't cross your path, you'll be eager to read Wendy Lichtman's "Knock on Wood," a selection that examines how and why people hold fast to certain superstitions.

Thomas Hayden's "Gotcha!" is an extensive piece that looks at famous hoaxes that have succeeded in the past and what contemporary hoaxes—or are they really hoaxes?—are circulating today.

Now that you have read the introduction to this chapter, go back and reread the quotations on p. 3. Then choose one of the quotations and write about whether you agree or disagree with it. Be sure to defend your opinion.

Just like in days long ago, stories with outlandish details and outcomes fascinate and terrorize contemporary society. Why are we so willing to believe the strange and even bizarre tales that come to us? In this essay, first published in the Los Angeles Times *in 1995, author **Neal Gabler** looks at some of the questions that surround urban legends.*

Starting Out...

Read the statements below and then circle A if you agree or D if you disagree.

A   D   Urban legends tell stories of anything that can happen because our world is utterly terrifying.

A   D   Disney cartoons are really complex expressions of fear.

A   D   In most urban legends, obstacles are overcome in the end.

Words to Watch

anomic: socially unstable, alienated, and disorganized

chimerical: highly improbable

contemporary: current, modern

cosmology: the study of the physical universe

crystallize: to give a definite, precise, and usually permanent form to

emasculation: the act of depriving a man of strength or vigor

exorcise: to free from evil spirits

exploitalk: a made-up word that combines "exploiting" (taking advantage of) and "talk"

Hades and the River Styx: in Greek mythology, the River Styx winds around Hades (hell) nine times

in flagrante delicto: Latin for "in the commission of the act" (in this case, the sexual act)

parse: to examine closely

Pierre: a hotel in New York City

prosaic: matter-of-fact, straightforward

treacly: overly sweet or sentimental

trope: a figure of speech using words in nonliteral ways, such as a metaphor

---

How Urban Myths Reveal Society's Fears
by Neal Gabler

The story goes like this: During dinner at an opulent wedding reception, the groom rises from the head table and shushes the crowd. Everyone naturally assumes he is about to toast his bride and thank his guests. Instead, he solemnly announces that there has been a change of plan. He and his bride will be taking separate honeymoons and, when they return, the marriage will be annulled. The reason for this sudden turn of events, he says, is taped to the bottom of everyone's plate. The stunned guests quickly flip their dinnerware to discover a photo—of the bride *in flagrante delicto* with the best man.

At least that is the story that has been recently making the rounds up and down the Eastern seaboard and as far west as Chicago. Did this really happen? A *Washington Post* reporter who tracked the story was told by one source that it happened at a New Hampshire hotel. But then another source swears it happened in Medford, Mass. Then again another suggests a banquet hall outside Schenectady, N.Y. Meanwhile, a sophisticated couple in Manhattan has heard it happened at the Pierre.

In short, the whole thing appears to be another urban myth, one of those weird tales that periodically catch the public imagination. Alligators swarming the sewers after people have flushed the baby reptiles down the toilet. The baby-sitter who gets threatening phone calls that turn out to be coming from inside the house. The woman who turns out to have a nest of black-widow spiders in her beehive hairdo. The man who falls asleep and awakens to find his kidney has been removed. The rat that gets deep-fried and served by a fast-food outlet. Or, in a variation, the mouse that has somehow drowned in a closed Coca-Cola bottle. These tales are preposterous, but in a mass society like ours, where stories are usually manufactured by Hollywood, they just may be the most genuine form of folklore we have. Like traditional folklore, they are narratives crafted by the collective consciousness. Like traditional folklore, they give expression to the national mind. And like traditional folklore, they blend the fantastic with the routine, if only to demonstrate, in the words of University of Utah folklorist Jan Harold Brunvand, the nation's leading expert on urban legends, "that the prosaic contemporary scene is capable of producing shocking or amazing occurrences."

Shocking and amazing, yes. But in these stories, anything can happen not because the world is a magical place rich with wonder—as in folk tales of yore—but because our world is so utterly terrifying. Here, nothing is reliable and no laws of morality govern. The alligators in the sewers presents an image of an urban hell inhabited by beasts—an image that might have come directly from Hades and the River Styx in Greek mythology. The baby-sitter and the man upstairs exploits fears that we are not even safe in our own homes these days. The spider in the hairdo says that even on our own persons, dangers lurk. The man who loses his kidney plays to our fears of the night and the real bogymen who prowl them. The mouse in the soda warns us of the perils of an impersonal mass-production society.

As for the wedding-reception tale, which one hacker on the Internet has dubbed "Wedding Revenge," it may address the greatest terror of all: that love and commitment are chimerical and even friendship is meaningless. These are timeless issues, but the sudden promulgation of the tale suggests its special relevance in the age of AIDS. When commitment means even more than it used to, and in the age of feminism, when some men are feeling increasingly threatened by women's freedom. Thus, the groom not only suffers betrayal and humiliation; his plight carries the hint of danger and emasculation, too. Surely, a legend for our time.

Of course, folklore and fairy tales have long subsisted on terror, and even the treacly cartoons of Walt Disney are actually, when you parse them, dark and complex expressions of fear—from Snow White racing through the treacherous forest to Pinocchio gobbled by the whale to Dumbo being separated from his mother. But these crystallize the fears of childhood, the fears one must overcome to make the difficult transition to adulthood. Thus, the haunted forest of the fairy tales is a trope for haunted adolescence; the witch or crone, a trope for the spent generation one must vanquish to claim one's place in the world; and the prince who comes to the rescue, a trope for the adult responsibilities that the heroine must now assume.

Though urban legends frequently originate with college students about to enter the real world, they are different from traditional fairy tales because their terrors are not really obstacles on the road to understanding, and they are different from folklore because they cannot even be interpreted as cautionary. In urban legends, obstacles aren't overcome, perhaps can't be overcome, and there is nothing we can do differently to avoid the consequences. The woman, not knowing any better, eats the fried rat. The baby-sitter is terrorized by the stranger hiding in the house. The black widow bites the woman with the beehive hairdo. The alligators prowl the sewers. The marriage in Wedding Revenge breaks up.

It is not just our fears, then, that these stories exploit. Like so much else in modern life—tabloids, exploitalk programs, real-life crime bestsellers—urban legends testify to an overwhelming condition of fear and to a sense of our own impotence within it. That is why there is no accommodation in these stories, no lesson or wisdom imparted. What there is, is the stark impression that our world is anomic. We live in a haunted forest of skyscrapers or of suburban lawns and ranch houses, but there is no one to exorcise the evil and no prince to break the spell.

Given the pressures of modern life, it isn't surprising that we have created myths to express our malaise. But what is surprising is how many people seem committed to these myths. The *Post* reporter found people insisting they personally knew someone who had attended the doomed wedding reception. Others went further: They maintained they had actually attended the reception—though no such reception ever took place. Yet even those who didn't claim to have been personally involved seemed to feel duty bound to assert the tale's plausibility.

Why this insistence? Perhaps the short answer is that people want to believe in a cosmology of dysfunction because it is the best way of explaining the inexplicable in our lives. A world in which alligators roam sewers and wedding receptions end in shock is at once terrifying and soothing—terrifying because these things happen, soothing because we are absolved of any responsibility for them. It is just the way it is.

But there may be an additional reason why some people seem so willing to suspend their disbelief in the face of logic. This one has less to do with the content of these tales than with their creation. However they start, urban legends rapidly enter a national conversation in which they are embellished, heightened, reconfigured. Everyone can participate—from the people who spread the tale on talk radio to the people who discuss it on the Internet to the people who tell it to their neighbors. In effect, these legends are the product of a giant campfire around which we trade tales of terror.

If this makes each of us a co-creator of the tales, it also provides us with a certain pride of authorship. Like all authors, we don't want to see the spell of our creation broken—especially when we have formed a little community around it. It doesn't matter whether these tales are true or not. What matters is that they plausibly reflect our world, that they have been generated from the grass roots and that we can pass them along.

In a way, then, these tales of powerlessness ultimately assert a kind of authority. Urban legends permit us to become our own Stephen Kings, terrorizing ourselves to confirm one of the few powers we still possess: the power to tell stories about our world.

From Where I Stand... (Journal Responses)

1. One interesting point in this selection was _____
   _____. It was interesting because
   _____.
2. After reading this selection, I wonder _____.
3. The part of this selection that enlightened me the most was
   _____
   _____. This is because _____.

JUST THE FACTS

1. The main point of this selection is a) some people said they had actually attended the wedding reception, but it never ever took place; b) people take a certain pride in devising urban legends; c) urban legends permit us to terrorize ourselves to

confirm one of the few powers we still possess: the power to tell stories about our world; d) urban legends have been around for many years.

2. In the "Wedding Revenge" urban legend, a) the bride is shown in a photo with the best man; b) the groom is shown in a photo with the maid of honor; c) the bride and groom ask for revenge against a rumor-spreading guest; d) the bride and groom announce that they have decided to part ways.

3. The author says that anything can happen in urban legends because a) people like to stretch their imaginations; b) the person who originates the legend secretly wants attention; c) our world is utterly terrifying; d) we like to think of the most outlandish outcomes possible.

4. The author says that the urban legend about the wedding "may address the greatest terror of all"; this terror is that a) love and commitment are chimerical; b) people cannot find safety in being in a crowd; c) people really never know what will be said about them in a large gathering; d) a ceremony can be ruined by just one ill-mannered guest.

5. The author says that a) urban legends provide an outlet for people who need to "visit the fantastic world"; b) urban legends give no lessons and impart no wisdom; c) some of those who believe urban legends are among the most powerful people in the world, and that is frightening; d) the urban legends that are true outnumber those that are false.

EXPANDING HORIZONS

1. Reread the "Wedding Revenge" urban legend. Then describe one character's reaction to the groom's announcement. You might choose to write from the point of view (the character who tells the story) of the bride, one of the bride's parents, the best man, or anyone else in attendance.

2. A number of variations of the "Wedding Revenge" story exist. Read about the history of the legend at www.snopes.com/weddings/embarrass/bothered.asp and then write a summary of your research.

3. The urban legend about alligators in sewers has a lengthy history. Read the site www.barrypopik.com/article/480/alligator-in-the-sewers-urban-myth to answer the following questions:

   When was an eight-foot alligator found in an East Harlem manhole?

   According to one legend, why were people not able to harvest the marijuana that had been flushed down toilets?

   References to alligators in the sewers of New York can be found in the novel
   _____ by _____
   _____.

   What joke did John T. Flaherty use for proving the absence of alligators in the sewers?

   The story about Charles Gidds, who picked up and suddenly dropped an alligator, came from the *New York Times*, in an issue dated _____
   _____.

4. The selection refers to urban legends about a rat that is fried and then served by a fast-food outlet. In 2005, a woman claimed to have found a finger in the chili that she

had purchased from a national fast-food chain. Research the events behind this story and then write a summary of your findings. Online sites to consult include these:

> www.msnbc.msn.com/id/7844274/
> www.boingboing.net/2005/04/22/wendys_finger_food_f.html
> kron4.com/Global/story.asp?S=3653156
> urbanlegends.about.com/b/a/160779.htm
> urbanlegends.about.com/b/a/162772.htm

5. The author talks about urban legends being "embellished, heightened, reconfigured." Choose an urban legend and rewrite it with more details or a different ending.

WRITE ON!

1. Gabler says, "We live in a haunted forest of skyscrapers or of suburban lawns and ranch houses." I agree/disagree (choose either "agree" or "disagree") with this statement because _____.

2. Relate the circumstances behind a time when you tried to explain a situation in a logical way, but the listener did not want to hear your views.

3. Many urban legends revolve around places or circumstances where people feel that they are safe, but they prove not to be. Write about at least three places where you would feel safe. Be sure to give your reasons as to why you feel safe in those places.

Below are two e-mails, either of which may sound familiar to you. The first one—and many variations of it—has been circulating on the Internet for a number of years. The second one is more recent, but the intent is the same—to establish a relationship with the reader so that confidential information will be sent overseas and then used to get (that is, to steal) money from the reader's bank account.

Starting Out...

In a small group, discuss the following questions. Elect one of your group members to act as secretary, or have each member of the group act as secretary for a separate question. At the end of the time designated by your instructor, share your group's answers with the rest of the class.

1. What's the meaning of the phrase "There's no such thing as a free lunch"? When was the last time you received anything free? What were the circumstances?

2. What is the ending of this frequently used phrase: "If it sounds too good to be true..."? Is there any truth in the phrase?

3. What's the most outrageous rip-off you've ever heard of? What made it so extreme? Do you know of anyone who fell for it? Why do you think that those behind it thought that they might be successful in duping others?

Words to Watch

backdrop: environment, conditions

CEO: the abbreviation for "Chief Executive Officer," the highest official in a company

civil servants: government employees

colleagues: coworkers, associates

commence: begin, start

discretion: caution, good judgment

endeavor: try, attempt

incidental: associated with

incurred: acquired, gotten, sustained

maturity: in financial terms, when money (usually a note or bond) is due

probate: legal establishment of the authority of a deceased person's will

revert: return, go back

suspense account: an account used to store short-term funds or securities until a permanent decision is made about how they are to be distributed

transfer: the moving (in this case, of money) from the account of one person to the account of another person

utmost: greatest, highest

If It Sounds Too Good to Be True...

by Howgul Abul Arhu and Wang Qin

From: Howgul Abul Arhu [mailto:howgul_abul_arhu2000@yahoo.com]
Sent: Wednesday, June 06, 1998 8:04 PM
To: dclark@pssd.com
Subject: confidential

Attention: The President/CEO
Dear Sir,

Confidential Business Proposal

Having consulted with my colleagues and based on the information gathered from the Nigerian Chambers Of Commerce And Industry, I have the privilege to request your assistance to transfer the sum of $47,500,000.00 (forty seven million, five hundred thousand United States dollars) into your accounts. The above sum resulted from an over-invoiced contract, executed, commissioned and paid for about five years (5) ago by a foreign contractor. This action was however intentional and since then the fund has been in a suspense account at The Central Bank Of Nigeria Apex Bank.

We are now ready to transfer the fund overseas and that is where you come in. It is important to inform you that as civil servants, we are forbidden to operate a foreign account; that is why we require your assistance. The total sum will be shared as follows: 70% for us, 25% for you and 5% for local and international expenses incidental to the transfer.

The transfer is risk free on both sides. I am an accountant with the Nigerian National Petroleum Corporation (NNPC). If you find this proposal acceptable, we shall require the following documents:

a. your banker's name, telephone, account and fax numbers
b. your private telephone and fax numbers—for confidentiality and easy communication
c. your letter-headed paper stamped and signed

Alternatively we will furnish you with the text of what to type into your letter-headed paper, along with a breakdown explaining, comprehensively, what we require of you. The business will take us thirty (30) working days to accomplish.

Please reply urgently.
Best regards
Howgul Abul Arhu

From: Wang Qin (wangqin61@totalmail.com)
Sent: Wednesday, June 06, 2004 8:04 PM
To: mthompson@uenet.com
Subject: for your eyes only

MR. WANG QIN
HANG SENG BANK LTD.
DES VOEUX RD. BRANCH,
CENTRAL HONG KONG,
HONK KONG.

Let me start by introducing myself. I am Mr. Wang Qin credit officer of the Hang Seng Bank Ltd. I have a concealed business suggestion for you.

Before the U.S and Iraqi war our client General Ibrahim Moussa who was with the Iraqi forces and also business man made a numbered fixed deposit for 18 calendar months, with a value of Twenty millions Five Hundred Thousand United State Dollars only in my branch. Upon maturity several notice was sent to him, even during the war early this year. Again after the war another notification was sent and still no response came from him. We later find out that the General and his family had been killed during the war in bomb blast that hit their home.

After further investigation it was also discovered that Gen. Ibrahim Moussa did not declare any next of kin in his official papers including the paper work of his bank deposit. And he also confided in me the last time he was at my office that no one except me knew of his deposit in my bank. So, Twenty millions Five Hundred Thousand United State Dollars is still lying in my bank and no one will ever come forward to claim it. What bothers me most is that according to the to the laws of my country at the expiration three years the funds will revert to the ownership of the Hong Kong Government if nobody applies to claim the funds. Against this backdrop, my suggestion to you is that I will like you as a foreigner to stand as the next of kin to Gen. Ibrahim Moussa so that you will be able to receive his funds.

WHAT IS TO BE DONE:

I want you to know that I have had everything planned out so that we shall come out successful. I have contacted an attorney that will prepare the necessary document that will back you up as the next of kin to Gen. Ibrahim Moussa, all that is required from you at this stage is for you to provide me with your Full Names and Address so that the attorney can commence his job. After you have been made the next of kin, the attorney will also fill in for claims on your behalf and secure the necessary approval and letter of probate in your favor for the move of the funds to an account that will be provided by you.

There is no risk involved at all in the matter as we are going adopt a legalized method and the attorney will prepare all the necessary documents. Please endeavor to observe utmost discretion in all matters concerning this issue. Once the funds have been transferred to your nominated bank account we shall share in the ratio of 70% for me, 25% for you and 5% for any expenses incurred during the course of this operation.

Should you be interested please send me your private phone and fax numbers for easy communication, you can write me via my private box (wangqin61@totalmail.com) and i will provide you with more details of this operation. Your earliest response to this letter will be appreciated.

Kind Regards

Mr. Wang Qin

From Where I Stand... (Journal Responses)

1. If I could meet one of the originators of this e-mail in person, I would tell him
   _____
   because _____.
2. Under what circumstances would you begin to believe an e-mail like this?
3. These e-mails asked for several pieces of personal information. What personal information would you not send over the Internet? Why?

JUST THE FACTS

1. The main idea of this selection is a) the writers say you can get rich quickly if you follow the instructions in the e-mails; b) you have friends or relatives in places all over the world; c) sometimes people will go out of their way to alert you to good things that can happen; d) friends from foreign lands want to come to visit you.
2. The first e-mail comes from a man who says he lives in a) Nicaragua; b) North Dakota; c) Nigeria; d) Norway.
3. One item of personal information that the first e-mail did *not* ask for was a) your banker's name; b) your banker's telephone numbers; c) your telephone number; d) your Social Security number.
4. The second e-mail comes from a man who says he lives in a) Hong Kong; b) Hawaii; c) Haiti; d) Holland.
5. The second e-mail claims that money was left in the account of a) a distant relative you never knew about; b) a man who was killed in the war; c) a woman who was interested in "good characters"; d) a family whose last descendant had specified that you "be notified immediately."

EXPANDING HORIZONS

1. One reason that these e-mails may have been difficult to read was because of the number of mistakes in grammar, mechanics, and punctuation. Rewrite the e-mails, using correct forms of conventional English.

2. Summarize the tips about the Nigerian scam that are found at the National Fraud Information Center's Web site at www.fraud.org/tips/internet/nigerian.htm.

3. Write a newspaper article that warns your readers about the dangers of replying to either of these e-mails, or any other e-mails that are hoaxes. Use the newspaper technique of answering the 5 Ws (the questions *who? what? when? where?* and *why?*).

4. At least one person has baited the scammer; that is, he knew that the original e-mail he received was a hoax, but he went ahead and sent a number of fraudulent replies. Read this account of his exploits at spl.haxial.net/nigerian-fraud/ and then summarize the various e-mail exchanges.

5. Write a thematic comparison of the two e-mails. In doing this, you compare (relate the similarities) and contrast (relate the differences) the two works.

Write On!

1. Write about some of your experiences with e-mail, citing instances of how e-mail has helped you or been a hindrance to you. Or, if you don't use e-mail, write your reasons why.

2. Take either of the e-mails and cite the many reasons why its information and requests are so preposterous.

3. Write about a time that someone offered you what you initially thought was a wonderful deal, but on reflection you found was too good to be true.

You probably know people—maybe you're even one yourself—who carry out superstitious moves without fail. Maybe they insist on leaving a house from the same door they entered, or maybe they always throw a pinch of salt over their shoulder for good luck, or they walk around a black cat so that it won't cross their path. Why so superstitious? This selection by **Wendy Lichtman,** *from the November 2000 issue of* Good Housekeeping, *takes a look at that question.*

Starting Out...

Make a list of at least five superstitions that have heard of, and then compare your list with others in the class. What is the most well-known superstition? What superstitions had you not heard of? How does your list compare with that of others who come from different parts of the country or the world?

Words to Watch

anesthetized: given a medical drug that brought on a loss of sensation

antidote: something that relieves or counteracts a problem

arcane: mysterious, secret

feng shui: the Chinese practice of positioning objects, based on a belief that patterns and flow have positive and negative effects

quirk: odd habit, peculiarity

Knock on Wood
by Wendy Lichtman

The morning of my son's jaw surgery I spent a lot of time choosing my socks. Digging through my dresser drawer, I was relieved to find a pair (gray with a tiny red print) that felt right. I'm too sophisticated to think a color can bring good luck, I told myself, but just in case, I'm wearing red.

Then I put on the necklace with the locket my son had given me when he was in second grade, slipped a small crystal into my pocket, and headed to the hospital.

I believe none of this, I thought, as I stood in the surgical waiting area trying to decide which seat would be best. For several minutes I examined that large beige room as if I were a student of the Chinese art of feng shui—about which I know absolutely nothing—and could decipher whether facing the windows or hallway, sitting next to a plant or near the phone, was most advantageous. Finally, after I found a spot directly across from the operating room—so I wouldn't have my back to my anesthetized son, so I'd have my heart facing him—I sat down.

Like many people, I was raised knocking on wood, tossing salt over my shoulder, and avoiding the path of black cats. But I knew that the more powerful magic, the arcane behaviors the adults in my family practiced, was what really could make the world a safer place. Biting my tongue after I spoke of some potential danger would prevent it, walking out the same door of a building that I had walked in would protect me for the entire day, and stepping onto an airplane with my right foot first would keep the thing flying.

Yet, by early adulthood I'd quit the tongue-biting, salt-tossing, wood-knocking business. "You don't really believe that it changes outcome, do you?" I asked my family at a large holiday dinner. "I can understand that it makes you feel as if you have some control, and that can be comforting," I admitted. "But this," I insisted, as I took the saltshaker and spilled a bit onto the tablecloth, "can't possibly cause something terrible to happen."

Across from me I saw my aunt Rosie reach up to tug on her left earlobe, which is what she does to keep us safe.

"I just don't believe we have the power to change the future by doing any of this nonsense," I announced. "I don't believe," I told my astonished family, "that it's safer to fly on a Tuesday."

"You don't need to believe it, sweetheart," my aunt Pearl reassured me as she took a pinch of the salt that I'd spilled and tossed it over her left shoulder. "I cover for you all the time."

So I was surprised, years later, when I was traveling with my infant son for the first time, that I froze at the doorway of the airplane. I'd been a mother only a few months then, and I was amazed by how much more full of danger the world seemed. Why take chances? I asked myself, as I held my baby close and did a tricky little two-step to make sure that I walked onto that plane with my right foot first.

And here I am now, I thought as I looked around the waiting room, wearing just the right socks.

"May I?" the woman sitting next to me asked, as she reached for the newspaper I'd placed on the table between us. While we chatted I saw that she was holding a small gray stone with a hole in the center. She rubbed the stone with her thumbs, she passed it from hand to hand, and when a doctor came to tell her that her husband had been moved to the recovery room, she closed the stone gently between her palms. Before the woman left the room, she turned to me. "Your son is in my prayers," she said.

And that was when I realized something else about superstition: It has become, for me, a doorway to prayer. When, in the early-morning darkness, I'd put on my socks and my necklace, then slipped the crystal into my pocket, and chosen my chair, I believe I was saying this: Please let him get through surgery; please help him heal.

I spoke to my aunt Rosie last week, knocked on wood when I reported that my son was doing well, and told her how superstitious I'd been while he was in surgery.

"Good," she said. "Because there have been times," my aunt told me quietly, "when I didn't pull my earlobe, and I really wish I had...."

From Where I Stand... (Journal Responses)

1. The part of "Knock on Wood" that I found the most interesting was _____ _____ because _____

2. One of the oddest superstitions that I have heard of is _____. _____; this is odd because _____.

3. I think that people who, like the author's aunt Rosie, carry out superstitions to a great degree, are _____ _____ because _____.

JUST THE FACTS

1. The main idea of this selection is a) superstitions are a part of life for many people; b) when superstitious people meet those who are not superstitious, anger and resentment can arise between both parties; c) people who are not superstitious lead much happier lives than those who follow superstitions; d) superstitions are mainly centered in the U.S., Canada, and Mexico.

2. The reader can infer that the author wore a particular locket on the day of her son's surgery because a) she knew that it would please her son; b) her husband had requested that she wear it; c) she thought it might bring good luck; d) she wanted it to be the first thing her son saw when he awoke from the surgery.

3. In the waiting room at the hospital, the author a) became angry when the surgery went over its scheduled two hours; b) sat with her heart facing the operating room; c) was aware that many people were watching her strange behavior; d) was disappointed that her best friend did not come to keep her company.

4. The author states that superstition, for her, has a) "become a doorway to prayer"; b) become "a constant source of irritation" with her husband; c) been an embarrassment when she was in the company of others; d) been the source of many discussions with a member of the clergy.

5. To keep the family safe, the author's Aunt Rosie a) always began to walk with her right foot; b) said a special prayer after each meal; c) led the family in an ancient song; d) tugged on her left earlobe.

EXPANDING HORIZONS

1. The cat, a focus of numerous superstitions, is also the subject of Glenda Moore's "Folklore and Superstition" at www.xmission.com/~emailbox/folklore.htm.

Read this site and then write about what you consider to be the most interesting parts of it.

2. Many sports have superstitions associated with them. Choose one of the sites below and then summarize what you learn. Alternately, you may find online or printed material that deals with another sport.

> sports in general: www.factmonster.com/spot/superstitions1.html
>
> golf: www.golfbtb.com/superstitions.htm
>
> sports and the number 13: www.infoplease.com/spot/superstitions2.html
>
> rodeo: rodeo.about.com/cs/rodeobasics/a/superstitions.htm

3. Write a letter to your son or daughter (or future son or daughter) explaining why he or she should or should not honor certain superstitions. Be sure to fully explain your reasons.

4. Take a completely off-the-wall point of view. Write what it is like from a cat's point of view to be the object of superstitions.

5. Take a look at "The Tradition of Superstitions" at www.brownielocks.com/superstitions.html and research the history behind certain superstitions. Then write a summary of some of these superstitions.

WRITE ON!

1. Suppose you have a very superstitious friend who asks you what you think about him or her following various superstitions (you can choose which superstitions your friend follows). Write what you think you would say to this friend.

2. Friday the thirteenth is approaching. Write a letter to the editor of your school newspaper, giving your views on whether or not this should be noted in the paper.

3. Talk with at least five other people about superstitions that they have heard of or practice. Then pick which is the most unusual and write about it.

This doctored photograph, which has been widely circulated on the Internet, shows a supposedly innocent tourist visiting the World Trade Center on the day of the attacks.

The photo is a hoax. Not only is the man's clothing wrong for the still-summer day, at the time of the attacks the observation deck of Tower 2 was not yet open (Tower 1 did not have an observation deck), the type of plane is wrong (the plane in the picture is a 757; both of the planes in the attacks were 767s), and the plane is approaching from the wrong direction.

Questions
1. If you could speak to the person who created this hoax and who sent it out on the Internet, what would you say? Why?
2. If one of your good friends e-mailed you a copy of this, would you set your friend straight about the fact that it is a hoax? Why or why not?

In this selection, U.S. News & World Report *senior writer **Thomas Hayden** takes a look at what may be—or may not be—present-day hoaxes. He relates some of the famous hoaxes that have fooled people in the past and wonders if modern man is still as gullible as those who have been tricked in the past.*

Starting Out...

Take a poll in your class or among a group of at least ten of your friends, asking the questions below. Then tabulate the results. To get the correct percentage, divide the number of particular responses by the total number of people who answered. For instance, if you poll thirteen people and five answer "yes" to a yes-or-no question, then the percentage of people who answered "yes" is 38 percent (five divided by thirteen). After you have calculated the percentages, create graphs that detail your results.

Have you ever been to a fortuneteller or psychic or played with a Ouija board?
    Yes   No

Have you ever had your palm read, had tarot cards read, or had tea leaves read for you?
    Yes   No

Have you ever used any other method to predict the future?
    Yes   No

Words to Watch

barker: an employee who stands outside a show and talks loudly to lure customers

chump: a sucker, a mark, a person easily fooled

debunked: exposed, discredited

deconstructs: takes apart

flimflam: nonsensical talk, rubbish, gobbledygook

mots juste: a French phrase meaning "appropriate words or expressions"

mountebank: a person who sells quack medicine from a platform

Ph.D.: the abbreviation for Doctor of Philosophy, the highest degree that a university awards

proliferate: increase or spread at a rapid rate

rube: an unsophisticated fellow, a hick

shelling: paying

snake oil: a worthless preparation marketed as something that cures many illnesses

a sucker born every minute: many people are easily fooled by others (this phrase is often incorrectly attributed to circus owner P. T. Barnum)

sucker-punched: unexpectedly hit

yowza: a slang word similar to "yes, sir"

Gotcha!
by Thomas Hayden

She strolls onto the stage as if into her own living room, casually elegant in a twinkling, black tunic top and matching trousers. "I love you, Sylvia!" cries an exuberant young woman, her enthusiasm rising above the applause of 2,400 paying audience members. Sylvia Browne—psychic, medium, prolific author—accepts the affirmation gracefully and takes the podium. "I want to talk to you about angels, about spirit guides, and about how to become more psychic." Shudder. This is precisely the conversation I've spent most of my life avoiding. But I was trapped in a sea of believers, and having paid $78.50 of *U.S. News*'s money for my seat in the Atlantic City Convention Center auditorium, I didn't dare attempt an escape.

What is a hoax, exactly? When does a good deal become too good to be true, and where does belief end and credulity begin? In the stories that follow, we present elaborate swindles, outrageous gags, and insidious disinformation campaigns. They're all hoaxes—proof there's a sap for every scam artist, and easy mark for every mountebank, a chump for every charlatan. The notion that the Eskimos have 100 words for "snow" isn't true—more urban legend than hoax—but English certainly has a telling number of *mots juste* for stretchers of the truth and the suckers who believe them. And it is a collaboration; history shows that a successful hoax often depends not so much on the guile of the hoaxer as on the gullibility of the hoaxed.

Life is full of decisions to believe or not to believe. When it comes to psychics, I'm quick to adopt a skeptical stance. Yet despite any number of analyses exposing the psychic's art as, at best, a clever party trick, many people—perhaps even you, dear reader?—clearly believe this stuff. Sylvia Browne's *Book of Dreams* (Dutton, $25.95), about connecting with loved ones on "the other side," is on the *New York Times* bestseller list. John Edward, who also offers a link to the dead, has a hit with his television show *Crossing Over*, and other dabblers in divination and necromancy are perennial favorites on TV talk shows. I went to see Browne not so much to test her psychic powers as to test my own ability to resist the temptation to believe in them, real or not. Sadly, my status as a hardened skeptic did not survive unblemished, but more on that later.

Scale o' lies.

The word *hoax* is thought to derive from the old magician's incantation "hocus pocus." Nailing down a precise definition is no easy task, but on the spectrum of mendacity, most hoaxes fall somewhere between a scam on one side and a practical joke on the other. Unlike urban legends, notes Alex Boese, who maintains the Web site museumofhoaxes.com, a hoax should be traceable back to a perpetrator who's knowingly trying to deceive the public. Boese, a Ph.D. student at the University of California–San Diego, has a book coming out this fall based on his hoax research. By coincidence—or is it!—he shares Browne's publishers. When tall tales, such as those spun by the infamous Charles Ponzi…are used to trick the unsuspecting out of their money, they also become fraud. But while some recent business dealings—Enron's accounting practices, that whole "new economy" thing—can certainly feel like hoaxes, they rarely rise above the level of dirty tricks or mass wishful thinking.

Whatever else can be said about hoaxes, they do have a wonderfully democratizing effect. Doctors, lawyers, scientists, even (who are we kidding; especially) the media, are all just as susceptible to polished patter and an appealing story as the rawest Victorian rube shelling out his wages for a barker's snake oil cure-all medicine. The "hook," as it's known in the trade, is often a plausible story, tailored to fit the victim's prejudices, or to play on greed, vanity, or desperation. In the early 20th century, a crudely faked fossil skull tricked anthropologists into believing that modern humans originated in England—an appealing thought to European scientists…. And in 1983, *Newsweek* and German magazine *Der Stern* paid millions to print excerpts from a bogus diary, purportedly the private musings of Adolf Hitler…. "People saw great big headlines and pats on the back, and perhaps something more substantive as well," says one former *Newsweek*er. "It was just too tempting to pass up." Sometimes, it turns out, believing is really just seeing what you want to be true.

Are we more vulnerable to hoaxes in the information age, or less so? With modern communications, hoaxes can be debunked as rapidly as they are created. Several Web sites track electronic hoaxes (hoaxbusters.ciac.org is a good one), but if the number of phony virus alert E-mails I receive is any indication, the Internet's power is more readily harnessed to proliferate hoaxes than to quash them. For the record, Bill Gates will not give you a thousand dollars for testing an E-mail tracking application, and you shouldn't trust that dude in Nigeria who swears he needs your help to transfer millions out of the country. With E-mail, notes Boese, "anybody can potentially have access to millions of people." Then that anybody happens to be a hoaxer, the results can be spread for years.

The events of September 11 have proved to be particularly rich fodder for Internet hoaxes. The most famous features a photo of a tourist on a World Trade Center observation deck, a mere instant before an airliner slams into the building. Even if the film could have survived the horrific fires that day, the image is an obvious fabrication. The airplane is approaching from the wrong direction, the WTC observation deck was closed when the attacks took place, and the tourist is wearing winter clothes on a warm day. The photo, phony as it was, worked as a hoax not because it was believable but because it captured the public mood perfectly; the hapless tourist stood in for all of us, sucker-punched out of the blue on a perfect late-summer morning.

Fertile ground.

Other 9/11 hoaxes were more sinister. False claims of lost relatives, designed to elicit sympathy or claim undeserved compensation, were the most tawdry.

A series of anthrax hoaxes, following the all too real postal attacks, exploited people's justifiable fear. And 21st-century spins on the notorious Protocols of the Elders of Zion hoax…abounded. That Israel was behind the attacks and that Jewish employees were warned to stay home that day are patently ridiculous claims. When lies are planted in a field of ugly prejudice, even the most insidious hoaxes can take root.

Other, more benign deceptions are designed to argue a point. In 1996, physicist Alan Sokal used a classic hoaxer's tool—impeccable credentials—to dupe the editors of *Social Text*, a respected academic journal of cultural studies. Any number of observers—not all of the cranky and conservative—maintain that the entire field of postmodern, post-structuralist theory belongs to another class of hoax, namely highfalutin flimflam. But Sokal went them one better. In his paper *Transgressing the Boundaries: Toward a Transformative Hermeneutics of Quantum Gravity*, Sokal argues that recent advances in quantum physics support the idea that physical reality is nothing more than a social construct. The editors didn't follow much of the science, they later admitted, but were pleased to publish a contribution from an established scientist. Too bad the article was a sham. In revealing his hoax, Sokal invited those who believe the laws of physics are cultural conventions to test them from his 21st-floor window. Sokal became a media darling—it's hard to resist a story with the punch line "take that, smarty-pants!" and used his exposure to call for greater intellectual rigor in academia.

In the hands of an expert, perpetrating a hoax can even become an art form. New York artist Joey Skaggs has convinced reporters that, among other things, he was a roving priest offering "religion for people on the go" with his tricycle-mounted "portofess" confessional and a Korean entrepreneur soliciting live dogs from animal shelters for his soup business. Skaggs is a hoaxing purist; he constructs his stories with a moral—usually a variation on the themes of questioning assumptions and revealing prejudice—and deconstructs his efforts at his Web site, joeyskaggs.com. "Revelation is the most important aspect of the process," he says. "That's the point where consciousness can change." You'd think the resulting embarrassment would sharpen reporters' skepticism, but ask Skaggs if he has ever fooled anyone twice and he laughs. "Twice is nothing," he says. "The media's job is to question a premise, but information overload and the strain to get a story first gets in the way of getting it right." For the record, he has fooled *U.S. News* only once—something about the Japanese snapping up geoduck clams—and that was way back in 1987.

Twain's tales.

The media have perpetrated their share of hoaxes, too. No less an icon than Mark Twain was famous for passing off tall tales (a gruesome massacre, a "petrified shah" found in the hills of Nevada) as reported fact in his newspapering days. But in the late 1990s, the novelist was outdone by an audacious young staff writer at the *New Republic*. Stephen Glass, the magazine said, invented all or part of some 27 separate stories he wrote for that magazine. A Vegas casino offering odds on a space shuttle malfunction? A New York bond trader so committed to watching the market tickers that he kept a portable urinal at his desk? A 15-year-old hacker extorting fast cars and pornography from a software firm? Fabrications all, but Glass's stories were so appealing that editors simply couldn't resist them—until an enterprising tech reporter, feeling scooped, blew the lid off Glass's hacker yarn. Twain parlayed his creative flair into one of the greatest literary careers of all time; the disgraced Glass dedicated himself to law school.

Many hoaxes seem obvious in retrospect. But surely reasonable people can disagree about whether Sylvia Browne and other high-profile psychics qualify as a hoax? Millions of people do seem to believe the improbable notion that these self-proclaimed seers can divine the future and speak with the dead. I caught up with Browne on a lecture tour to see if I could figure out why.

All sorts of deceit is on offer in Atlantic City—I passed up a come-on, several hustles, and a scam on the way to the convention center—but Browne claims to offer the real deal. She's a gracious woman, with a gravelly voice and a knowing, world-weary air, and generously invited me backstage. I introduced myself as a journalist but didn't reveal that my magazine was working on an issue about hoaxes. (This was not in itself a hoax on my part, just a cheap deception.) A few minutes into the interview, Browne started "reading" me. "Watch out for your right ear," she warned. "You could be getting an infection." (Plausible enough—a good, safe opener.) "You've got a problem with your neck and shoulder." (Often true, but what ill-postured reporter, frantically scribbling all this into a notebook, *wouldn't* have neck and shoulder problems?) She moved on to specifics: "There's a problem with the disk between the fourth and fifth vertebrae in your lower back." *Shiver.* I had spent the entire preceding week flat on my back with lower-back pain—could she be on to something? Well, maybe statistics. "About 80 percent of herniated disks occur between those vertebrae" or the next disk down, says Scott Boden, a professor of orthopedic surgery at the Emory University School of Medicine in Atlanta. Given the prevalence of disk problems, he says, Browne's diagnosis "would be statistically safe."

The reading continued; I'm a perfectionist (my editors would be pleased), and I'll soon move. I confess, I felt another chill, even as she raised a knowing eyebrow. I am moving this month, and given the lousy housing options in Washington D.C., I'll probably keep leapfrogging. The parting shot: "Oh, and your love life sucks." *Sheesh.* Strictly speaking, my love life doesn't suck, it simply doesn't exist, but close enough. She conjured vague notions of someone short and blond though, with greenish eyes. (Yowza—finally we get to the "tell 'em what they want to hear" part!) But I don't get out enough, she chided, and can't just sit around waiting for something good to happen.

The final chastisement is central to Browne's appeal—safe predictions and comforting messages combined with tough love. "I don't care if you feel miserable," she tells the audience later that night. "Smile anyway.... Get over it." Sound advice, and it comes with full theological backing. Think your life is tough? It should be—we're in hell! But don't worry, this life is just a way to test our strength and fortify our spirits before returning to heaven. This is liberation theology for the daytime-TV crowd—the hard times will soon be over and your deceased loved ones are happy, so stop whining, get off the couch, and go help someone.

Good show.

Despite the tingles of recognition I felt during her reading, I didn't leave feeling convinced of Browne's powers. But neither did I feel ripped off—she puts on a good show. (I might have felt differently if I'd paid the $700 fee for a private telephone consultation, but with the waiting list full until 2005, I didn't have a chance to find out.) One woman, whose husband died in the World Trade Center attacks, told me that despite her family's misgivings, Browne's message gave her a sense of peace and closure, noting, "If you don't need it, you won't come looking for it."

And that—whether Browne is for real or not—points to the first law of constructing a hoax; find a need and fill it with a good story, and the world will beat a path to your 1-900 number.

Given the current spate of "accounting irregularities," you might think we'd learn to be a little more skeptical. And yet, pulling off a hoax is sometimes so simple, it can even happen by accident. Just ask Paul Guinan, a Portland, Ore., artist whose Web site (www.bigredhair.com/boilerplate) features a "mechanical man" named Boilerplate, supposedly created in the 1880s. The site, a joke from start to finish, includes photos of the charming robot meeting Pancho Villa and journeying to Antarctica. Guinan was shocked—and a little chastened—to find his innocent site duped many visitors, including historians. "I felt both pride and embarrassment that I fooled all these people," he says. "If I can do it, I guess anyone can." A sucker born every minute? Shoot, if you believe that lowball estimate, I'd like to talk with you about buying the Eiffel Tower.

From Where I Stand... (Journal Responses)

1. I think that certain psychics can/cannot (choose either "can" or "cannot") get in touch with spirits because _____.
2. I think getting to the bottom of hoaxes is easier/harder (choose either "easier" or "harder) today than 50 years ago because _____.
3. I think the difference between a tall tale and a hoax is _____
_____.

JUST THE FACTS

1. The main point of this selection is a) the author, who was skeptical about the powers of a psychic, felt neither convinced of her powers nor ripped off; b) the author,

who was skeptical about the powers of a psychic, had his mind changed after the psychic talked with him about a little-known part of his childhood; c) the author felt completely ripped off after his session; d) the psychic felt that she had been cheated.

2. Hayden says that the "hook" of a tale is often a plausible story that a) fits the victim's prejudices or plays on greed, vanity, or desperation; b) takes place in a setting that the victim finds believable; c) has just a small element of something that the victim can find familiar; d) is terrifying enough that the victim leaves with a "sense of the unknown."

3. Bill Gates giving you $1,000 for testing an e-mail tracking application and a Nigerian man saying he needs your help to transfer millions out of the country are examples of a) e-mail hoaxes; b) how the Internet has been put to good use; c) deeds that began as urban legends but turned into real situations; d) how the Internet has been used by people all over the world.

4. The last bit of information that Browne told Hayden was that Hayden's a) current love was someone short and blond, with green eyes; b) love life would quickly take a turn for the worse with his wife; c) love life sucked; d) former girlfriend would make a surprise reappearance in his life.

5. The "cheap deception" that Hayden pulled on Browne was that he a) told a lie about his current address; b) didn't reveal that he was working on a magazine issue about hoaxes; c) told Browne that he was 35, when he was actually 38; d) told Browne that he couldn't afford to pay for a private session.

EXPANDING HORIZONS

1. Hayden thinks that the phrase "a sucker born every minute" is too conservative an estimate. What do you think? In what cases do you ever see people being taken advantage of?

2. When Hayden finally met Sylvia Brown in person, he introduced himself as a journalist but did not say that the article he was writing was about hoaxes. Do you think that this was ethical or not? Defend your position.

3. Hayden says the word *hoax* is thought to derive from the old magician's incantation "hocus pocus." The history of a word is called its *etymology*. An unabridged dictionary will trace a word's etymology as far back as possible. In the dictionary, the etymology will appear inside brackets, usually at the end of the definitions. The first entry inside the brackets tells the language that the word most recently came from, followed by the word in that language, which is written in italics. If that word, in turn, evolved from an earlier language and word, that will be cited next; the original definition of the word will also be listed. The word *history*, for example, might have an entry for its etymology that looks like this:

[Lat. *histoira*, Gk., *histr*, learned man]

This tells the reader that the modern word *history* developed from the Latin word *histoira*, which in turn came from the Greek word *histr*, which meant "learned man."

To determine various language abbreviations, you'll sometimes need to check the key (located in different places, depending on the dictionary).

Find the interesting etymologies for these words:

appendix	ballot	biscuit	candidate	elite	gymnasium
assassin	berserk	bulimia	denim	escape	liberty

library	pagan	regret	sinister	victim	zero
malaria	pay	robot	thermostat	window	
opportunity	planet	second	trivia	witness	

4. Hayden reports about New Yorker Joey Skaggs, a man who has made a career out of carrying out hoaxes. Visit Skaggs's Web site www.joeyskaggs.com/; click on "Dogma" and read Skaggs's explanation for why he does what he does. Then write letter of response, pointing out positions with which you agree or disagree. Be sure to support your opinion.

WRITE ON!

Suppose a friend pays for you to have several sessions with a psychic. Write a response to these questions:

1. First, state whether or not you believe in psychics, and state why.
2. If you believe in psychics, cite three questions you would ask. Why would you ask these particular questions?
3. If you don't believe in psychics, cite three questions would you ask in order to try to trick the "psychic." Do you think you would be successful? Why or why not?

READ ON!

Brunvand, Jan Harold. *Encyclopedia of Urban Legends*. New York: W. W. Norton & Company, 2002.

——. *Too Good to Be True: The Colossal Book of Urban Legends*. New York: W. W. Norton & Company, 2001.

Collis, Harry. *101 American Superstitions: Understanding Language and Culture through Superstitions*. New York: McGraw-Hill, 1998.

"Common E-mail Hoaxes." www.3oddballz.com/hoaxes/.

Craughwell, Thomas J. *The Cat in the Dryer: And 222 Other Urban Legends*. New York: Black Dog & Leventhal Publishers, 2002.

"Don't Spread that Hoax!" www.nonprofit.net/hoax/.

Fiery, Ann, and Ulriksen, Mark. *The Completely and Totally True Book of Urban Legends*. Philadelphia: Running Press Book Publishers, 2001.

"The Folklorist.com: A Website Devoted to the Study of the Human Condition." thefolklorist.com/.

"Futile Attempt: Superstitions." www.geocities.com/sonhedaze/third.html.

"OldSuperstitions.com: The Largest List of Superstitions on the Web." www.oldsuperstitions.com/.

Roeper, Richard. *Urban Legends: The Truth Behind All Those Deliciously Entertaining Myths That Are Absolutely, Positively, 100% Not True*. Franklin Lakes, New Jersey: New Page Books, 2001.

"Silly Superstitions." www.islandnet.com/~luree/silly.html.

"Superstitions: Old Wives Tales, Folklore, Bizarre Beliefs, Taboos, Omens, Lucky & Unlucky Things." www.corsinet.com/trivia/scary.html.

"Urban Legends and Superstitions." urbanlegendsonline.com/.

How would you describe what's going on in this photograph? In what time period would you place this photo, and why? What specific items or visual clues lead you to believe this? Write a sentence in which you describe a peculiar part of this image—without mentioning the rest of the image. Then, exchange sentences with a classmate; can you guess what the other's sentence is describing? Why or why not?

CHAPTER TWO

POPULAR CULTURE
What's Hip and
What's Hopped—and
Who Cares?

Country music is three chords and the truth. —*Harlan Howard*

Damn T.V.... Ruined my imagination and my ability to...ummm...ya...you know...
—*Bart Simpson*

I think that parents only get so offended by television because they rely on it as a babysitter and the sole educator of their kids. —*Trey Parker and Matt Stone*, South Park

In feature films the director is God; in documentary films God is the director. —*Alfred Hitchcock*

In the future, everybody will be famous for fifteen minutes. —*Andy Warhol*

It's a marvelous feeling when someone says "I want to do this song of yours" because they've connected to it—That's what I'm after. —*Mary Chapin Carpenter*

Just the thought of a rap version of Beethoven's *Fifth Symphony* or "Achy, Breaky Heart" is bound to make people smile. —*Anthony Kennedy*

MTV is the lava lamp of the 1980's. —*Doug Ferrari*

Our culture is obsessed with the people we see on television and watch in the movies.
—*Ryan Seacrest*

Please, young people...Elvis has left the building. —*Horace Lee Logan*

Pop culture is not about depth. It's about marketing, supply and demand, consumerism.
—*Trevor Dunn*

Television has proved that people will look at anything rather than each other. —*Ann Landers*

The whole pop culture cache is done and it's hard for us to get our artists into those general circulation publications. —*Branford Marsalis*

There's never a new fashion but it's old. —*Geoffrey Chaucer*

This isn't brain surgery; it's just television. —*David Letterman*

Popular Culture: What's Hip and What's Hopped— and Who Cares?

Quick! Can you identify

_____ a movie that's playing in the theaters now?

_____ a singer you'd be likely to hear on a popular radio station?

_____ at least one program that's going to be on TV tonight?

_____ clothes that are stylish?

_____ current players in one or more national or collegiate sports teams?

_____ the author or plot of a book on the best-seller list?

_____ a jingle that goes with a company's ads?

_____ a way to make purchases from the Internet?

If you answered yes to at least one of those questions, then—whether you admit it or not—you're part of popular (pop) culture.

Pop culture involves what many people find to be entertaining and appealing—personally, locally, nationally, and internationally. Countless aspects of pop culture are so pervasive that, even if they don't appeal to you, you're aware of them unless—to use a current cliché—you've been living under a rock.

This chapter is an overview of various segments of pop culture that are in vogue today, but what's hot now may or may not have the staying power to be part of pop culture tomorrow. While experts find that predicting the next "new thing" is difficult, maybe after reading this section you'll have a brainstorm about future pop culture.

The selections in the chapter focus on various facets of popular culture. First, take a look around the classroom and see how many people are wearing what may be the most ubiquitous U.S. fashion statement: blue jeans. These have long been a part of American culture (indeed, now of the culture of most parts of the world), and the interesting history behind them is highlighted in the first selection of this chapter, "Blue Jeans: An American Phenomenon."

Through a more recent phenomenon of popular culture, the Internet, a number of services and businesses have begun. One of these, eBay, was founded in 1995 and has found its way into the daily lives of many shoppers around the world. John Marr relates how online shopping has changed his life in "Confessions of an eBay Addict."

No discussion of pop culture would be complete without a look at the movies. Since their inception, one of the most popular genres of films has been action movies, which usually pit the good guys against the bad guys. In "Go Ahead, Make Her Day," however, film critic and author Richard Corliss takes a look at how the "guys" have turned into the "gals" in some current action films.

Another major part of pop culture is music, and certainly American music takes many forms. Jazz and the blues are distinctly American music styles that have become popular all across the world. "St. Louis Blues," by W. C. Handy, addresses the age-old problem of the seemingly never-ending sadness felt when a lover breaks up and leaves with someone else.

The final selection addresses television, perhaps the most popular medium in pop culture. Since the inception of television in the middle part of the twentieth century, game shows have been shown in one form or another. John Teti's "Regis Makes Contestants, ABC Rich on 'Millionaire'" looks at the sometimes checkered history of television game shows.

Now that you have read the introduction to this chapter, go back and reread the quotations on p. 31. Then choose one of the quotations and write about whether you agree or disagree with it. Be sure to defend your opinion.

*Blue jeans have long been part of the fashion statements for many, if not most, Americans. These days, the majority of people have several pairs of jeans that they wear for casual attire, and a growing number of businesses often allow their employees to wear jeans to work. This selection, by **Marjorie Dorfman**, examines how jeans came to be such an integral part of American pop culture.*

Starting Out...

Look around the classroom and determine what percent of the class is wearing jeans today. To find this percentage, take the number wearing jeans and divide it by the total number of people in the class.

Words to Watch

accolades: praise, honors

capitalism: the economic system in which the means of production are privately owned, and where investment and goods and services are determined by supply and demand in a market

forthright: straightforward, candid

free enterprise: freedom of private businesses to operate competitively for profit with minimal government regulation

fustian: made from a coarse, sturdy cloth of cotton and flax

haute couture: exclusive fashions

ideological: having to do with a set of beliefs that form the basis of a political, economic, or other system

individualism: distinctiveness, uniqueness

personify: characterize, typify

ponderable: considerable enough to be carefully thought out

psyche: spirit or soul

symbolized: represented

transcended: exceeded, gone beyond

unpretentious: plain, natural

via: by way of, by means of

Blue Jeans: An American Phenomenon
by Marjorie Dorfman

What do Elvis Presley, James Dean, Marlon Brando and all the 19th century cowboys and gold rush miners have in common? Their blue jeans, that's what! To the cowboys and miners, the pants were durable work clothes that molded to their individual body shapes to become a "personal garment." To the "rebel" movie icons of the 1950s, jeans symbolized individualism and social revolt. Today, they are an ageless phenomenon and they personify all that is good about America and its democratic values of independence and equality. Their worldwide popularity since the 1960s has made them the most universally worn item of clothing in the world today, crossing class, gender, age, regional, national and even ideological lines.

In 1962 *American Fabrics* magazine referred to denim as an "honest, substantial, forthright and unpretentious fabric." I could understand such accolades if a textile could apply for a job, but after all, an equal opportunity employer does have his or her limitations! Still, denim and blue jeans have come a long way from Levi Strauss's original purpose, work pants for the California coal miners in the mid nineteenth century. The Bavarian peddler imported the cotton fabric with blue dyed thread from the French city of Nimes and it is presumed that this is where the term "denim" comes from. Whatever its origins, denim is here to stay and blue jeans have become an established attitude about clothing and lifestyle.

How the word "jeans" came to mean pants made out of denim is a question almost as ponderable and rewarding as which came first, the chicken or the egg. There seem to be two schools of thought on the subject and neither can be proven absolutely true. One idea is that the word might be a derivation of "Genoese," meaning the type of fustian pants worn by sailors from Genoa, Italy. The other theory stems from the fact that jean and denim fabrics were both used for work wear for many decades and "jeans pants" was a common term for pants made from jean fabric. Before 1873, Strauss bought "jean pants" to sell in California. When denim became even more popular for work wear, the word "jeans" was still used as the term for the denim version of these pants. It doesn't really matter, does it? They are here and so are you and I. ("Maybe millions of people go by...")

In 1872 a poor tailor from Reno, Nevada, named Jacob Davis shared an idea with Levi Strauss to improve the strength of the work pants he made for his customers by adding metal rivets. In 1873 the two men patented the improvement in "Fastening Pocket Openings." Levi brought Davis to San Francisco to oversee the first manufacture of their copper riveted "waist overalls" made from brown cotton duck and blue denim. Knowing that the riveted pants were going to be perfect for work wear, Levi and Jacob decided to make them out of denim rather than jeans because denim seemed the sturdiest fabric of the two. This decision would forever rock the textile world in a way that even Elvis Presley couldn't. (He could rock, but you know what I mean!)

Jeans are still in the workplace today, where once the suit, shirt and tie was king. It's really only the tools we need for work that have changed over the years. Instead of a pick and shovel or a tired horse with no jeans of his own, we use telephones, pens, paper and computer keyboards. Still we wear the same thing: jeans, jeans, jeans! From a garment associated exclusively with work, jeans have progressed to one associated with leisure sportswear and even haute couture status via designer labels. They have transcended even the garment world, making guest appearances and disguising themselves as perfume fragrances such as Versace's "Black Jeans" for him and "Baby Rose Jeans" for her.

Scratch N'Sniff jeans reach yet another smelly audience, presenting to the weary world and anyone else willing to smell, a wide array of scents such as Ammonia, Ashtray, Sweat, Peanut Butter and Watermelon, just to mention a few. These Scratch N'Sniff jeans keep the concept of teenagers, capitalism, free enterprise and aerosol sprays alive and well in America. There truly seems no end to the versatility and expansion of the concept of "blue jeans."

Today Levi-Strauss and Company makes jeans in approximately 108 sizes and 20 different finishes. There are 37 separate sewing operations involved in making a single pair of Levis. The double row of stitching on the back pockets known as the Arcuate design is the oldest apparel trademark still in use today. It was first used in 1873. During World War II, this design was painted on the pockets due to government rationing of thread. At that time, denim was considered "essential to defense" and only those individuals specifically designated could wear it! Where do blue jeans and denim go from here? I hope they stay exactly where they are, or at least not too far away. Blue jeans will always be a part of the American psyche, like "The Star Spangled Banner" and apple pie. I wouldn't have it any other way. Would you?

From Where I Stand... (Journal Responses)

1. I currently own about _____ [state the number] pairs of jeans, and I enjoy wearing jeans the most when I go to _____ [state a place].
2. The most I would pay for a pair of jeans is _____ [state an amount]; I would not pay more because _____.
3. One place that I think is inappropriate to wear jeans is

    _____
    _____ because _____.

JUST THE FACTS

1. The main idea of this selection is a) the Levi Strauss Company is responsible for jeans; b) denim is a sturdy material that is appropriate for many fashions; c) jeans have been part of the American culture for many years; d) when people wear jeans, they make a fashion statement.

2. The Levi Strauss Company's original purpose for jeans was a) work pants for coal miners; b) work pants for farm workers; c) covering for wagons traveling across the prairies; d) material used in making sails for oceangoing vessels.
3. An improvement that Jacob Davis suggested was to a) manufacture jeans in both men's and women's sizes; b) add metal rivets; c) sell jeans already hemmed; d) market jeans to children as well as adults.
4. Arcuate is a) the name of a rival company that makes jeans; b) the finish that is used to make the denim more durable; c) one of the main distribution centers for jeans; d) a design of stitching.
5. The selection mentions that during World War II, a) electricity was rationed; b) paper was rationed; c) thread was rationed; d) heating oil was rationed.

EXPANDING HORIZONS

1. Go to the Web site of the Levi Strauss Company at www.levistrauss.com/about/ and then click on "History" on the left-hand side. From there, select a decade to research. When you have finished, summarize what you have learned about the decade you studied.
2. The selection says that "the Arcuate design is the oldest apparel trademark still in use today." Suppose you have been given the job of designing a new trademark for a brand of jeans. What would your trademark be? Why would you choose that design?
3. The selection mentions rationing of thread during World War II. Out of necessity, many other items were rationed then. Research rationing during this time and then summarize what you learn. Online sites to consult include:

    www.straightdope.com/classics/a1_382b.html
    www.nps.gov/pwro/collection/website/rationing.htm
    www.rootsweb.com/~nyfulton/Salute/WWIIrations.htm

4. Tailor Jacob Davis suggested adding metal rivets to jeans, which proved to be a significant contribution. Research more about Davis and write a short biography of him. Online sites to consult include these:

    baseportal.com/cgi-bin/baseportal.pl?htx=/zpub2000/sfentries&cmd=list&range
    =0,50&Title~=J&cmd=all&Id=204
    www.5minuteenglish.com/sep17.htm

WRITE ON!

1. Defend or refute this statement from the selection: "Today, [jeans]...personify all that is good about America and its democratic values of independence and equality."
2. Some designer jeans cost more than $250. If you found a pair that fit well and looked good on you but cost $200, would you think those jeans would be worth the money? Why or why not?
3. In 1969 a writer for *American Fabrics* magazine declared, "Denim is one of the world's oldest fabrics, yet it remains eternally young." What does the writer mean by that? Do you agree or disagree with the writer? Why or why not?

Shopping has long been a part of the culture of many—if not most—Americans; in recent years, the Internet has also become a part of the culture of many—if not most—Americans. The confluence of these two areas of pop culture was inevitable. Customers can of course buy any number of products directly from company Web sites, but online auction sites, such as commercial giant eBay, have become incredibly popular. This article, from the March 1999 issue of Bad Subjects: Political Education for Everyday Life, *takes a look at how shopping on eBay changed the life of writer **John Marr.***

Starting Out...

Poll ten people, using the questions below. Then compile your results into a graph or chart.

1) Do you think that purchasing from the Internet is safe?

 yes no not sure

2) Have you ever purchased anything from eBay or another online auction site?

 yes no

3) Have you ever sold anything through eBay or another online auction site?

 yes no

Words to Watch

automaton: machine

Beaver & Wally's: a reference to the two sons in the television show *Leave It to Beaver,* which aired in the late 1950s and early 1960s

call to arms: a rallying term used by supporters of a cause; a battle cry

catch-as-catch can: an idiom meaning "try to get something any way possible"

Franklin Mint: a company that makes many types of collectible items

screen name: a name selected by an Internet user; usually not the person's real name

search function: an feature on an Internet site; it lets a user type in a category; then only items in that category are listed on the computer screen

serendipity: fate, chance

Skinner Box: invented by psychologist B. F. Skinner, a box used to gather information about the behavior of rats and pigeons

Adam Smith: an eighteenth-century economist known as "the father of economics"

thrifted: a made-up word meaning "bought at a thrift shop"

tiki: a Polynesian figurine

virtual: carried on by means of a computer or computer network

waiting for lightning to strike: an idiom meaning "waiting for something to happen"

yeech: slang for "gosh" or "for heaven's sake"

Confessions of an eBay Addict
by John Marr

Hello.

My name is John Marr.

And I'm an eBay addict.

It started innocently enough. A few friends told me about this great website where you could find all kinds of neat old junk. It wasn't the electronic equivalent of the local antique collective where dealers, living in absolute horror of anyone ever finding any kind of a bargain, slap $20 price tags on any book published before 1975. It was an auction site. Sellers put stuff on the electronic block. Potential buyers bid. And courtesy of the electronic invisible hand, the authority of hundreds of so-called "Official Price Guides" is decimated. Adam Smith would be proud.

So I logged on to eBay (www.ebay.com). At first, I was staggered by the sheer volume of crap (more than 1.4 million items on the block at any one time as of this writing). There was everything from bootlegged computer software to Franklin Mint-style pseudo-collectibles. Zeroing in on the mystery subcategory under the "Books," I found plenty of junk, from Agatha Christie paperbacks to endless volumes featuring plucky female private eye protagonists. Yeech. At least the prices seemed sane (one of the cheap pleasures of eBay is watching the neglect of items with ridiculously high minimum bids). But finding the good stuff seemed problematical. Scrolling through a junk shop 50 items at a time is no way to shop no matter how fast your connection is.

Then I discovered the search function.

I was forevermore lost.

eBay combines the appeal of the grungy, catch-as-catch-can merchandise of the garage sale with the convenience of keyword searching. Toss in the frequent illusion (and occasional realization) of a bargain and the heady passion of the auction. The resulting combination is lethal for anyone who has difficulty passing up a thrift store. For sane and sensible used-goods shoppers out for a deal on a used DVD player, this is not a problem. But for all you compulsive collectors, passionate packrats, junk store junkies, welcome to your Skinner Box.

I'm not going to tell you what I'm looking for because I don't want to give anyone ideas. Let us just say it is a very special type of magazine. In an instant, I had 75 of them on my screen, most with pleasingly low bids. This was about 74 more than I'd find in a month of rummaging through used bookstores and dealer's catalogs. The only frustration? You have to register to bid (a process that takes overnight) and several of the more tasty auctions were ending in a few hours. The torment!

As soon as I had my screen name and my password, I started bidding. At first, it was nirvana. It's overwhelming to see arcane items that you've been hunting for months, if not years, popping up on your screen. It was such a heady experience being able to search for anything that I immediately forgot half the stuff I was looking for. I have since remembered.

Of course, eBay doesn't totally replace the pleasures of real (as opposed to virtual) shopping. Some things are lacking, most notably serendipity and the chance discovery of the thing you can't live without that you never knew existed. No matter how high-powered your modem, rummaging at random through eBay waiting for lightening to strike just isn't the way to go. But if you know exactly what you're looking for, a quick search through eBay is like distilling the contents of a thousand junk shops into one almost pure page of a specialty store.

The single item that convinced me of the possibilities of eBay was a humble alarm clock. Many years ago, I thrifted a '50s alarm clock. It was nothing fancy, but it kept good time, filled my room with a comforting retro ticking sound, and never failed to wake me in the morning. Best of all, I subsequently discovered it was a twin to the clock on Beaver & Wally's nightstand. Now that's a timepiece!

One sad day it broke. The local clock repair shops laughed at me. Even if parts were available, repairing such junk was beneath them. So I tried to replace it. For years I searched antique stores, junk shops, and thrift stores without once finding one remotely resembling my beloved cream-colored ticker. In desperation (one does have to get up in the morning, after all) I purchased pallid substitute after pallid substitute. But a gaping void remained on my nightstand.

Twins of my beloved clock pop up every week on eBay. I now have two in cream, another in black, and am actively bidding on a few larger models in the same style.

This is one of the deadliest features of eBay. It's far too easy to find far too many things. Your normal collector of slightly off-the-beaten track stuff is protected from himself by the nature of the market. The stuff just doesn't pop up that much. Collecting can continue indefinitely at a slow and steady pace without thought to budgetary limitations or space constraints. But eBay is like a mall, complete with a specialty store catering to the most arcane collectors. It's not how much you can find—it's how much you can afford. Collectors are noted neither for their discipline or restraint. It's easy to wake up one day to discover your previously healthy bank balance has been transformed into a mushrooming accumulation of alarm clocks, beer signs, or tiki mugs.

Bargains can be had on eBay. But it's easy to get sucked into paying more than you wanted in the heat of the auction. Bidding can get bloody. eBay uses what is known as a "Vickery Auction." Like a traditional auction, the computer always shows the amount of the current high bid. But there's no need (save in the waning moments of a crucial auction) to sit by your screen constantly upping your bid. Instead of simply making a bid, you indicate the maximum amount you're willing to bid. (eBay swears this isn't revealed until after the auction closed.) The winner is the person with the highest maximum bid. But this isn't necessarily what they have to pay. The amount of the winning bid is figured at one increment (usually 50 cents or a dollar) above the maximum bid of the second highest bidder. If no one else bids, you get the item for the amount of the minimum bid set for the auction (see footnote).

This is a rational system for a perfect automaton. You figure how much the item is worth to you and bid that amount. If you get it, fine. If not, on to the next auction. But I am far from a perfect automaton, and I highly doubt anyone else on eBay is either. Because of the nature of the bidding, you don't know the opposition's maximum; you just know (thanks to a helpful email from eBay) that the bid is now $1 more than what you thought you were willing to pay. A marginal value fallacy sets in. If you're willing to pay $20, why not $21? And if $21 is not too much, neither should $22. Who can, when caught in the grips of lust for stuff, let a single measly dollar get in between them and the object of their desire?

Not me. When eBay emails me the dreaded notification that I have been outbid, I consider it a call to arms. Damn the budget. I must counterattack and up my maximum, repeatedly if necessary. For crucial auctions, I've been known to hover over my computer in the waning moments, ready to respond or stealthily sneak in that last minute bid that takes the field. If I fail—and sometimes sanity does prevail—there is the consolation of knowing I drove the price up for the other guy. If I succeed, well, at least I wind up with some pretty cool stuff, even if it means paying $30 for something that, at first bidding, I thought was only worth $15.

This is why I find myself in an apartment rapidly filling up with old magazines, cheap rusty alarm clocks, and other assorted debris of days gone by. My checking account is barren, my hand is developing mouse-related carpal tunnel syndrome. The mail guy at work is getting visibly pissed as the packages arrive on an almost daily basis.

I am an eBay addict. And I'm proud of it.

Footnote: There are also the much reviled "reserve price auctions" where the seller reserves the right to not sell the item if bidding doesn't reach a specified level.

From Where I Stand... (Journal Responses)

1. If I had enough money, I'd like to collect _____

_____

because _____.

2. I prefer to shop online/in person (choose either "online" or "in person") because

_____.

3. A time when I paid too much for something was when _____.

JUST THE FACTS

1. The main idea of this selection is a) eBay has asked Marr to be a spokesperson for the company; b) Marr has made many new friends through his eBay sales; c) Marr has become a real fan of eBay; d) Marr has suffered "withdrawal pangs" since he stopped shopping on eBay.

2. On eBay, Marr was "lost forever" when he discovered a) a woman whom he fell in love with; b) the search function; c) additions to his collection of old maps; d) his credit card had been used illegally.

3. Initially, Marr was looking on eBay for a special type of a) computer; b) jewelry for his wife; c) cell phone; d) magazine.

4. Marr says the single item that convinced him of the possibilities of eBay was a) several old records he had been searching for; b) a type of a camera that he had used as a boy; c) an alarm clock; d) tickets to a sold-out sporting event.

5. Marr says that a drawback to eBay is a) that it's easy to get sucked into paying more than a person wanted to pay; b) having to wait for the item to be mailed; c) knowing that someone you haven't met has your credit card information; d) not being able to talk with the seller face-to-face.

EXPANDING HORIZONS

1. This article is enhanced by Marr's use of alliteration (the repetition of beginning consonant sounds). Find at least three examples of alliteration.

2. Besides eBay, a number of other online auctions are accessible. Take a look at one or more of them and compare them to eBay (www.ebay.com/). Some that you might look at are:

    auctions.yahoo.com/
    www.ubid.com/
    auctions.overstock.com/
    www.auctiondollar.com/
    www.msbid.com/
    www.ibidfree.com/

3. Auction sites such as eBay often have strange items up for sale: a haunted funeral home, a play head of M. C. Hammer inside a loaf of bread, 25 packets of itching powder, the "ghost of [an] infamous homicide detective," a flashlight that attaches over

the wearer's ear. Take a look at some of the odd items currently for sale on eBay or other auction sites and then write a short story that centers around one of them. To find weird items on eBay, go to everythingelse.ebay.com/, then click on "Weird Stuff," "Slightly Unusual," "Really Weird," "or Totally Bizarre."

4. Read an article about recent selling and buying trends on eBay, then summarize what you have learned. You might look at one of these articles:

"'RV' Tops eBay Search Terms" money.cnn.com/2004/12/30/news/fortune500/ebay_indicator/

"The Year According to eBay" www.usatoday.com/tech/news/2004-12-29-ebay_x.htm

WRITE ON!

This article was written in 1999. Pretend you are John Marr and write a sequel to this article (use the present year). Answer the following questions:

1. Are you still an eBay addict? If so, what have you bought lately?

2. If not, why not? What made you stop?

3. What do you think would make more people become eager customers of eBay? Why?

Action movies have long been one of the most popular forms of entertainment all over the world. In the past, the action has revolved around male figures, heroes who often have to rescue female figures. In this article by **Richard Corliss,** *originally published in* Time *magazine in 2001, the author takes a look at recent changes in both movies and television—changes that focus on female action figures.*

Starting Out...

Put a check beside any of the following films or television shows that you have seen, and be prepared to give your opinion of them:

_____ *Buffy the Vampire Slayer*

_____ *Powerpuff Girls*

_____ *Dark Angel*

_____ *Josie and the Pussycats*

_____ *Crouching Tiger, Hidden Dragon*

_____ *Charlie's Angels*

_____ *Barbarella*

_____ *Lara Croft: Tomb Raider*

_____ XFL games

_____ MTV's *Jackass*

Words to Watch

coiffures: hair-dos

élite: best, most selective

frenetic: frantic, hectic

greenlighted: authorized, gave the go-ahead

icons: those who are the object of great devotion, idols

jape: escapade, adventure

juxtaposition: the act of positioning close together or side-by-side

le mot du jour: French for "the word of the day"

levitation: the phenomenon of a person or thing rising into the air by apparently supernatural means

maven: a person who has special knowledge or experience, an expert

mogul: tycoon, head of business

poignancy: a quality that arouses emotions (especially pity or sorrow)

sci-fi spoof: a science-fiction film that makes fun of something

skeptics: those who doubt or question generally accepted ideas

swain: boyfriend, beau

Go Ahead, Make Her Day
by Richard Corliss

It used to be the heroine's job to get in trouble and the hero's job to get her out of it. How many films ended with the good guy and the bad guy battling it out while the sweet young thing shivered to one side, never thinking to pick up a plank and help out? You've come a long way, baby. Flick on the TV, and see women—young women, almost always—kicking and thinking and winking at both the old notion of femininity and the aging precepts of feminism. Buffy the Vampire Slayer (in her fifth season on the WB) saves her classmates from Evil, when she's not cracking a book or a joke. The Cartoon Network's *Powerpuff Girls*, "the most élite kindergarten crime-fighting force ever assembled," protect Townsville with their magical powers. Max, the bionic babe on Fox's *Dark Angel*, occasionally lets a mere man help her save the world, after which she suavely extracts herself from his adoration. "What's the plan?" asks her enraptured swain of the moment, who doesn't deserve to be in her car pool, let alone her gene pool. Max's blunt reply: "I'm the plan."

Fact is, TV has long been a woman's medium. Movies are guy space. So consider the release next month of *Josie and the Pussycats*, a live-action version of the comic book and '70s TV cartoon series, and this summer's *Tomb Raider*, with Angelina Jolie as supervixen Lara Croft. Consider, and savor, the success of *Crouching Tiger, Hidden Dragon*, the all-time top-grossing foreign-language film that was set to hit the $100 million mark at the North American box office last weekend. Ang Lee's martial arts fantasy features two strong women, a 30ish warrior (Michelle Yeoh) and a willful teen (Zhang Ziyi) just discovering to what uses, good or ill, she may put her powers of physical levitation and female cunning.

"It's a mythic epic narrative which has as its center a female consciousness," says James Schamus, one of the film's writers and producers. "In all the great epics, from the Iliad on, the protagonists have been masculine, their destinies a masculine destiny. Now a real shift is taking place, in which some collective identities—those created for the whole culture regardless of gender—are female."

The women of the *Charlie's Angels* movie, which has earned $125 million since its November debut, might not seem to have kinship with *Crouching Tiger*'s stately stunners. This colorful jape propels Cameron Diaz, Drew Barrymore and Lucy Liu through its empty-calorie plot with the force of a hurricane blow-dryer. The stars giggle, wear swank togs, toss their coiffures in luxurious slo-mo. Diaz shakes her booty a lot. And skeptics may laugh their booty off when told that the Angels are icons of empowerment.

Yet they do fly through the air, giving the bad guys foot-facials (*Charlie's* stunt maven, Yuen Cheung-yan, is the brother of Yuen Wo-ping, who choreographed *Tiger*). And to Barrymore, who produced it, Charlie's is a tribute to today's woman: able, independent and cute—not so much femi-nist as femi-nice. "We wanted the Angels to be strong, but not masculine," says scriptwriter John August. "They aren't afraid of their sexuality, but they don't use it as power. Drew and I agreed they should be recognizable 'girls.' And she doesn't mind the word girls."

Didn't "girls" used to be a dirty word? To today's in-charge Hollywood woman, it's *le mot du jour*. "We're very girlie," says Nancy Juvenon, Barrymore's partner in Flower Films, which will produce a remake of the Jane Fonda sex sci-fi spoof *Barbarella*, with Barrymore in the title role. (Flower has three projects in the works; that makes Barrymore, 26, a baby mogul, or mo-girl.) Now the un-chic phrase, the F word, is feminism, because it connotes a starchy righteousness. "A bad thing about old-style feminism," says Amy Pascal, the Columbia Pictures chairman who greenlighted *Charlie's*, "was that you could be a brain surgeon but you couldn't be a sexy brain surgeon. Finally some woman said, 'I want to be both.' Men get to be sexy and successful. Feminism should include sexuality."

It surely does for Max (played by Jessica Alba, a kind of Angelina Jolie Jr.); she sizes up a man by scanning him from head to crotch. Other Max attributes were once the prerogative of heroic males: a gravity, a radiating inner ache, a past and a quest. She's lonely on top, flirting with potential mates but searching for a mother. In this sense she is a big sullen sister to Blossom, Bubbles and Buttercup, the Powerpuff Girls. They too are the spawn of a biological experiment. (They also levitate, like the *Tiger* women.) And though the show is perky, and its pace frenetic, the Girls carry the burden of others' expectation. When things go wrong, the Townsville adults chant, "Your fault! Your fault!" There is a poignancy to the Girls' perfection.

"I wanted the heroes to be strong, tough and cool," says Craig McCracken, the show's creator. "The juxtaposition of their being really cute and really strong seemed more interesting than if they had been muscley guys. People are starting to accept that girls are cool, and girlie things are cool." Schamus, who has daughters ages 4 and 8, thinks the Powerpuff Girls offer positive action role models: "My daughters are provided with more tools to gain confidence in the mastery of their own lives."

We will let others decide if this new trend is progressive or helpful to female viewers—let alone to unenlightened males, who have long appreciated the spectacle of women fighting (it used to be called mud wrestling). But the action woman is certainly a corrective to a zillion idiot action films and XFL games and episodes of *Jackass*. Women of any age hardly get a break in pop culture. So you go, girlie.

From Where I Stand... (Journal Responses)
1. (If you are female): When someone refers to me as a "girl," I feel _____
_____because
_____.

2. (If you are male): I would feel _____ referring to a female as a "girl" because _____.

3. Given the choice, I prefer to watch television/go to the movies (choose either
"watch television" or "go to the movies") because _____.

JUST THE FACTS

1. The main idea of this selection is a) females are getting more parts as action figures in both movies and television; b) male action figures are more readily accepted than female figures; c) in movies, heroines get in trouble and heroes save them; d) martial arts figures can attract women as well as men.

2. John August, scriptwriter for *Charlie's Angels*, said those behind the film wanted the Angels a) to appeal to both male and female audiences; b) to show that they were capable of wild stunts; c) to be strong but not masculine; d) to use their sexuality as power.

3. For today's in-charge Hollywood woman, *le mot du jour* is a) feminism; b) girls; c) woman; d) entrepreneur.

4. Craig McCracken, the Powerpuff Girls' creator, said that a) people are starting to accept that girls are cool; b) the Powerpuff Girls have been chosen as role models for many Girl Scout groups; c) his sons had readily accepted the show; d) no one had ever asked him why the girls were so powerful.

5. According to the author, the action woman a) is the new superhero who will dominate domestic and foreign films; b) will probably never be as popular as the action man; c) is a figure who will be popular for just a short time; d) is a corrective to a zillion idiot action films.

EXPANDING HORIZONS

1. Pick one of the films mentioned in the selection (*Josie and the Pussycats; Crouching Tiger, Hidden Dragon; Charlie's Angels; Barbarella;* or *Lara Croft: Tomb Raider*) and write a movie review of it.

2. Conduct a poll in your class to see which genre of movies is the most popular: action, adventure, comedy, crime/gangster, drama, epics/historical, horror, musical, romance, science fiction, war, Western, or documentary.

3. A word's *denotation* is its literal definition, what you would find in a dictionary. Its *connotation*, however, is the impression that a word gives beyond its defined meaning. For example, the denotation of the word *home* is "the place where one lives"; its connotation suggests security, warmth, and, usually, family. Describe your connotation of these words:

girl   girlie   boy   man   feminism   masculinity

4. This selection says, "In all the great epics, from the Iliad on, the protagonists have been masculine, their destinies a masculine destiny." Read about the Iliad and write a summary of what you learn. Online sites to consult include these:

   www.enotes.com/iliad/
   luna.cas.usf.edu/~demilio/2211unit1/iliadplt.htm
   www.sparknotes.com/lit/iliad/summary.html
   classics.uc.edu/~johnson/epic/ilsum.html

5. If you were the head of a major movie or television studio, what kind of movies or shows would you greenlight? Why do you think the public needs more of this type of entertainment?

WRITE ON!

The author writes, "Flick on the TV, and see women—young women, almost always—kicking and thinking and winking at both the old notion of femininity and the aging precepts of feminism." Address one of these questions:

1. How do you define "femininity"?
2. How do you define "feminism"?
3. Would you like to see middle-aged or older women in action roles? Why or why not?

Has someone ever broken up with you to be with another person? This univesal and timeless problem has happened to almost everyone at one time or another. If you turn on the radio, you'll hear many songs that lament the loss of a loved one. But what if you had lived 100 years ago? You couldn't turn on the radio (it hadn't yet been invented), but many of the popular songs of the time focused on the same problems that confront people today. "St. Louis Blues," first published in 1914, is one of those songs. Here's one adaptation, which so famously recounts a woman's distress after her lover leaves her for someone else.

Words to Watch

apron strings: domination, power

Kentucky colonel: an honorable title (not a military rank) given by approval of the governor of Kentucky

powder: make-up

rock and rye: an American liquor made with rye whiskey and rocky candy syrup

store-bought: purchased (in this case, rather than grown)

St. Louis Blues
by W.C. Handy

I hate to see that evenin' sun go down,
I hate to see that evenin' sun go down,
'Cause my baby has done left this town.

If I'm feelin' tomorrow, just like I feel today,
If I'm feelin' tomorrow, like I feel today,
I'll pack my trunk and make my get-away.

St. Louis woman, with all her diamond rings,
Stole that man of mine, by her apron strings;
If it wasn't for powder, and her store-bought hair,
That man I love wouldn't've gone nowhere! Nowhere!

I've got the St. Louis blues, just as blue as I can be;
Lord, that man's got a heart like a rock cast in the sea,
Or else he wouldn't have gone so far from me!

Gee, I love that man like a school boy loves his pie,
Just like an old Kentucky colonel loves his rock and rye,
I guess I'll love that man until the day I die.

QUESTIONS

1. "St. Louis Blues" was one of the first blues songs to succeed in the popular culture of its day, almost 100 years ago. The genre of the blues, however, was not without its detractors. Just like hip-hop music is often frowned upon today (and, similarly, rock and roll was frowned upon in its early days), 100 years ago many people disapproved of blues music. Pick a type of music that you like and write a letter to someone defending your musical tastes.

2. Listen to a version of "St. Louis Blues" at www.archive.org/details/OriginalDixielandJazzBandwithAlBernard and write a musical review of it.

3. You're probably aware that an apostrophe often signals that letters are omitted. Usually this comes in a contraction, such as *isn't* (the apostrophe showing the *o* of *not* is omitted). In the song, note the apostrophe in the words *evenin'* and *feelin'*. This also shows that something has been omitted (in this case, the *g* at the end of the word), and Handy used it to try to mimic the way the woman would have spoken or sung the words. Write a few sentences of a recent conversation that you've had, using apostrophes for both common contractions and dropped letters.

Are you familiar with the television show Who Wants to be a Millionaire? *How about* Jeopardy!, The Price is Right, *or* Wheel of Fortune? *This article, written in 1999 when Millionaire was at its prime-time height, takes a look at popular past and present television game shows. Are you eager to learn about their long and sometimes checkered history? Is that your final answer?*

Starting Out...
If the television is on and you have the time, would you watch the game shows listed below or would you switch channels?

_____ watch	_____ switch channels	*Who Wants to Be a Millionaire?*
_____ watch	_____ switch channels	*Jeopardy!*
_____ watch	_____ switch channels	*The Price is Right*
_____ watch	_____ switch channels	*Wheel of Fortune*
_____ watch	_____ switch channels	*Deal or No Deal*
_____ watch	_____ switch channels	*Family Feud*

Words to Watch

attrition: gradual decrease in number or strength

emcee: master of ceremonies, the host of an event who introduces others

faltering: performing with a loss of effectiveness

futuristic: advanced, innovative, ultramodern

icon: one who is the object of great attention and devotion

irrelevance: something unrelated to a matter being considered

melodrama: a drama characterized by exaggerated emotions, and stereotypical
characters and conflicts

moniker: name

mundane: ordinary, boring

old hat: an idiom meaning "behind the times" or "old-fashioned"

plight: dilemma, troubles

prestige: esteem, high status

prolific: productive, creative

sham: fraud, hoax

venerable: respected, honored

Regis Makes Contestants, ABC Rich on "Millionaire"

by John Teti

From "Twenty-One" to "Greed," game shows have gone
from primetime fixtures to daytime has-beens and back.

The TV game show. Despite its obvious entertainment value, this genre has seen more ups and downs than a drunk on a roller coaster in its over fifty years on the air. But the recent success of "Who Wants to Be a Millionaire?"

on ABC this summer changed all that, transforming the game show from its former status as a novelty to a high-profile network ratings-grabber.

What took so long? To find out, let's take a brief look at the history of game shows, in which scandals, attrition and Ricki Lake all contribute to the genre's troubled past.

In the '50s, game shows were at the height of their popularity as the big-money quiz show ruled the prime-time airwaves. The June 1955 introduction of "The $64,000 Question" on CBS kicked off the craze.

The producers created the show with the idea of spectacle in mind. To this end, they created a format in which contestants only answered questions in their field of expertise. This way, questions that were moderately difficult for contestants were unimaginably hard for viewers, giving them the feeling that they were watching spectacular genius.

The melodrama of "risking it all" for the bigger money was the other important component that made "The $64,000 Question" a success, but such melodrama also damaged game shows' popularity for good. "Twenty-One," a Jack Barry & Dan Enright production, was created for NBC in response to CBS's hit. But "Twenty-One" couldn't naturally create tension and spectacle as "The $64,000 Question" did.

To compensate for their mundane format, Dan Enright made one of the most historic decisions in game show history—he rigged "Twenty-One." Enright figured that by supplying answers to certain contestants, he could make underdogs into superstars, boosting the ratings in the process.

It worked. The first celebrity Enright created was Herbert Stempel, but when better-looking, more charming and even more lovable Charles Van Doren tried out for the show, Enright got rid of Stempel in a hurry.

As Van Doren became more of a nationwide phenomenon (even making the cover of "Time" magazine), Stempel became more irate at his plight. Eventually, Stempel decided to blow the whistle by telling the press that "Twenty-One" was a sham. In late August 1958, the headlines read "Twenty-One Fixed!" By the end of the year, quiz shows had disappeared from television.

They were replaced by game shows that remained truer to that moniker by adapting board games or used similarly complex sets of rules. Visible elements of chance became more significant as shows desperately tried to demonstrate that they were not rigged. Despite these efforts, game shows would never attain their original prestige and popularity, but instead would be relegated to daytime television alongside soap operas.

It was during the '60s through '80s that the great game show producers determined the course of the industry. Mark Goodson and Bill Todman were probably the most prolific and accomplished game show producers. They created such games as "Password," "Family Feud" and the pop-culture icon "The Price is Right." Other venerable game creators included Bob Stewart ("The $10,000/ $25,000/... Pyramid") and Merv Griffin ("Wheel of Fortune," "Jeopardy!").

The one problem with these legendary producers? They're all old men. Of the four producers above, one is dead (Todman), two are retired (Goodson, Stewart) and one is too busy attending to his hotel and media empires to think of new game shows (Griffin).

Since the late '80s, shows have gradually disappeared from the air with nothing to replace them. Nobody was creating new games. In fact, the few new games that were created were just repackaging for old games. This trend is still visible—today's "Jeopardy!," "Hollywood Squares" and "Family Feud" are all copies of the originals.

Where were all the new producers? Didn't anybody know how to think of a game that would be fun to watch and play along with at home? Perhaps, but by the '90s, nobody cared about games.

The new craze was talk shows—the trashier, the better. Phil Donahue and Sally Jesse Raphael gave rise to Jerry Springer and Ricki Lake. Game shows were old hat; hair-trigger tempered divorcées and the cheating, cross-dressing spouses they once loved were what modern audiences wanted.

By the mid-'90s, the only established game shows on television were the few that were considered American traditions: "The Price is Right," "Wheel of Fortune," and "Jeopardy!"

One TV executive was disgusted with this trend, and he decided to do something about it. Earlier this year, Michael Davies, a producer for ABC, saw a popular British game show called "Who Wants to Be a Millionaire?" and decided that it would work just as well here in the States. ABC was not so convinced, but they gave Davies two weeks at the end of August—traditionally the time for some of the lowest TV ratings of the year. The network considered the show's limited run nothing more than an experiment.

Davies' version of "Who Wants to Be a Millionaire?" premiered with Regis Philbin as emcee, a futuristic, high-tech set and the largest jackpot in primetime history.

Viewers loved it; ABC saw August ratings higher than ever before. Some insiders said that Davies and Philbin had rescued the faltering network from a decline into irrelevance. The FOX network immediately set to work on a copycat, "Greed: The Multi-Million Dollar Challenge," which premiered last Thursday.

Has "Millionaire" restored the game show to its original prestige? No, because TV is a very different medium today. While "Millionaire" relies on spectacle to a certain degree as "The $64,000 Question" and "Twenty-One" did, the new show works because it uses "common" American citizens that viewers relate to instead of revering. The thrill of thinking, "That could be me!" as contestants climb the ladder to the million-dollar jackpot keeps people tuning in.

Will game shows ever disappear altogether from television? I doubt it. Game shows combine two things that Americans love: play and money. As long as producers keep coming up with new ways to make that combination, audiences will watch.

From Where I Stand... (Journal Responses)

1. If the FCC (Federal Communications Commission) determined that a game show was rigged, I think the punishment should be _____ because _____.
2. I think the best game show that has ever been on television was/is (choose either "was" or "is") _____ because _____.
3. If I could be a contestant on any game show (past or present), I would choose _____ _____ because _____.

Just the Facts

1. The main idea of this selection is a) in the last fifty years, many game shows have been discovered to have been rigged; b) game shows appeal to certain parts of the population but not to everybody; c) in television history, game shows have had great popularity and then have had their popularity diminish; d) many people find game shows insulting because of the way the contestants are treated.
2. Television game shows were at the height of their popularity in the a) 1950s; b) 1960s; c) 1980s; d) 1990s.
3. Dan Enright, Herbert Stempel, and Charles Van Doren became famous for a) tying for most money won in a single game; b) popularizing a new format of game shows; c) being involved in rigging a game show; d) being famous producers of a number of hit game shows.
4. Mark Goodson, Bill Todman, Bob Stewart, and Merv Griffin became famous for a) competing as a team and winning over two million dollars; b) reporting on game shows in both newspapers and magazines; c) being involved in rigging a game show; d) being famous producers of a number of hit game shows.
5. The author says that *Who Wants to Be a Millionaire?* works because a) Regis Philbin is such a good host; b) viewers can relate to the "common" American citizens on it; c) the prize money is so large; d) the format is one that is easy to follow.

Expanding Horizons

1. The 1994 move *Quiz Show*, directed by Robert Redford, is based on the scandal that arose from the game show *Twenty-One*. View this movie and then write a review of it.
2. Take a look at the latest news from game shows at www.tvgameshows.net/, then write a summary of what you learn.
3. Read more about the scandal that surrounded *Twenty-One* and write a biography of either Herbert Stempel or Charles Van Doren or write a summary of what happened on the show. Online sites to consult include these:

> Herbert Stempel: www.pbs.org/wgbh/amex/quizshow/peopleevents/pande01.html
> Charles Van Doren: www.pbs.org/wgbh/amex/quizshow/peopleevents/pande 02.html
> *Twenty-One*: www.biography.ms/Twenty_One_(game_show).html

4. Think of a television show that you dislike (it can be a show that's currently broadcast or one that's off the air). Write a letter to the head of the network, giving reasons why you dislike the show so much.

WRITE ON!

Write about what could be done to improve television. Questions you might consider include these:

1. What shows or types of shows need to be taken off the air?
2. What type of show does television need more of?
3. How could scheduling of shows be improved?
4. Even though commercials are necessary to pay for much of what is shown on television, how could they be changed to enhance the time you watch TV?

READ ON!

Ad Flip: The World's Largest Archives of Classic Print Ads. www.adflip.com/.

All Music Guide. www.allmusic.com/.

Billboard magazine. www.billboard.com/bb/index.jsp.

Bogart, Leo. *Over the Edge: How The Pursuit of Youth by Marketers and the Media Has Changed American Culture.* Chicago: Ivan R. Dee, 2005.

Browne, Ray B., and Browne, Pat, eds. *The Guide to United States Popular Culture.* Bowling Green, OH: Bowling Green State University Popular Press, 2001.

CineMedia: The Internet's Largest Film and Media Directory. www.cinemedia.org/welcomes/you.html.

Cirelli, Michael, and Sitomer, Alan. *Hip-Hop Poetry and the Classics.* Beverley Hills, CA: Milk Mug Publishing, 2004.

Cullen, Jim, ed. *Popular Culture in American History.* Malden, MA: Blackwell Publishers, 2001.

Dean, William D. *The American Spiritual Culture: And the Invention of Jazz, Football, and the Movies.* New York: Continuum, 2002.

"Fashion Models and Postmodern Consumer Society." www.eng.fju.edu.tw/Literary_Criticism/feminism/women/model.html.

"The Greatest Films." www.filmsite.org/.

"History of Film Theme Page." www.cln.org/themes/history_film.html

Neal, Mark Anthony. *Soul Babies: Black Popular Culture and the Post-Soul Aesthetic.* New York: Routledge, 2002.

Perone, James E. *Music of the Counterculture Era.* Westport, CT: Greenwood Press, 2004.

"Resource Center for Cyberculture Studies." www.com.washington.edu/rccs/.

Rolling Stone magazine. www.rollingstone.com/.

Shuker, Roy. *Understanding Popular Music.* London, New York: Routledge, 2001.

Vanderbilt University Television News Archive. tvnews.vanderbilt.edu/.

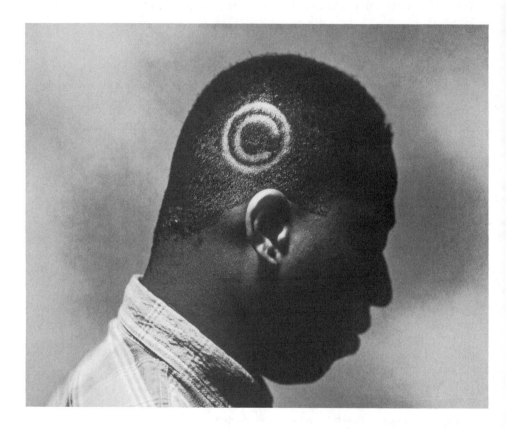

The symbol that is shaved into the man's head denotes a copyright, the legal right given to an author, composer, playwright, publisher, or distributor to exclusive publication, production, sale, or distribution of a literary, musical, dramatic, or artistic work. Write about the significance of the copyright symbol on the man. What does it imply? In what ways are we all alike and in what ways are we different? Write about what defines you and what makes you different from everyone else.

CHAPTER THREE

IDENTITY

You Are Unique, Just Like Everyone Else

A man cannot be comfortable without his own approval.   —*Mark Twain*

An identity would seem to be arrived at by the way in which the person faces and uses his experience.   —*James Arthur Baldwin*

Be as you wish to seem.   —*Socrates*

Don't back down just to keep the peace. Standing up for your beliefs builds self-confidence and self-esteem.   —*Oprah Winfrey*

It is better to be hated for what you are than to be loved for what you are not.   —*Andre Gide*

Know thyself.   —*Inscription at Delphi in ancient Greece*

Men can starve from a lack of self-realization as much as they can from a lack of bread.   —*Richard Wright*

Men's minds are too ready to excuse guilt in themselves.   —*Titus Livius*

Never envy people unless you are willing to swap identities with them.   —*Anonymous*

One of the most wonderful things in nature is a glance of the eye; it transcends speech; it is the bodily symbol of identity.   —*Ralph Waldo Emerson*

One's real life is often the life that one does not lead.   —*Oscar Wilde*

The value of a human being can be found in the degree to which he has attained liberation from the self.   —*Albert Einstein*

This above all: to thine own self be true.   —*Polonius, in Shakespeare's* Hamlet

Those people who are uncomfortable in themselves are disagreeable to others.   —*William Hazlitt*

Identity: You Are Unique, Just Like Everyone Else

What puts the "I" in your *i*ndividual *i*dentity? If you were asked to define yourself, what would you say? How are you like others? More importantly, what particular characteristics make you different from everybody else? If your friends or relatives were asked to define you, would they name the same characteristics that you cited?

What has changed about the way you approach life now as compared to five or ten years ago? Are you more self-confident? Are you more aware of what makes you a unique being? Do you handle yourself better when you're in a crowd or in a situation that you find intimidating?

When asked to talk about themselves, some people initially speak in terms of their work ("My name is Samuel, and I'm an engineer at Hall and Company"). Others define themselves in terms of their relationship to others ("I'm Clara, Cecil's wife and Claudia's mother"). Still others name some physical possession they are associated with ("I'm Pamela, and I live in the green Queen Anne house across the street").

But many factors other than these make us individuals and give us our sense of identity. Of course, your physical characteristics set you apart from others, but you can also look at crucial times when you were growing up. In what ways were you shaped by the way your parents or guardians reared you? What other influential adults from your life when you were young, like teachers, members of the clergy, or neighbors, helped to shape who you are today?

And what about your education? Can you list any past experiences in school that had an influence on your adult life? What educational experiences outside of school have affected you?

What features of your personality are important in your identity? Are you trusting or suspicious of others? Do you consider yourself generous or thrifty— or somewhere in between? Do you go out of your way to make friends, or do you wait for others to approach you? Do you usually take control of situations or wait for someone to tell you what should be done? Do you tend to question authority or assume that the powers that be are often right?

When did you develop the style of dress that you now prefer? Does the way you dress say anything about the individual you are? What about the way you conduct yourself around others; how has this changed over time? Do you feel more comfortable being alone or in a group? Do you work better alone or in a group? At a party, do you tend to stay to yourself or to mingle?

Strange as it may seem, your identity might even be influenced by your name. Has anyone ever commented on your name? Are you comfortable with your name or nickname?

This chapter includes selections that examine what identity is, how different people react to similar situations, how we are affected by the way others treat us, and how individuals are both unique and alike.

Now that you have read the introduction to this chapter, go back and reread the quotations on p. 57. Then choose one of the quotations and write about whether you agree or disagree with it. Be sure to defend your opinion.

Elizabeth Cady Stanton, *first involved in the abolitionist movement and later a famous suffragette, published her autobiography when she was an octogenarian. In this chapter she looks back at a time when, as a young girl, she wanted to take the place—at least, in her father's eyes—of her brother who had died.*

Starting Out...

Circle A if you agree with the statement or D if you disagree.

A D   Parents should always share their grief with their children.

A D   Children sometimes misinterpret what their parents say to them.

A D   Sometimes an adult who is not a family member can have a greater influence on a child than a parent has.

Words to Watch

bequeath: leave in a will after one dies

cortège: funeral procession

exhortation: urgent appeal

gave vent to: an idiom meaning "expressed an emotion"

grammar: in this case, a book of grammar

lexicon: dictionary

suffragette: a supporter of giving women the right to vote

vexation: annoyance, irritation

Eighty Years and More: Reminiscences 1815–1897
by Elizabeth Cady Stanton

Chapter II
School Days

When I was eleven years old, two events occurred which changed considerably the current of my life. My only brother, who had just graduated from Union College, came home to die. A young man of great talent and promise, he was the pride of my father's heart. We early felt that this son filled a larger place in our father's affections and future plans than the five daughters together. Well do I remember how tenderly he watched my brother in his last illness, the sighs and tears he gave vent to as he slowly walked up and down the hall, and, when the last sad moment came, and we were all assembled to say farewell in the silent chamber of death, how broken were his utterances as he knelt and prayed for comfort and support. I still recall, too, going into the large darkened parlor to see my brother, and finding the casket, mirrors, and pictures all draped in white, and my father seated by his side, pale and immovable. As he took no notice of me, after standing a long while, I climbed upon his knee, when he mechanically put his arm about me and, with my head resting against his beating heart, we both sat in silence, he thinking of the wreck of all his hopes in the loss of a dear son, and I wondering what could be said or done to fill the void in his breast. At length he heaved a deep sigh and said: "Oh, my daughter, I wish you were a boy!" Throwing my arms about his neck, I replied: "I will try to be all my brother was."

Then and there I resolved that I would not give so much time as heretofore to play, but would study and strive to be at the head of all my classes and thus delight my father's heart. All that day and far into the night I pondered the problem of boyhood. I thought that the chief thing to be done in order to equal boys was to be learned and courageous. So I decided to study Greek and learn to manage a horse. Having formed this conclusion I fell asleep. My resolutions, unlike many such made at night, did not vanish with the coming light. I arose early and hastened to put them into execution. They were resolutions never to be forgotten—destined to mold my character anew. As soon as I was dressed I hastened to our good pastor, Rev. Simon Hosack, who was always early at work in his garden.

"Doctor," said I, "which do you like best, boys or girls?"

"Why, girls, to be sure; I would not give you for all the boys in Christendom."

"My father," I replied, "prefers boys; he wishes I was one, and I intend to be as near like one as possible. I am going to ride on horseback and study Greek. Will you give me a Greek lesson now, doctor? I want to begin at once."

"Yes, child," said he, throwing down his hoe, "come into my library and we will begin without delay."

He entered fully into the feeling of suffering and sorrow which took possession of me when I discovered that a girl weighed less in the scale of being than a boy, and he praised my determination to prove the contrary. The old grammar which he had studied in the University of Glasgow was soon in my hands, and the Greek article was learned before breakfast.

Then came the sad pageantry of death, the weeping of friends, the dark rooms, the ghostly stillness, the exhortation to the living to prepare for death, the solemn prayer, the mournful chant, the funeral cortège, the solemn, tolling bell, the burial. How I suffered during those sad days! What strange undefined fears of the unknown took possession of me! For months afterward, at the twilight hour, I went with my father to the new-made grave. Near it stood two tall poplar trees, against one of which I leaned, while my father threw himself on the grave, with outstretched arms, as if to embrace his child.

At last the frosts and storms of November came and threw a chilling barrier between the living and the dead, and we went there no more.

During all this time I kept up my lessons at the parsonage and made rapid progress. I surprised even my teacher, who thought me capable of doing anything. I learned to drive, and to leap a fence and ditch on horseback. I taxed every power, hoping some day to hear my father say: "Well, a girl is as good as a boy, after all." But he never said it. When the doctor came over to spend the evening with us, I would whisper in his ear: "Tell my father how fast I get on," and he would tell him, and was lavish in his praises. But my father only paced the room, sighed, and showed that he wished I were a boy; and I, not knowing why he felt thus, would hide my tears of vexation on the doctor's shoulder.

Soon after this I began to study Latin, Greek, and mathematics with a class of boys in the Academy, many of whom were much older than I. For three years one boy kept his place at the head of the class, and I always stood next. Two prizes were offered in Greek. I strove for one and took the second. How well I remember my joy in receiving that prize. There was no sentiment of ambition, rivalry, or triumph over my companions, nor feeling of satisfaction in receiving this honor in the presence of those assembled on the day of the exhibition. One thought alone filled my mind. "Now," said I, "my father will be satisfied with me." So, as soon as we were dismissed, I ran down the hill, rushed breathless into his office, laid the new Greek Testament, which was my prize, on his table and exclaimed: "There, I got it!" He took up the book, asked me some questions about the class, the teachers, the spectators, and, evidently pleased, handed it back to me. Then, while I stood looking and waiting for him to say something which would show that he recognized the equality of the daughter with the son, he kissed me on the forehead and exclaimed, with a sigh, "Ah, you should have been a boy!"

My joy was turned to sadness. I ran to my good doctor. He chased my bitter tears away, and soothed me with unbounded praises and visions of future success. He was then confined to the house with his last illness. He asked me that day if I would like to have, when he was gone, the old lexicon, Testament, and grammar that we had so often thumbed together. "Yes, but I would rather have you stay," I replied, "for what can I do when you are gone?" "Oh," said he tenderly, "I shall not be gone; my spirit will still be with you, watching you in all life's struggles." Noble, generous friend! He had but little on earth to bequeath to anyone, but when the last scene in his life was ended, and his will was opened, sure enough there was a clause saying: "My Greek lexicon, Testament, and grammar, and four volumes of Scott's commentaries, I will to Elizabeth Cady." I never look at these books without a feeling of thankfulness that in childhood I was blessed with such a friend and teacher.

From Where I Stand… (Journal Responses)
  1. I think that Elizabeth's father should have _____
     because _____.
  2. A time when I was not recognized for my achievements came when _____
     _____.
  3. A time when I was a child and tried to comfort an adult came when _____
     _____.

JUST THE FACTS

1. The main idea of this selection is that Elizabeth Cady Stanton a) found someone who believed in her; b) tried to please her father; c) became interested in the abolitionist movement; d) became interested in the suffrage movement.
2. A tragedy occurred with the death of Elizabeth's a) mother; b) father; c) sister; d) brother.
3. Elizabeth's father told her that he wished she a) would reconsider her decision to go to college; b) were a boy; c) could stay at home with the family; d) would be "a voice of reason."
4. Elizabeth decided to study a) German; b) Greek; c) French; d) Spanish.
5. Simon Hosack was a) the slave Elizabeth helped to escape; b) the man Elizabeth fell in love with; c) Elizabeth's pastor; d) opposed to women having the right to vote.

EXPANDING HORIZONS

1. Read another chapter from Elizabeth Cady Stanton's autobiography and compare it with this chapter. Her book is available online at www.blackmask.com/thatway/books154c/eigstan.htm.
2. Elizabeth Cady Stanton is best remembered for her part in the women's suffrage movement. Read biographies of her and summarize her work in this movement. Online sources include these:
   www.nps.gov/wori/ecs.htm
   digital.library.upenn.edu/women/stanton/years/years-II.html
   www.americanswhotellthetruth.org/pgs/portraits/E_Cady_Stanton.html
3. In her studies, Elizabeth learned Greek. Research Greek letters, how they are written, their names, their equivalent English letters at this site: www.ibiblio.org/koine/greek/lessons/alphabet.html.
4. Elizabeth also learned how to ride a horse. Research riding methods used today and summarize what you learn. Online sites to consult include these:
   www.ehow.com/how_10761_learn-ride-horse.html
   www.lifestyleblock.co.nz/articles/Horses/06_Learn_to_Ride.htm

WRITE ON!

1. Elizabeth thought that studying Greek and learning about horses would make her more like a boy. Given the same circumstances today, what do you think young Elizabeth would elect to study?

2. In the twenty-first century, what classes do you think that all young men should take in school? What about all young women? Why?

3. Think of a person—not a family member—who has had a positive effect on your life. Write some of the circumstances behind why you chose that person.

I'm Nobody! Who Are You?
by Emily Dickinson

Words to Watch
banish: expel, send away   **bog:** swamp, marsh

I'm Nobody! Who are you?
Are you—Nobody—Too?
Then there's a pair of us?
Don't tell! They'd advertise—you know!

How dreary—to be—Somebody!
How public—like a Frog—
To tell one's name—the livelong June—
To an admiring Bog!

Questions

1. Think about a time when you felt like an outsider, and then you suddenly found someone to connect with. That is what happens in this poem. In the first line, the speaker says that she's "nobody" and asks another person if he or she is "nobody, too."

2. Because the two "nobodies" have found each other, they really aren't nobodies anymore. The speaker says that they must keep their friendship a secret or else "they'd banish us." Write about who "they" might be.

3. Write about whether you agree or disagree that having a friend—even it it's someone you've just met—is more important than being in the limelight. Alternately, write about whether you find it "dreary to be somebody" or you prefer to be in the limelight.

4. Emily Dickinson lived a very curious life. Read short biographies of her and then summarize what you learn. Online sites to consult include these:

    www.online-literature.com/dickinson/
    www.americanpoems.com/poets/emilydickinson/
    womenshistory.about.com/library/bio/bldickinson.htm
    www.cswnet.com/~erin/edbio.htm

*Just how opposite is the opposite sex? Do you think that babies are born with "blank slates," so the adults in their lives can influence their personalities and behavior as the children grow? What effect does play have to do with social-ization of children? In this selection, science writer **Deborah Blum** addresses these and other fascinating questions.*

Starting Out...
Circle A if you agree with the statement or D if you disagree.

A D   Little boys who ask for a soldier equipped with battle cannons for their birthday should get the present.

A D   Little boys who ask for a Barbie or other doll for their birthday should get the present.

A D   Levels of testosterone shoot up before competition.

Words to Watch

adrenal gland: either of two glands, one located above each kidney

analogous: similar in such a way as to permit drawing a comparison

androgens: hormones, such as testosterone, that control masculine characteristics

chicken-or-egg aspect: having to do with the question "Which came first—the chicken or the egg?" That is, a situation in which one cannot provide either item because one lacks the other

congenital adrenal hyperplasia: an inherited condition that affects the adrenal glands

continuum: a continuous extent, succession, or whole

dismembering: pulling off the limbs of

gender neutrality: free from reference to gender or sex, as in the term *police officer* (instead of *policewoman* or *policeman*)

gravitate: to be attracted as if by an irresistible force

in utero: in the uterus, the female organ in which a fertilized egg develops

neuroscientist: a scientist studying the nervous system

neurotransmitters: a chemical substance that transmits nerve impulses

phallic symbols: forms considered to be representations of the penis

splitting hairs: an idiom meaning "focusing on details that are not important"

testosterone: a hormone produced primarily in the testes and responsible for male secondary sex characteristics

What's the Difference Between Boys and Girls?

by Deborah Blum

A funny thing happened when we left "puppy dogs' tails" and "sugar and spice" behind. Scientists discovered that it's not just our culture that makes rules about gender-appropriate behavior—it's our own body chemistry.
—*Science*, cover story

My four-year-old son asked for a Barbie this year. His blue eyes were hopeful, his small face angelic. His mother was suspicious.

Between this child and his older brother, our house is a Toys R Us warehouse of heavily muscled action figures, dinosaurs with jagged teeth, light-up swords and leaking water pistols. Complaint is constant—Oh, Mom, you're no fun—over my refusal to buy more additions to the arsenal. My older son at one point began to see weapons in household objects the way adults dream up phallic symbols. "Shoot her with the toothbrush," he once shouted to a companion as they chased the cat around the house.

"Why do you want the Barbie, honey?" I asked.

"I wanna chop her head off."

There I was again, standing at the edge of the great gender divide, the place and the moment where one becomes absolutely sure that the opposite sex is, in fact, opposite. I know of no way for women of my generation, raised to believe in gender neutrality, to reach this edge faster than through trying to raise children.

"I did not do this," a friend insisted on the day her son started carefully biting his toast into the shape of a gun. "I think my daughter has a pink gene," a British journalist confided recently, as she confessed that her daughter has not only a Barbie collection but all the matched plastic purses and tiny high-heeled shoes. I don't think in pastels myself. I think jungle-green, blood-red. Most of all, I think there's a reason—a reasonable biology—to the differences we see in little boys and girls, men and women, males and females.

We are, I hope, moving past the old politically correct notion that we are pure culture, that children are born blank slates to be influenced—or, worse, manipulated—by the adults around them. There's a straightforward reason why we are a male-female species: Reproductively, it works. We are all born with bodies designed to be the same (breathe, circulate blood) and to be different (produce sperm, produce eggs, produce milk, produce none). There's an internal biology—structural and behavioral—that supports those differences. It's not all of who we are, but it's a part. When is biology the primary influence? Where does culture overtake it, and at what point, in the startlingly fluid landscape of human behavior, does one alter the other?

One of my favorite illustrations of the way culture fine-tunes us for gender roles has to do with the Barbie versus Godzilla effect. It turns out that lots of little boys ask for dolls and other so-called girl toys. They aren't encouraged, though; parents really hesitate to buy their children "gender inappropriate" toys. In a study involving almost 300 children, researchers found that if little boys asked for a soldier equipped with battle cannons for their birthday, they got it some 70 percent of the time. If they asked for a Barbie doll, or any of her plastic peers, the success rate was 40 percent or less. Can you think of a child who wouldn't figure out in, oh, a day, how to work that system?

Marc Breedlove, a neuroscientist at the University of California, Berkeley, points out that splitting apart biology and culture is analogous to splitting hairs. But scientists try to separate the strands anyway, exhaustively exploring early development. A few ambitious scientists have even looked for prebirth differences, arguing that it's difficult to slap too much cultural attitude onto a fetus. It turns out that boy fetuses are a little more active, more restless, than girl fetuses. And in the first year after birth, toy preferences already seem distinct: Boy infants rapidly engage with more mechanical or structural toys; little girls of a few months gravitate toward toys with faces, toys that can be cuddled.

The world of play—the toys we gravitate to, how we play with them, how we play in general—has now become serious business to scientists. Today's hottest theory of play is that it's a practice run at the challenges of adult life. Through games, the experts tell us, we learn the art of measuring the competition, how to win and lose gracefully (we hope), which leads pretty directly into how to build friendships. In scientific terms, we learn socialization.

"Play offers a non-life-threatening way of asserting yourself," says Christine Drea, a researcher. "By playing, you learn skills of managing competition and aggression." We are a social species. We find isolation destructive, and we establish patterns of childhood play that reflect adult social structures. In humans, our patterns tend to conform to our chemistry: Human males are likely to produce seven to 10 times more testosterone, for example, than females.... And so, you would correctly predict, little boys tend to be more rough-and-tumble than little girls. That's true, in fact, for the entire realm of primates (monkeys, apes, man).

Back in the late 1970s, Robert Goy, a psychologist at the University of Wisconsin, first documented that young male monkeys consistently played much more roughly than juvenile females. Goy then went on to show that if you manipulate testosterone level—raising it in females, cutting it off in males—you reverse those effects, creating sweet little boy monkeys and rough-and-tumble girls. We don't experiment with human development this way, obviously. But there are naturally occurring genetic variations that make closely comparable points. As mentioned earlier, human males circulate higher levels of testosterone. There's a well-known exception, however, called congenital adrenal hyperplasia (CAH), in which a baby girl's adrenal gland inadvertently boosts testosterone levels. Researchers have found that CAH girls, in general, prefer trucks and cars and aggressive play. That doesn't mean they don't join in more traditional girl games with friends—but if left to choose, they prefer to play on the rowdy side of the street.

Higher testosterone levels are also responsible for another characteristic: competitiveness. In fact, testosterone is almost predictable in this regard. It shoots up before a competition; that's been measured in everything from chess matches to soccer games to courtroom battles to brawls. It stays up if you win, drops if you lose. Its role, scientists think, is to get you up and running and right on the competitive edge.

Even in preschool, boys and girls fall into very different play patterns. Boys tend to gather in larger, competitive groups. They play games that have clear winners and losers and bluster through them, boasting about their skills. Girls, early on, gather in small groups, playing theatrical games that don't feature hierarchy or winners. One study of children aged three to four found they were already resolving conflict in separate ways—boys resorting to threats, girls negotiating verbally and often reaching a compromise.

There are some provocative new insights into that verbal difference. Recently, researchers at Emory University have found that little female monkeys are much quicker to pick up "verbal" skills than little boy monkeys. Sound familiar? The small female monkeys do more contact calling (cooing affectionately) than their male counterparts. And it appears, again, that this is related to their mothers' prenatal hormones. Some very preliminary tests suggest that females exposed to androgens early in their fetal development become more like male monkeys: They are less likely to use language to express themselves.

In humans, too, we look for natural biological variations. In general, girls have sharper hearing than boys—the tiny hair cells that register sound waves vibrate more forcefully. These are ears tuned for intense communication. (The rare exception tends to be in boy-girl twin pairs. Those girls are more likely to have ears built a little more like their brothers'—less active hair cells, notched-down response. Researchers looking at this suspect a higher exposure to androgens in utero.) There's something about the biology of the egg-producing sex that seems to demand more acute communication abilities.

Of course, there's a whole range of personalities and behaviors that don't fall into any of the obvious stereotypes. What about tomboys, those exuberant girls who prefer softball to tea parties? What about the affectionate sweetness of little boys, who—away from the battle zone of their friends and brothers—turn out to be surprisingly cuddly and clingy? What about the female stiff, the chatty male, and so on, into infinity? The quick answer: Sex differences are group differences, overall patterns.

The complex of genes and hormones and neurotransmitters and internal chemistry that may influence our behaviors varies from person to person and is designed to be flexible. There's nothing in average, everyday biology that forbids either the truck-loving girl or the boy who likes to play house, the aggressive, competitive adult woman or the nurturing, stay-at-home man. Human biology makes room for every possible type of personality and sexuality in the range between those stereotypes.

And finally, the way we behave can actually influence our biology. The link between testosterone and competition makes this point perfectly. Yes, corporate lawyers tend to have higher testosterone levels than ministers. But there's a chicken-or-egg aspect to this. Is the lawyer someone born with a high testosterone level? Or is it the profession that pushed it up? Or some combination of both? It's worth noting that the parallel works in men and in women; women in competitive jobs have more testosterone; men who stay home with their children have less.

Nothing in biology labels behaviors as right or wrong, normal or abnormal. Any stereotypes we impose on children—and, by extension, adults—are purely cultural, not biological. For example: Little boys are noisy and rambunctious; we tend to equate that with being emotionally tough. But what science actually tells us is the exact opposite. Little boys, we're learning, need a lot of emotional support. One revealing study of children of depressed and withdrawn mothers, done at U.C. Berkeley, found that a lack of affection actually lowered the IQ of little boys. Laura Allen, a neuroscientist at the University of California, Los Angeles, explains it like this: "I think boys need more one-on-one attention. I think affection may change the sex hormone level in the brain, which then affects brain development." Both the Berkeley study and a more recent federal daycare study find a different pattern in girls. They're emotionally sturdier—I think most of us have already figured this out—and their healthy development seems most harmed by being restricted. It's confinement that seems to drive down IQ in our daughters.

What's the real difference between boys and girls? More, and less, than we thought. With rare exceptions, the anatomy of gender is straightforward, separate. But the chemistry of gender is more complex. It's a continuum, I think, and we can each find a place within the wide band of "normal." What's more, we can change our place. And we can influence our children's places—not by force but by guidance.

And so, if you're wondering, I did not buy my son the doll. I'm too grown up these days to approve of dismembering pricey toys. I did let him pick out a scaled-down Barbie, instead of a toy car, in one of those fast-food kid's meal promotions. It turned out to be cream and gold in appearance, annoyingly indestructible, and he lost interest. These days, he likes to make books and draw pictures of blood-dripping dinosaurs. Me? I pass him the red crayons.

From Where I Stand... (Journal Responses)

1. I think that the most money that should be spent for a toy for a child whom I'm close to is _____
because _____.

2. If a male child whom I am close to asked me to buy him a doll, I would/would not (choose either "would" or "would not") because _____
_____.

3. When I was a child, one of my favorite toys was _____
_____ ; I liked
it because _____.

JUST THE FACTS

1. The main idea of this selection is that boys and girls a) have more—and fewer—differences that previously thought; b) can be "programmed" to think like the opposite sex; c) have different levels of testosterone and hormones; d) must be given the toys that they request in order to lead normal lives later in life.

2. The author's son said he wanted a particular toy so that he could a) take it to play with his friend Sam; b) complete the set he had already started; c) let his friends in kindergarten see what the toy looked like; d) chop off its head.

3. The author cites a survey that found that boys who asked for soldiers for their birthday got the toy about a) 70 percent of the time; b) 60 percent of the time; c) 50 percent of the time; d) 40 percent of the time.

4. The selection states that girl infants often lean toward a) mechanical or structural toys; b) toys that have specific colors; c) toys with faces or that can be cuddled; d) toys that have soothing sounds.

5. Researchers have found that CAH (congenital adrenal hyperplasia) girls, in general, prefer a) toys that are pink or baby blue; b) toys that have faces and can be cuddled; c) dolls made of soft material; d) trucks and cars and aggressive play.

EXPANDING HORIZONS

1. "Nature versus nurture" is a phrase used to describe debates over the degrees to which a person's inherited makeup (that is, a person's nature) and a person's life experiences, education, or training (that is, nurturing) influence his or her traits or attributes. Read one of the following articles about this subject and write a summary of it:

    www.alternet.org/mediaculture/20593/

    observer.guardian.co.uk/science/story/0,1596,796600,00.html

    folk.uio.no/roffe/faq/node11.html

2. Visit the National Toy Hall of Fame at www.strongmuseum.org/NTHoF/NTHoF.html; then click on at least three of the toys to read more in-depth material. Summarize what you learn.
3. Take a look at toy trivia at www.thelittlewoodshop.co.uk/toy-trivia.php; then explain which two pieces of trivia you found the most interesting.
4. The author writes of "gender neutrality." Advocates of gender neutrality in language argue that gender-specific words and phrases are sexist and should be changed in order to not favor one sex over the other. The terms "aviatrix" and "poetess," for example, have all but disappeared in favor of "aviator" and "poet." Take a look at these sentences that use gender-specific words or phrases (in italics below) and determine what gender-neutral words or phrases could be substituted.

   The *policeman* came to my rescue after the wreck.

   Thank goodness for the *fireman* who extinguished the fire quickly.

   One *stewardess* in particular was helpful during my first flight.

   Has the *postman* delivered today's mail?

   The meeting was called to order by the *chairman*.

   The *male nurse* helped Mom after her surgery.

WRITE ON!

1. Suppose you have at least $1000 to spend on toys for a child—your own child, a niece or nephew, or another child whom you've become close to. What particular toys would you choose, and why would you choose them?
2. Think back to your childhood and relate how competitive—either in play or in the classroom—you were. Give specific examples.
3. In Shakespeare's *Romeo and Juliet*, Juliet says, "What's in a name? That which we call a rose by any other name would smell as sweet…" Explain what she means by this and then either defend or refute her statement.

Can names serve as any indication about a person's future? In this selection, which appeared in the March 5, 2006, edition of the Evansville (IN) Courier & Press, *columnist **Rich Davis** looks at how he eventually came to appreciate his name, and he presents questions about some common and not-so-common names.*

Starting Out...

Read the following statements and then circle A if you agree or D if you disagree.

> A D A person's first name can determine what others think about him or her.
>
> A D What a person is named can determine what happens to him or her later in life.
>
> A D I like my first and middle names.

Words to Watch

a la: in the style of, in the manner of

Baghdad: an allusion (reference) to the U.S. war in Iraq

barbs: insults, digs

blast: attack, assault

conventional: traditional, unadventurous

from the same cloth: an idiom meaning "very similar to"

loosen her grip on the pocketbook: an idiom meaning "become not as stingy" or "spend some money"

magical carpet ride: an allusion (reference) to a flying carpet, featured in the Arabian Nights stories, that takes people anywhere they want to go

mellowing: gaining wisdom or tolerance, usually from maturity

misgivings: doubts, suspicions

Nomen est omen: Latin for "Names are destiny"

planted: placed, gave to

rolled off his tongue: an idiom meaning "sounded" or "was easy to say"

sportier: flashier, jazzier

this bites: slang for "this is very annoying or unpleasant"

Titanic: the ill-fated ship that sank on its first voyage in 1912

Names Are Destiny? Tell That to "Richie"

by Rich Davis

My older brother John Paul surprised me recently when he said he wished he had my middle name—Powell. He liked the way it rolled off his tongue, the fact that it was our grandfather's middle name.

In the days before kids became walking report cards (The lower the pants, the lower the grades?) and Baghdad was still a magical carpet ride, Grandpa Davis was the best part of a Sunday visit to our grandparents' house, with its gloomy drapes, old piano and Yorkshire pudding.

Grandpa was from Wales. He came to this country to mine coal in Southern Illinois, sending for his blue-eyed English bride in 1912. Grandma was booked on the *Titanic*, but a lucky, last-minute illness put her on a later ship.

Grandpa would tell Grandma to loosen her grip on the pocketbook long enough to give us ice cream money. Tall and dignified, and with a nice singing voice, he was from the same cloth as the miners in the 1941 movie "How Green Was My Valley." Suspenders, pocket watch, pipe tobacco.

I was named after him—Richard Powell.

To be frank, I hated the name, as well as the nickname—Richie—an uncle planted on me. In college I finally became Rich, free of the "Richie Rich" and "Itchy Richie" barbs from pals with more desirable names: Greg, Doug, Jeff.

There were times I wondered if my life would have been different had I been named Scott or Mike or something sportier. Would I have been more athletic, more popular, more confident? Treated more favorably by teachers?

The Romans have a saying: "Nomen est omen." Names are destiny. But do we grow into our names, or do they shape us? Did Oprah Winfrey, Leonardo DiCaprio or Keanu Reeves ever have misgivings?

Before you blast me with something that rhymes with Richie, please know that today I feel honored to be named after my grandfather— and glad he didn't have a really strange name, such as Avis. Then I'd be Avis Davis.

Maybe this mellowing comes from reading tabloid headlines at check-out counters. Demi Moore's daughters are Scout, Rumer and Tallulah Belle. Julia Roberts' twins are Phinnaeus and Hazel. Nicolas Cage named his son Kal-el (a la Superman). Gwyneth Paltrow's little girl is Apple—as in computer or "this bites"? Celebrities don't seem to be following www.babycenter.com, which indicates the most popular names in 2005 were Aidan, Jacob, Ethan, Nicholas, Matthew, Ryan, Tyler, Jack, Joshua and Andrew. And for girls, Emma, Emily, Madison, Kaitlyn, Sophia, Isabella, Olivia, Hannah, Makayla and Ava.

While my parents were conventional (kids named Sue, John, Richard and Christine), it was more interesting up the block at the Zavich household. Mr. and Mrs. Zavich were Yugoslavian immigrants who ran a bakery on Main Street. Each Zavich child's name began with V, from Vlado and Vello to Vida and Vera, until they apparently ran out of Vs and named the youngest Nancy.

From Where I Stand... (Journal Responses)
1. One aspect of "Names Are Destiny? Tell That to 'Richie'" that I'd like to learn more about is _____.
2. If I had a new baby (choose either "boy" or "girl"), I would name the child _____ because _____.
3. The funniest/most appropriate/most inappropriate/weirdest (choose either "funniest," "most appropriate," "most inappropriate," or "weirdest") name I ever heard was _____ because _____.

JUST THE FACTS

1. The main idea of this selection is the author a) has come to appreciate his name; b) wishes that he had "a more exotic name like Kal-el"; c) resents being insulted by his family about his name; d) has convinced his wife that his children's names should all begin with "V."
2. The author says that he was surprised when his brother a) named his son after the author; b) asked to be called by a new nickname; c) said he wished he had the author's middle name; d) named his daughter after Oprah Winfrey.
3. The author was named after a) President Richard Nixon; b) his grandfather; c) his father's brother (his Uncle Richard); d) the actor Richard Gere.
4. One of the popular baby names in 2005 was *not* a) Emma; b) Jacob; c) Apple; d) Isabella.
5. The author writes of a family that a) nicknamed each of their children after one of the Seven Dwarves; b) used Billy or Billie as a middle name for each of the children; c) gave both of their children a first name, followed by three middle names; d) named most of their children with a name that began with "V."

EXPANDING HORIZONS

1. Choose one of the following to write about:
   - why you were given the name you have (ask parents, other relatives, or older friends)
   - why one of your friends was given the name he or she has
   - how you decided on the name of one of your children
2. Visit www.mit.edu/~perfors/hotornot.pdf to read Amy Perfors's article "The Effect of Sound Symbolism on Perception of Facial Attractiveness." Then summarize what you learn.
3. Davis uses imagery (words that appeal to various senses) when he describes the family's Sunday visits to his grandparents' house: "its gloomy drapes, old piano and Yorkshire pudding." Think of a home you visited in your childhood and write about it, describing as many of the sights, sounds, smells, and tastes as you can remember.
4. Interview as many of your older relatives as possible to create your own family tree. When you are speaking to relatives, ask for any interesting stories that they may have about your ancestors, and write a summary of the best story you learn. Then download a family tree form at genealogy.about.com/library/free_charts/ Family_Tree.pdf and fill it in with as much information as you can.

5. Read "What's in a Name: Highlights from Our 2005 Baby Name Survey" at www.babycenter.com/refcap/pregnancy/babynaming/1447507.html and summarize the results from the survey.

WRITE ON!

1. Your cousin Emily and her husband are expecting a child at the same time you are. Emily has written to you that she wants to call her baby the same name that you've already picked out for your new offspring. Write a letter to your cousin, explaining your feelings about what she has written.
2. You have recently discovered that you're about to become a parent. Write your reasons why you do or do not want to know the sex of the baby before he or she arrives.
3. A friend of yours has given you (or your child) a nickname that you despise. Write a letter to that person, detailing your reasons why you dislike the name and explaining why you prefer not to be called by that name.

READ ON!

"Baby Name Traits." www.americanbaby.com/ab/babynames/traits.jhtml.

"Baby Names." www.americanbaby.com/ab/babynames/popularNames.jhtml.

Blum, Deborah. *Sex on the Brain: The Biological Differences Between Men and Women.* New York: Viking, 1997.

"Deborah Blum." en.wikipedia.org/wiki/Deborah_Blum.

Dickson, Paul. *What's in a Name? Reflections of an Irrepressible Name Collector.* Springfield, MA: Merriam-Webster, 1996.

Goo, Sara Kehaulani. 2004. "Sen. Kennedy Flagged by No-Fly List." *Washington Post* August 20. www.washingtonpost.com/wp-dyn/articles/A17073-2004Aug19.html

Gordon, Ann D., ed. *The Selected Papers of Elizabeth Cady Stanton and Susan B. Anthony.* New Brunswick, NJ: Rutgers University Press, 1997.

Higgins, David James Monroe. *Portrait of Emily Dickinson; The Poet and Her Prose.* New Brunswick, NJ: Rutgers University Press, 1967.

Norman, Teresa. *A World of Baby Names.* New York: Berkley Pub. Group, 1996.

"The Poetry of Emily Dickinson: Complete Poems of 1924." www.bartleby.com/113/.

Salsini, Barbara. *Elizabeth Stanton, A Leader of the Women's Suffrage Movement.* Charlotteville, NY: SamHar Press, 1972.

Schneier, Bruce. 2004. "U.S. 'No-Fly' List Curtails Liberties." *Newsday* August 25. www.schneier.com/essay-052.html.

"Scientists' Nightstand: The Bookshelf Talks with Deborah Blum." www.americanscientist.org/template/ScientistNightstandTypeDetail/assetid/25044.

"Sexy Names (And Some Unsexy Ones Too)." library.thinkquest.org/4626/sexy.htm.

Stanton, Elizabeth Cady. *Eighty Years and More: Reminiscences, 1815–1897.* Amherst, NY: Humanity Books, 2002.

"What Should You Name Your Baby?" www.americanbaby.com/ab/quiz.jhtml?quizId=/templatedata/ab/quiz/data/33.xml.

The woman pictured in this advertisement from the 1950s is opening tin cans of strange food, such as baked eel, fried ants, broiled sparrow, and pickled squid. Have you ever seen any of those foods for sale today? Have you ever eaten any of those foods? Which of those foods is the most and least appealing to you? Suppose you were at a restaurant, and you were being offered these items at no charge. Write about why you would or would not try those foods. Be sure to support your preferences with clear-cut examples.

CHAPTER FOUR

FOOD, GLORIOUS FOOD

Ask not what you can do for your country. Ask what's for lunch.   —*Orson Welles*

Chemically speaking, chocolate really is the world's perfect food.   —*Michael Levine*

Eat breakfast like a king, lunch like a prince, and dinner like a pauper.   —*Adelle Davis*

Eat not to dullness; drink not to elevation.   —*Ben Franklin*

Food is our common ground, a universal experience.   —*James Beard*

Good food ends with good talk.   —*Geoffrey Neighor*

I am not a glutton—I am an explorer of food.   —*Erma Bombeck*

I don't even butter my bread; I consider that cooking.   —*Katherine Cebrian*

Never eat more than you can lift.   —*Miss Piggy*

One should eat to live, not live to eat.   —*Benjamin Franklin*

Part of the secret of success in life is to eat what you like and let the food fight
it out inside.   —*Mark Twain*

Red meat is not bad for you. Now blue-green meat, that's bad for you!   —*Tommy Smothers*

Tell me what you eat, and I will tell you what you are.   —*Anthelme Brillat-Savarin*

When women are depressed, they either eat or go shopping. Men invade another country. It's a
whole different way of thinking.   —*Elaine Boosler*

Your body is precious. It is our vehicle for awakening. Treat it with care.   —*Buddha*

Food, Glorious Food

We're usually consumed (pardon the pun) with food at least three times a day, and our connections with food are almost always present. Even our language is peppered (ha! ha!) with food references. If something can be done easily, it's a piece of <u>cake</u>. A favorite youngster is the <u>apple</u> of your eye. Is your boss coming to visit you soon? Look out for the big <u>cheese</u>, and be sure to try to <u>butter</u> him or her up. In other familiar food idioms, you can

- bring home the <u>bacon</u> for your family,
- be cool as a <u>cucumber</u> in a difficult situation,
- tell yourself not to cry over spilled <u>milk</u> when you've made a mistake,
- cut the <u>mustard</u> in a new job,
- <u>eat</u> <u>crow</u> (or humble <u>pie</u> or <u>dirt</u> or your own <u>words</u>) when you're wrong,
- hope that you can have your <u>cake</u> and eat it too,
- take criticism with a grain of <u>salt</u>,
- realize that a fellow student is in the <u>soup</u> for having cheated on a test,
- have your finger in the <u>pie</u> in lots of student organizations,
- put your thoughts in a <u>nutshell</u>,
- think certain comedian is <u>nutty</u> as a <u>fruitcake</u> or out to <u>lunch</u>,
- hope that your new invention sells like <u>hotcakes</u>,
- <u>stew</u> in your own <u>juice</u> when you don't do your homework,
- drive a <u>souped</u>-up car,

. . . the list, obviously, goes on and on. Are all these idioms making your mouth water?

Our familiarity with food references also relates to ads for certain foods, and we easily recognize the icons that accompany many popular brands. For instance, what fun little characters do you think of if someone mentions Keebler products? And what famous man do you picture if you decide on KFC (Kentucky Fried Chicken) for tonight's dinner? In "Food Icons: Immortal in the Eyes of The Television Beholder," Marjorie Dorfman examines other mascots that have long been associated with food products.

Even though food nourishes and entertains us, it can also bring us problems. For instance, we've all had times when we were embarrassed by our own cooking or disgusted by the food we were served. Laurie Colwin's "Repulsive Dinners: A Memoir" might remind you of some eating experience that you have had to suffer through.

The abundance and availability of food—particularly of fast food—have created predicaments that often arise when we choose the wrong food or consume too much food. Eric Schlosser's "Throughput" takes a look at some problems associated with the fast-food industry.

Now that you have read the introduction to this chapter, go back and reread the quotations on p. 77. Then choose one of the quotations and write about whether you agree or disagree with it. Be sure to defend your opinion.

Popular author **Laurie Colwin** *(1944–1992) wrote about food, home and family, love, marriage, and other human relationships. She was a magazine columnist (Gourmet) and the author of five novels, three volumes of short stories, and two collections of food writing. Her 1988 book* Home Cooking: A Writer in the Kitchen *is part memoir, part cookbook, and contains the humorous selection "Repulsive Dinners: A Memoir."*

Starting Out...

Form a small group in your class and discuss this question:

> What was the most disgusting meal that you have ever had in someone else's home?

Think about what was served (or supposed to be served) at the meal, how you reacted to the meal, how the other guests reacted to the meal, and how the dinner ended.

After everyone has related his or her worst experience, take a vote in the group to see whose story is the most disgusting.

Words to Watch

abounds: is plentiful

cerise: a deep to vivid purplish red

champion: supporter, fan

coup de grâce: finishing stroke or decisive event

flat: the British term for "apartment"

frankincense: a resin formerly valued for both worship and embalming

from soup to nuts: an idiom meaning "including everything"

galingale: an aromatic root formerly used in medicine and cooking

Hampstead: an area of London, England

hors d'oeuvre: appetizer, starter

medieval: relating to the Middle Ages, the period in European history often dated C.E. 476 to 1453

pie: in the U.K., a dish containing meat and baked in pastry-lined pan often with a pastry top

salmonella: bacteria found in undercooked poultry or eggs, a common cause of food poisoning

seedy: seamy, sordid, disrespectable

Shepherd's Bush: an area in London, England

Repulsive Dinners: A Memoir
by Laurie Colwin

There is something triumphant about a really disgusting meal. It lingers in the memory with a lurid glow, just as something exalted is remembered with a kind of mellow brilliance. I am not thinking of kitchen disasters—chewy pasta, burnt brownies, curdled sauces: these can happen to anyone. I am thinking about meals that are positively loathsome from soup to nuts, although one is not usually fortunate enough to get either soup or nuts.

Bad food abounds in restaurants, but somehow a bad meal in a restaurant and a bad home-cooked meal are not the same: after all, the restaurant did not invite you to dinner.

My mother believes that people who can't cook should rely on filet mignon and boiled potatoes with parsley, and that they should be on excellent terms with an expensive bakery. But if everyone did that, there would be fewer horrible meals and the rich, complicated tapestry that is the human experience would be the poorer for it.

My life has been much enriched by ghastly meals, two of the awfulest of which took place in London. I am a great champion of English food, but what I was given at these dinners was neither English nor food as far as I could tell.

Once upon a time my old friend Richard Davies took me to a dinner party in Shepherd's Bush, a seedy part of town, at the flat of one of his oldest friends.

"What is he like?" I asked.

"He's a genius," Richard said. "He has vast powers of abstract thought." I did not think this was a good sign.

"How nice," I said. "Can he cook?"

"I don't know," Richard said. "In all these years, I've never had a meal at his house. He's a Scot, and they're very mean."

When the English say "mean," they mean "cheap."

Our host met us at the door. He was a glum, geniusy-looking person and he led us into a large, bare room with a table set for six. There were no smells or sounds of anything being cooked. Two other guests sat in chairs, looking as if they wished there were an hors d'oeuvre. There was none.

"I don't think there will be enough to go around," our host said, as if we were responsible for being so many. Usually, this is not the sort of thing a guest likes to hear but in the end we were grateful that it turned out to be true.

We drank some fairly crummy wine, and then when we were practically gnawing on each other's arms, we were led to the table. The host placed a rather small casserole in the center. We peered at it hopefully. The host lifted the lid. "No peeking," he said.

Usually when you lift the lid of a casserole that has come straight from the oven, some fragrant steam escapes. This did not happen, although it did not immediately occur to me that this casserole had not come straight from the oven, but had been sitting around outside the oven getting lukewarm and possibly breeding salmonella.

Here is what we had: the casserole contained a layer of partially cooked rice, a layer of pineapple rings and a layer of breakfast sausages, all of which was cooked in a liquid of some sort or other. Each person received one pineapple ring, one sausage and a large heap of crunchy rice. We ate in perfect silence, first in shock, then in amazement, and then in gratitude that not only was there not enough to go around, but that nothing else was forthcoming. That was the entire meal.

Later as Richard and I sat in the Pizza Express finishing off a second pie, I said: "Is that some sort of Scottish dish we had tonight?"

"No," Richard said. "It is a genius dish."

Several years later on another trip to London, Richard and I were invited to a dinner party in Hampstead. Our host and hostess lived in a beautiful old house but they had taken out all the old fittings and the place had been redesigned in postindustrial futuristic.

At the door, out hostess spoke these dread words: "I'm trying this recipe out on you. I've never made it before. It's a medieval recipe. It looked very interesting."

Somehow I have never felt that "interesting" is an encouraging word when applied to food.

In the kitchen were two enormous and slightly crooked pies.

"How pretty," I said. "What kind are they?"

"They're medieval fish pies," she said. "A variation on starry gazey pie." Starry gazey pie is one in which the crust is slit so that the whole baked eels within can poke their nasty little heads out and look at the pie crust stars with which the top is supposed to be festooned.

"Oh," I said, swallowing hard. "In what way do they vary?"

"Well, I couldn't get eels," said my hostess. "So I got squid. It has squid, flounder, apples, onions, lots of cinnamon and something called galingale. It's kind of like frankincense."

"I see," I said.

"It's from the twelfth or thirteenth century," she continued. "The crust is made of flour, water, salt and honey."

I do not like to think very often about that particular meal, but the third was worse.

It took place in suburban Connecticut on a beautiful summer evening. The season had been hot and lush, and the local markets were full of beautiful produce of all kinds. Some friends and I had been invited out to dinner.

"What will we have, do you think?" I asked.

"Our hostess said we weren't having anything special," my friends said. "She said something about an 'old-fashioned fish bake.'"

It is hard to imagine why those four innocent words sounded so ominous in combination.

For hors d'oeuvres we had something which I believe is called cheese food. It is not so much a food as a product. A few tired crackers were lying around with it. Then it was time for dinner.

The old-fashioned fish bake was a terrifying production. Someone in the family had gone fishing and had pulled up a number of smallish fish— no one was sure what kind. These were partially cleaned and not thoroughly scaled and then flung into a roasting pan. Perhaps to muffle their last screams, they were smothered in a thick blanket of sour cream and then pelted with raw chopped onion. As the coup de grâce, they were stuck in a hot oven for a brief period of time until their few juices ran out and the sour cream had a chance to become grainy. With this were served boiled frozen peas and a salad with iceberg lettuce.

Iceberg lettuce is the cause of much controversy. Many people feel it is an abomination. Others have less intense feelings, but it did seem an odd thing to have when the market five minutes away contained at least five kinds of lettuce, including Oakleaf, Bibb and limestone.

For dessert we had a packaged cheesecake with iridescent cherries embedded in a topping of cerise gum and a light tan coffee.

As appears to be traditional with me, a large pizza was the real end of this grisly experience.

But every once in a while, an execrable meal drags on way past the closing times of most pizzerias. You straggle home starving, exhausted, abused in body and spirit. You wonder why you have been given such a miserable dinner, a meal you would not serve to your worst enemy or a junkyard dog. You deserve something delicious to eat, but there is nothing much in the fridge.

You might have egg and toast, or a glass of hot milk, or toasted cheese, but you feel your spirit crying out for something more.

Here is the answer: rösti. Rösti is a Swiss grated potato dish. In reality it is an excuse for eating a quarter of a pound of butter. While your loved one is taking a hot shower or mixing a drink, you can get to work.

Take off your coat and plunge one large Idaho potato into boiling water. By the time you have gotten into your pajamas and hung up your clothes, it is time to take it out—seven minutes, tops. This seems to stabilize the starch.

Gently heat a large quantity (half a stick) of unsalted butter in a skillet. It should foam but not turn brown. Grate the potato on the shredder side of the grater, press into a cake and slip into the butter. Fry till golden brown on both sides.

The result is somewhat indigestible, but after all, you have already been subjected to the truly indigestible. You will feel better for it. You and your companion—or you yourself (this recipe makes two big cakes: if you are alone, you can have both all to yourself)—will begin to see the evening's desecrations as an amusement.

Because you *are* the better for your horrible meal: fortified, uplifted and ready to face the myriad surprises and challenges in this most interesting and amazing of all possible worlds.

From Where I Stand… (Journal Responses)

1. I think Colwin's statement "There is something triumphant about a really disgusting meal" is true/false (choose either "true" or "false") because _____
   _____.

2. I enjoy/do not enjoy (choose either "enjoy" or "do not enjoy") cooking because
   _____.

3. I like to eat at the home of (name a friend or relative) because _____
   _____.

JUST THE FACTS

1. The sentence that best expresses the main idea of this selection is a) usually when you lift the lid of a casserole that has come straight from the oven, some fragrant steam escapes; b) somehow I have never felt that "interesting" is an encouraging word when applied to food; c) there is something triumphant about a really disgusting meal; d) iceberg lettuce is the cause of much controversy.

2. At the first dinner party, the "glum, geniusy-looking" host a) said there wouldn't be enough food to go around; b) told the guests they would have to leave because he had an emergency; c) apologized when the guests were horrified after the family cat jumped on the table and began eating the casserole; d) bored the guests while trying to impress them with his knowledge of Shakespeare's plays.

3. At the second dinner party, the one in Hampstead, a) the host became ill as he was serving the food; b) the hostess left the dinner table and did not return for more than an hour; c) the host and hostess began arguing with each other; d) the hostess announced that she was trying out a medieval recipe.

4. At the third dinner party, the one in Connecticut, a) one of the guests dominated the conversation so much that the others were "bored to tears"; b) a terrible snowstorm dictated that the party be cut short; c) guests were served fish that had been partially cleaned, not thoroughly scaled, then flung into a roasting pan; d) one guest

embarrassed the host and hostess when he objected loudly to the wine that they served with the meal.

5. After leaving the dinner disasters that she described, Colwin ate a) pizza; b) a huge bowl of her favorite cereal; c) soda crackers; d) popcorn and apples.

EXPANDING HORIZONS

1. This selection is an excerpt from Colwin's *Home Cooking: A Writer in the Kitchen*. Read another selection from this book (perhaps "Alone in the Kitchen with an Eggplant" or "Stuffed Breast of Veal: A Bad Idea") and write a summary of it. You can also consult *More Home Cooking*, the sequel to *Home Cooking: A Writer in the Kitchen*, which was published posthumously in 1993.

2. Colwin wrote a number of articles for *Gourmet* magazine. Pick an article in a recent copy of *Gourmet*, *Bon Appétit*, *Cooking Light*, *Food and Wine*, *Cook's Illustrated*, or *Vegetarian Times*. Read one of the articles in the magazine and write a summary of it.

3. In this selection, Colwin shared her recipe for rösti, a Swiss grated potato dish. Pick a favorite recipe of your own and write it in a similar style.

4. In a short personal narrative, write about one of your own cooking experiences. You could choose to write about how you learned to cook, your favorite meal to cook, a cooking disaster or triumph that came from your hands, or another cooking-related topic.

5. Even though people from the United States and the United Kingdom speak (and write) the same language, a number of differences can be found between American English and British English. The famous English writer Oscar Wilde once said, "The Americans are identical to the British in all respects except, of course, language." Some of these differences are in spelling, such as these:

American	British
color	colour
flavor	flavour
recognize	recognise
patronize	patronise
check	cheque
defense	defence
tire	tyre
jail	gaol

Differences also exist in definitions of words. In Colwin's selection, for example, she visited a British "flat," which would be called an apartment in the U.S. Use reference materials to find out what these British words mean in American English:

aubergine	car park	courgettes	frock
bin liner	car silencer	crisps	gear box
biscuit	chemists	demister	hob
bonnet	chips	dodgy	holiday
boot	coach	dummy	hoover
braces	conserves	dustbin	indicators
candy floss	cot	football	jelly

jumper	porridge	starters	tram
lift	pram	suspenders	treble
lorry	pudding	sweet	trousers
motorway	queue	tinned	tube
nappies	recovery	torch	vest
petrol	solicitor	trainers	washing up

After you have mastered these words, take the online quiz at iteslj.org/v/e/ck-british-american.html to further check your skills at American English vs. British English.

WRITE ON!

1. Describe your idea of a perfect meal. Be sure to use imagery, words that help the reader see, smell, taste your food (or even hear and touch it, depending on your food choices).
2. Compare a place (either a home setting or a restaurant) where you like to eat with one that you'd prefer never to set foot in again.
3. Write a short piece of fiction in which your main character has to eat a disgusting meal. You might include details about what led him or her to this meal, what the meal consisted of, whether your character said anything about the meal while he or she was eating it, and what happened when your character left the meal.

*All of us who watch television—and who doesn't?—have become accustomed to being showered with commercials. Some of these advertisements feature people or animals so charming and appealing that their image stays with us long after the commercials have run their course and then disappeared from TV. Here author **Marjorie Dorfman** recalls some of her favorite TV icons.*

Starting Out...

Below is a list of eight advertising icons used by the food industry. Put a check mark beside the icon if you can picture it as it appeared on television or in printed ads, or if you can recall what the icon said in advertisements.

_____ Tony the Tiger

_____ The Pillsbury Doughboy

_____ Charlie the Tuna

_____ The Jolly Green Giant

_____ Mr. Clean

_____ Elsie the Cow

_____ The Campbell Kids

_____ Chiquita Banana

Words to Watch

alas: unfortunately, sadly

fickle: indecisive, changeable

icon-dom: a coined word meaning "a state or condition of being an icon"

icons: images, representations, symbols

jaunty: dashing, jolly, lively

lilting: a cheerful manner of speaking in which the pitch of the voice pleasantly varies

machinations: schemes, plots

moot point: a debatable question, an issue open to argument

obscurity: anonymity, insignificance

realm: area, sphere

rebuke: scolding, chiding

spokes-cartoon: a coined word taken from "spokesperson"; a cartoon that speaks on behalf of a company

sultry: expressing or arousing desire

tenacity: stubbornness, obstinacy

Tony the Tiger, The Pillsbury Doughboy, Charlie the Tuna, The Jolly Green Giant, Mr. Clean, Elsie the Cow, The Campbell Kids: figures (icons) used in television ads

Food Icons: Immortal in the Eyes of the Television Beholder

by Marjorie Dorfman

To be somebody you must last.

—Ruth Gordon

How have food icons sustained their popularity throughout the years? Why don't they age the way that we do? Tony The Tiger looks the same as when I was five years old and both The Pillsbury Doughboy and Charlie The Tuna bear not a single wrinkle upon their well advertised brows! Read on for their secrets and a smile or two.

From the valley of the Jolly Green Giant and the floors of Mr. Clean to the pastures of Elsie The Cow and the kitchen of The Campbell Kids lies the fickle realm of television advertising where cartoons are born and cultural food icons are made. There's a thin line between a trademark and a food icon and it's one that not all cartoons pass with flying or other colors. Most of the more famous television food icons began their lives as animated trademarks; that is, they were used to represent a specific product. Born on the high-powered wings of the media (although not able to leap tall buildings in a single bound), these symbols have maintained the growing tide of their own fame. How many can recall the pleasing voice and face of Miss Chiquita Banana, luring us into the healthful world of the banana? Who could ever forget Charlie The Tuna, Tony The Tiger and The Pillsbury Doughboy? They too belong in the realm of television cultural food icons, but the question is: How did they get there in the first place?

Chiquita Banana is the oldest of the lot mentioned above. (I should never say that about a "fellow" female, but the truth is the truth.) She dates back to 1941 when Dik Brown, the same artist who produced the Campbell Soup Kids, created her. She helped teach consumers about the nutritional value of bananas and how to ripen them. The first live "lady of fruit" was Miss Patty Clayton in 1944. The most famous Miss Chiquita was Elsa Miranda (no relation to Carmen) who made numerous personal appearances in 1945 and 1946.

Miss Chiquita first appeared on labels to identify the Chiquita Brand bananas in 1963. Her likeness remained unchanged for years and she eventually reached the ranks of media immortality (icon-dom). Until 1987 she was a sexy banana lady, but still a cartoon. And then all that changed. Whether or not bananas pass through puberty may always remain a moot point, but artist Oscar Grillo, who created the Pink Panther, most definitely transformed Miss Chiquita into a sultry yellow lady with a mission. You can hear her lilting pleas for all humans to eat bananas in her own seductive words at www.chiquita.com.

Charlie The Tuna, that striving go-getter fish of the 1960s, is another character forever immortalized by the powers that media be. He made his debut on American television in a commercial for Starkist in 1961. All his machinations to be selected by Starkist for lovers of fine tuna have always resulted in failure and the salty old soul has always been forced to bear the rebuke in actor Herschel Bernardi's voice: "Sorry Charlie. Starkist doesn't want tuna with good taste. Starkist wants tuna that tastes good."

In Pago Pago, American Samoa, the home of the Starkist canning factory, Charlie lives on in the form of a statue dedicated to his image. In case you can't find him, he's the jaunty-looking tuna on top of the pedestal wearing glasses and a red hat. A sign below him reads: "Home of Charlie The Tuna." Perhaps it is his tenacity and our need to root for the underdog that keeps Charlie forever in our hearts. Or maybe, alas, it's simply clever advertising. I'm afraid that only his ad agency knows for sure!

Back in 1952, the Kellogg Company held a contest to see who would represent their new cereal called: "Sugar Frosted Flakes of Corn." The contestants were Katie The Kangaroo, Elmo The Elephant, Newt the Gnu and Tony The Tiger. Tony was declared the winner, although it was nip and tuck with Katie the Kangaroo for a while. In 1953, Tony became the sole spokes-cartoon for Kellogg's "Sugar Frosted Flakes" cereal. Tony Jr. (originally referred to as "boy" and later as "son") made appearances along with Tony Sr. who obviously had paternity denial issues for awhile.

Thurl Ravenscroft, whose career in radio, film and television has spanned more than 60 years, is and always has been the voice behind Tony the Tiger. Thurl had been well known in the field of jingles and commercials as part of a quartet known as The Mellomen. Kellogg sent him a sample script along with a character description and his active imagination did the rest! The pay-off line was always: "Tony, are Frosted Flakes any good?" And Tony would always say: "Good? Why they're great!" It was Thurl who came up with the much more explosive and effective: "Gr-r-r-r-eat!!"

The Pillsbury Doughboy was created by an ad agency called Leo Burnett. Pacific Data Images, a pioneer in the work of computer graphics for film and video, created the animated version of the lovable figure for the commercials. In October of 1965, the 14 ounce, 8 ¾ inch character made his television debut advertising Crescent Rolls. His original voice was that of actor Paul Fries (1920–86). The Doughboy's co-star in the commercial was Maureen McCormick. He started his career with another name: Poppin' Fresh. He is all dough with blue eyes and always wears a baker's hat and scarf. His hometown is Minneapolis; he loves to bake and twenty years ago he had a wife and two children.

A mock funeral from a master of puns added the following paragraphs about his passing in the spring of 2002:

"The Pillsbury Doughboy died yesterday of a yeast infection and complications from repeated pokes in the belly. He was 71.

"Doughboy was buried in a lightly greased coffin. Dozens of celebrities turned out to pay their respects, including Mrs. Butterworth, Hungry Jack, the California Raisins, Betty Crocker, the Hostess Twinkies and Captain Crunch. The gravesite was piled high with flours. Aunt Jemima delivered the eulogy and lovingly described Doughboy as a man for all seasonings who never knew how much he was kneaded.

"Doughboy rose quickly in the show business, but his later life was filled with turnovers. He was not considered a 'very smart cookie,' wasting much of his dough on half-baked schemes. Despite being a bit flaky sometimes, he was still considered a roll model for millions.

"Doughboy is survived by his wife, Play-Dough, two children, John Dough and Jane Dough; plus they had one in the oven. He is also survived by his elderly father, Pop Tart.

"The funeral was held at 3:50 for about twenty minutes."

Napoleon once said (and he should know) that glory is fleeting, but obscurity is forever. It is not known if the sister saying "beauty fades, but stupid is forever" came from his mouth as well. Regardless, the man had a point. Time passes and what remains is only the whisper of recall to remind us of what once was. Miss Chiquita, the Campbell Kids, Tony The Tiger, Charlie The Tuna and The Doughboy are all mini legends in their own special way. They are all impressed deeply within my mind's eye where cultural icons never die and don't even get the chance to fade away!

Note: Elsie the Cow is a trademark of Borden's Milk Co., Charlie The Tuna is a trademark of Starkist Tuna Co., Tony The Tiger is a trademark of Kellogg's Foods, and The Doughboy is a trademark of Pillsbury.

From Where I Stand... (Journal Responses)
1. The most humorous part of this article was _____.
   It was humorous because _____.
2. My favorite current food icon on television or in print ads is _____.
   I like it because _____.
3. I think this article should have included information about (name a food icon)
   _____ because
   _____.

JUST THE FACTS

1. The main idea of this selection is a) Kate the Kangaroo was once in the running to be the character representing Frosted Flakes; b) Charlie the Tuna and the Pillsbury Doughboy were both conceived by the same advertising agency; c) Thurl Ravenscroft was the man behind Tony the Tiger; d) advertising icons can remain in our minds for a long time.

2. The oldest food icon mentioned in the article was a) Charlie the Tuna; b) Chiquita Banana; c) Tony the Tiger; d) the Pillsbury Doughboy.

3. In 1952, Kellogg Company determined who would represent their new "Sugar Frosted Flakes of Corn" cereal by a) using the name of the son of the president of Kellogg Company; b) using the first name of the movie star who was most popular at the time; c) holding a contest; d) pulling the name out of a hat.

4. From the article, you can infer that the author a) thinks that most of the food icons are too silly for adults to take seriously; b) would like to visit a museum of the icons; c) has fond memories of the icons; d) wished that she had collected copies of the ads the icons appeared in.

5. One of the food icons that was not mentioned was a) Ronald McDonald; b) Chiquita Banana; c) Elsie the Cow; d) the Campbell Soup Kids.

EXPANDING HORIZONS

1. The article mentions a number of real-life people associated with various food icons: Dik Brown, Miss Patty Clayton, Elsa Miranda, Oscar Grillo, Paul Fries, Maureen McCormick, Herschel Bernardi, Thurl Ravenscroft, and Leo Burnett. Research any of these people and write a short biography of his or her life.

2. The article cites several companies that are still in business. Research any of these companies and write a short summary of your findings. Online sites include these:

   The Jolly Green Giant: www.greengiant.com/
   Mr. Clean: www.homemadesimple.com/mrclean/
   The Campbell's Kids: www.campbellsoup.com/default.aspx
   Chiquita Banana: www.chiquita.com
   Kellogg Company: www.kelloggs.com/company/
   Borden's Milk Company: www.bordenonline.com/
   Starkist Tuna Company: www.starkist.com/

3. The author writes of the statue in American Samoa of Charlie the Tuna. Research this statue and the company and write a summary of your research. Online sites to consult include these:

   www.susanscott.net/OceanWatch2003/may16-03.html
   www.terragalleria.com/pacific/american-samoa/pagopago/picture.samo-3937.html
   www.house.gov/apps/list/press/as00_faleomavaega/pr030616.html

4. The "funeral piece" about the Pillsbury Doughboy contained a number of homonyms (words that sound alike but are spelled differently). For instance, the sentence "The gravesite was piled high with flours" contains the homonym "flours" instead of "flowers." Find at least two more homonyms in the funeral piece.

5. The "funeral piece" also contains several puns (plays on words). As an example, the piece says that the later life of Doughboy "was filled with turnovers." The word "turnovers" is a play on two different meanings of the word: 1) an abrupt change, and 2) a small pastry. Find at least two other examples of puns in the piece.

WRITE ON!

1. Write a short letter to a company that sponsors a current television icon used for advertising. In the letter, give your opinion of the icon. What makes this icon especially entertaining or clever or annoying or influential?

2. Think of one of your favorite foods. Use your creativity to think of an icon for that food. What would the icon look like? If you're artistic, draw a picture of your icon. What would you have it say in its advertisements?

3. Think of an advertisement (not necessarily one that used an icon) that is at least ten years old. Why do you think you remember that particular ad? What makes it stand out in your mind?

How to Eat a Poem
by Eve Merriam

Don't be polite.
Bite in.
Pick it up with your fingers and lick the
juice that may run down your chin.
It is ready and ripe now, whenever you are.
You do not need a knife or a fork or a spoon
or plate or napkin or tablecloth.
For there is no core
or stem
or rind
or pit
or seed
or skin
to throw away.

Questions

1. In this poem, Eve Merriam uses a metaphor, a comparison of two unlike things without using the word *like* or *as*. What is Merriam comparing in this poem?
2. Do you think that her comparison is valid? Why or why not?
3. What does Merriam mean when she says a poem "is ready and ripe now, whenever you are"?

***Eric Schlosser's** first book,* Fast Food Nation: The Dark Side of the All-American Meal, *offers a behind-the-scenes look at a number of problems with the fast-food industry. This excerpt describes some typical labor practices in a number of today's popular restaurants.*

Starting Out...

Think about a time that you were a teenage worker and relate some of your experiences.

- How were you treated when you were first hired and as you gained experience?
- What difference, if any, was there between your treatment by coworkers and by those in authority?
- What did you consider to be your best skill as a worker? Why?

Words to Watch

baby-boom: the generation of children born between the end of WWII (1945) and the middle of the 1960s

condiments: sauces or relishes, like mustard or ketchup

division of labor: assignment of specific tasks to workers

ethos: a group's distinctive spirit or character

fast asleep: an idiom meaning "sleeping deeply"

franchises: types of businesses in which one company pays another to sell goods or services in some specific area

franchisees: people who are authorized to sell a company's goods or services

hold down the fort: an idiom meaning "keep the place running by themselves"

labor practices: customary or compulsory procedures of employment

marginalized: living in a lower or outer edge, as of specific groups of people

mass production: the manufacture of goods in large quantities by means of machines, standardized design and parts, and, often, assembly lines

rite of passage: something that a person goes through in reaching adulthood

Speedee Service System: the McDonald brothers' name for the way that food was prepared, using an assembly line (one worker performing the same job)

throughput: the speed and volume of materials being sold or manufactured

wiped out: an idiom meaning "extremely tired"

Throughput
by Eric Schlosser

Every Saturday Elisa Zamot gets up at 5:15 in the morning. It's a struggle, and her head feels groggy as she steps into the shower. Her little sisters, Cookie and Sabrina, are fast asleep in their beds. By 5:30, Elisa's showered, done her hair, and put on her McDonald's uniform. She's sixteen, bright-eyed and olive-skinned, pretty and petite, ready for another day of work. Elisa's mother usually drives her the half-mile or so to the restaurant on the south side of Colorado Springs, in a largely poor and working-class neighborhood. Throughout the day, sounds of traffic fill the house, the steady whoosh of passing cars. But when Elisa heads for work, the streets are quiet, the sky's still dark, and the lights are out in the small houses and rental apartments along the road.

When Elisa arrives at McDonald's the manager unlocks the door and lets her in. Sometimes the husband-and-wife cleaning crew are just finishing up. More often, it's just Elisa and the manager in the restaurant, surrounded by an empty parking lot. For the next hour or so, the two of them get everything ready. They turn on the ovens and grills. They go downstairs into the basement and get food and supplies for the morning shift. They get the paper cups, wrappers, cardboard containers, and packets of condiments. They step into the big freezer and get the frozen bacon, the frozen pancakes, and the frozen cinnamon rolls. They get the frozen hash browns, the frozen biscuits, the frozen McMuffins. They get the cartons of scrambled egg mix and orange juice mix. They bring the food upstairs and start preparing it before any customers appear, thawing some things in the microwave and cooking other things on the grill. They put the cooked food in special cabinets to keep it warm.

The restaurant opens for business at seven o'clock, and for the next hour or so, Elisa and the manager hold down the fort, handling all the orders. As the place starts to get busy, other employees arrive. Elisa works behind the counter. She takes orders and hands food to customers from breakfast through lunch. When she finally walks home, after seven hours of standing at a cash register, her feet hurt. She's wiped out. She comes through the front door, flops onto the living room couch, and turns on the TV. And the next morning she gets up at 5:15 again and starts the same routine.

Up and down Academy Boulevard, along South Nevada, Circle Drive, and Woodman Road, teenagers like Elisa run the fast food restaurants of Colorado Springs. Fast food kitchens often seem like a scene from *Bugsy Malone*, a film in which all the actors are children pretending to be adults. About two-thirds of the nation's fast food workers are under the age of twenty.

Teenagers open the fast food outlets in the morning, close them at night, and keep them going at all hours in between. Even the managers and assistant managers are sometimes in their late teens. Unlike Olympic gymnastics—an activity in which teenagers consistently perform at a higher level than adults—there's nothing about the work in a fast food kitchen that requires young employees. Instead of relying upon a small, stable, well-paid, and well-trained workforce, the fast food industry seeks out part-time, unskilled workers who are willing to accept low pay. Teenagers have been the perfect candidates for these jobs, not only because they are less expensive to hire than adults, but also because their youthful inexperience makes them easier to control.

Business historian Alfred D. Chandler has argued that a high rate of "throughput" was the most important aspect of these mass production systems. A factory's throughput is the speed and volume of its flow—a much more crucial measurement, according to Chandler, than the number of workers it employs or the value of its machinery. With innovative technology and the proper organization, a small number of workers can produce an enormous amount of goods cheaply. Throughput is all about increasing the speed of assembly, about doing things faster in order to make more.

Although the McDonald brothers had never encountered the term "throughput" or studied "scientific management," they instinctively grasped the underlying principles and applied them in the Speedee Service System. The restaurant operating scheme they developed has been widely adopted and refined over the past half century. The ethos of the assembly line remains at its core. The fast food industry's obsession with throughput has altered the way millions of Americans work, turned commercial kitchens into small factories, and changed familiar foods into commodities that are manufactured.

At Burger King restaurants, frozen hamburger patties are placed on a conveyer belt and emerge from a broiler ninety seconds later fully cooked. The ovens at Pizza Hut and at Domino's also use conveyer belts to ensure standardized cooking times. The ovens at McDonald's look like commercial laundry presses, with big steel hoods that swing down and grill hamburgers on both sides at once. The burgers, chicken, French fries, and buns are all frozen when they arrive at McDonald's. The shakes and sodas begin as syrup. At Taco Bell restaurants the food is "assembled," not prepared. The guacamole is not made by workers in the kitchen; it's made at a factory in Michoacán, Mexico, then frozen and shipped north. The chain's taco meat arrives frozen and precooked in vacuum-sealed plastic bags. The beans are dehydrated and look like brownish corn flakes. The cooking process is fairly simple. "Everything's add water," a Taco Bell employee told me. "Just add hot water."

Although Richard and Mac McDonald introduced the division of labor to the restaurant business, it was a McDonald's executive named Fred Turner who created a production system of unusual thoroughness and attention to detail. In 1958, Turner put together an operations and training manual for the company that was seventy-five pages long, specifying how almost everything should be done. Hamburgers were always to be placed on the grill in six neat rows; French fries had to be exactly 0.28 inches thick. The McDonald's operations manual today has ten times the number of pages and weighs about four pounds. Known within the company as "the Bible," it contains precise instructions on how various appliances should be used, how each item on the menu should look, and how employees should greet customers. Operators who disobey these rules can lose their franchises. Cooking instructions are not only printed in the manual, they are often designed into the machines. A McDonald's kitchen is full of buzzers and flashing lights that tell employees what to do.

At the front counter, computerized cash registers issue their own commands. Once an order has been placed, buttons light up and suggest other menu items that can be added. Workers at the counter are told to increase the size of an order by recommending special promotion, pushing dessert, pointing out the financial logic behind the purchase of a larger drink. While doing so, they are instructed to be upbeat and friendly. "Smile with a greeting and make a positive first impression," a Burger King training manual suggests. "Show them you are GLAD TO SEE THEM. Include eye contact with the cheerful greeting."

The strict regimentation at fast food restaurants creates standardized products. It increases the throughput. And it gives fast food companies an enormous amount of power over their employees. "When management determines exactly how every task is to be done...and can impose its own rules about pace, output, quality, and technique," the sociologist Robin Leidner has noted, "[it] makes workers increasingly interchangeable." The management no longer depends upon the talents or skills of its workers—those things are built into the operating system and machines. Jobs that have been "deskilled" can be filled cheaply. The need to retain any individual worker is greatly reduced by the ease with which he or she can be replaced.

Teenagers have long provided the fast food industry with the regimentation of its workforce. The industry's rapid growth coincided with the baby-boom expansion of that age group. Teenagers were in many ways the ideal candidates for these low-paying jobs. Since most teenagers still lived at home, they could afford to work for wages too low to support an adult, and until recently, their limited skills attracted few other employers. A job at a fast food restaurant became an American rite of passage, a first job soon left behind for better things. The flexible terms of employment in the fast food industry also attracted housewives who needed extra income. As the number of baby-boom teenagers declined, the fast food chains began to hire other marginalized workers: recent immigrants, the elderly, and the handicapped.

English is now the second language of at least one-sixth of the nation's restaurant workers, and about one-third of that group speaks no English at all. The proportion of fast food workers who cannot speak English is even higher. Many know only the names of the items on the menu; they speak "McDonald's English."

The fast food industry now employs some of the most disadvantaged members of American society. It often teaches basic job skills—such as getting to work on time—to people who can barely read, whose lives have been chaotic or shut off from the mainstream. Many individual franchisees are genuinely concerned about the well-being of their workers. But the stance of the fast food industry on issues involving employee training, the minimum wage, labor unions, and overtime pay strongly suggests that its motives in hiring the young, the poor, and the handicapped are hardly altruistic.

From Where I Stand... (Journal Responses)
1. The most boring job I have ever had was _____.
   It was boring because _____.
2. The job in which I was the most underappreciated was _____. I
   was underappreciated because _____.
3. To show employees that they are appreciated, companies/managers (choose either
   "companies" or "managers") should _____.

JUST THE FACTS

1. The main idea of this selection is a) fast-food restaurants are becoming more popular in almost every American city; b) in restaurants that have a drive-through window, the "throughput" is a slang term for what is put in the customers' hands after the bill is paid; c) the "throughput" should reflect how satisfied a customer is with his or her service; d) teenagers, who account for most fast-food workers, must deliver a high rate of "throughput."

2. According to the article, the number of America's fast-food workers who are teenagers is about a) two-thirds; b) one-half; c) one-fourth; d) one-third.

3. Within the McDonald's company, "the Bible" is the a) list of people who complain and what they complain about; b) list of people who have asked for a promotion or a transfer to another location; c) operations manual with instructions about use of appliances, how menu items should look, and how employees should greet customers; d) record of current prices for all meals.

4. "McDonald's English" is a) the term given to what is spoken by employees who cannot speak English; b) a list of several options about how employees should greet customers; c) a list of options of what an employee should say if a customer complains; d) a slang term for any of the English muffin options that are offered for breakfast.

5. Eliza performs many chores before the restaurant opens for business, but one of them is not a) turning on the ovens and grills; b) checking the newspaper to see if

the current McDonald's ad is correct; c) getting food and supplies for the morning shift; d) getting the paper cups, wrappers, cardboard containers, and packets of condiments.

EXPANDING HORIZONS

1. This passage contains three literary techniques: imagery, alliteration, and ono-matopoeia.
   - Imagery is the use of a word or group of words that appeals to at least one of the senses: sight, taste, touch, hearing, and smell. For instance, the sentence "In the autumn, Pattye always drinks apple cider after she rakes the leaves" contains imagery because you the reader can taste the apple cider and see Pattye raking the leaves (and perhaps even smell the leaves).
   - Alliteration is the repeating of beginning consonant sounds in words that are beside or close to each other (Are you going to the Final Four, Phil?).
   - Onomatopoeia occurs when the sound of a word echoes what the word means. *Buzz, swish, crackle,* and *hum* are all examples of onomatopoetic words because you can hear what the word means when you say it.

   In the first paragraph, Schlosser uses imagery, alliteration, and onomatopoeia in portraying a certain sound. Identify the words and phrases that the author uses for these literary techniques.

2. In paragraph two, note that Schlosser begins the last eight sentences with "They" instead of changing his sentence structure. Why do you think that he chose to compose the last part of the paragraph that way? (Hint: Think about what the paragraph is talking about.) Also, he used the word "frozen" six times in that same paragraph? Why?

3. The term "throughput" is applied in other businesses besides the fast-food industry. Using the Internet, find and summarize articles dealing with throughput in other commercial ventures.

4. Schlosser quotes sociologist Robin Leidner, the author of *Fast Food, Fast Talk: Service Work and the Routinization of Everyday Life.* Read a few chapters of Leidner's book and cite specific points in these chapters; then write why you agree or disagree with these points.

5. Using the Internet or other research tools, investigate the cost and start-up requirements for Wendy's, Taco Bell, Pizza Hut, Domino's, or any other chain in your area.

WRITE ON!

1. Write what your typical work day consists of.
2. Write what your typical work day would consist of if you had the job of your dreams.
3. Write a letter to your supervisor stating what changes at work would make you a better worker or would make for a better workplace. Be sure to explain your opinions.

READ ON!

"A Brief History of McDonald's." www.mcspotlight.org/company/company_history.html.

Bourdain, Anthony. *Kitchen Confidential: Adventures in the Culinary Underbelly.* New York: Bloomsbury, 2000.

Brown, Alton. *I'm Just Here for the Food: Food + Heat = Cooking.* New York: Stewart, Tabori & Chang, 2002.

"ChefTalk Cooking Forums." cheftalkcafe.com/forums/index.php.

Colwin, Laurie. *More Home Cooking: A Writer Returns to the Kitchen.* New York: HarperCollins, 1993.

"Diary of an Itinerant Chef." www.movable-feast.com/.

"Epicurious.com: The World's Greatest Recipe Collection." www.epicurious.com/.

Fisher, M. F. K. *The Art of Eating.* Indianapolis: Hungry Minds, Inc., 1990.

Hughes, Holly, ed. *Best Food Writing 2005.* New York: Marlowe & Company, 2005.

Ikerd, John. "The New American Food Culture." www.kerrcenter.com/nwsltr/2005/spring2005/food_culture.htm.

Johnson, Robin. "Miscellaneous Food Jingles." www.geocities.com/foodedge/jingles5.html.

"Legislation Could Limit 'Junk Food' Advertising Aimed at Children." *Food & Drink Weekly.* March 21, 2005. www.findarticles.com/p/articles/mi_m0EUY/is_11_11/ai_n13482067#continue.

McGee, Harold. *On Food and Cooking: The Science and Lore of the Kitchen.* New York: Charles Scribner's Sons, 2004.

Murray, Bridget. "Fast-Food Culture Serves Up Super-Size Americans." *Monitor on Psychology.* Dec. 2001. www.apa.org/monitor/dec01/fastfood.html.

Oliver, Lynne. "The Food Timeline." www.foodtimeline.org/.

Reichl, Ruth. *Tender at the Bone: Growing Up at the Table.* New York: Random House, 1998.

——. *Comfort Me with Apples: More Adventures at the Table.* New York: Random House, 2001.

Super Size Me. 2004. Dir. Morgan Spurlock. Perf. Morgan Spurlock, John Banzhaf, Bridget Bennett, Kelly Bennet. The Con.

Trager, James. *The Enriched, Fortified, Concentrated, Country-Fresh, Lip-Smacking, Finger-Licking, International, Unexpurgated Foodbook.* New York: Grossman Publishers, 1970.

U.S. Department of Labor, Bureau of Labor Statistics. "Chefs, Cooks, and Food Preparation Workers." bls.gov/oco/ocos161.htm.

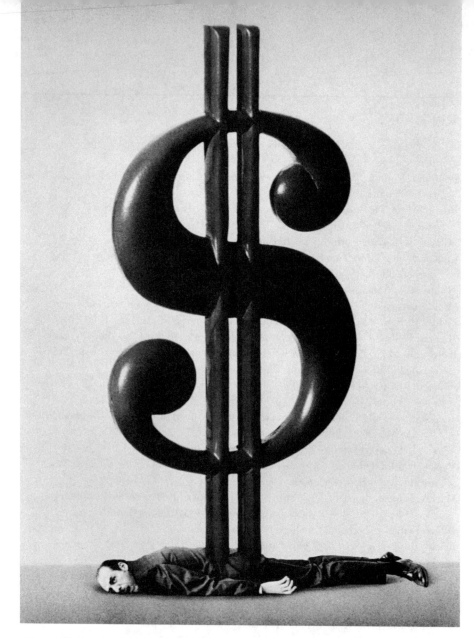

What will you spend your money on this week? Create a graph that you think will accurately account for your spending (include a section labeled "miscellaneous" for those items that are very small). Then keep a log for the next week about what your actual expenditures are and compare it with what you created on the graph.

Look at the picture above and think about its symbolism. Now look back at your log and write about whether or not you feel that you're in a similar situation.

CHAPTER FIVE

MONEY MATTERS

Business, you know, may bring money, but friendship hardly ever does   —*Jane Austen*

Honesty pays, but it don't seem to pay enough to suit some people.   —*Kin Hubbard*

I am opposed to millionaires, but it would be dangerous to offer me the position.   —*Mark Twain*

It is an unfortunate human failing that a full pocketbook often groans more loudly than an empty stomach.   —*Franklin Delano Roosevelt*

Life shouldn't be printed on dollar bills.   —*Clifford Odets*

Money is always there but the pockets change.   —*Gertrude Stein*

Money is the root of all evil, and yet it is such a useful root that we cannot get on without it any more than we can without potatoes.   —*Louisa May Alcott*

Money often costs too much.   —*Ralph Waldo Emerson*

Neither a borrower nor a lender be.   —*William Shakespeare*

Only when the last tree has died and the last river been poisoned and the last fish been caught will we realize we cannot eat money.   —*Cree Indian Proverb*

The easiest way for your children to learn about money is for you not to have any.   —*Katharine Whitehorn*

There are no pockets in a shroud.   —*Author Unknown*

There are people who have money and people who are rich.   —*Coco Chanel*

There is a very easy way to return from a casino with a small fortune: go there with a large one.   —*Jack Yelton*

We can tell our values by looking at our checkbook stubs.   —*Gloria Steinem*

Money Matters

Joe and Jane are two students who are engaged to be married. One day Jane noted that Joe had something on his mind, and she said to him, "Penny for your thoughts."

He replied that he thought it was time they discussed their different approaches to money. Showing Jane his bank statement, Joe said he felt like a million bucks because he was in the black. Jane's statement, on the other hand, revealed she was in the red and that with each major purchase she went farther in the hole.

Looking at her financial situation, Jane said, "I need some cold hard cash—in fact, I need to make it hand over fist."

When Joe asked her why she was so deep in the hole, Jane tried to pass the buck. After all, she declared, if everything nowadays didn't cost an arm and a leg, she wouldn't have to pay through the nose and feel as if she always had to pinch pennies until her next paycheck.

Then Joe put in his two cents about Jane's problems. He told her that during that week she should salt away part of her earnings. He also added that, if she paid cash on the barrelhead instead of using her credit cards, she might end up with money to burn after a short time—maybe she could even build up a little nest egg.

Jane replied that she always paid the interest on the credit cards, but Joe wondered if she was being penny-wise and pound foolish not paying off her credit cards every month. Jane said she couldn't do that for love or money....

At this point, it's up to you to write more about Joe and Jane, their money problems, and how they resolve them—if they do. Will you continue to use money-related idioms like those in the story? American English certainly has many of them; in fact, you could say that they're a dime a dozen.

Money is such a vital a part of everyday lives that it's no wonder we have so many concerns about it. Unwise monetary habits, like running up huge credit card debts for what we need...or what we *think* we need...or what we just want, potentially lead to years of interest payments and often raise the real cost of what we buy. Also, love of money can also be the root of evil and trouble for others in the form of identity theft.

Take all these reading selections at face value and you're sure to learn something new—you can bet your bottom dollar on that.

Now that you have read the introduction to this chapter, go back and reread the quotations on p. 101. Then choose one of the quotations and write about whether you agree or disagree with it. Be sure to defend your opinion.

College students may face a number of challenges if they take advantage of the credit card offers that come their way. **Ray Martin,** *financial advisor for* The CBS Early Show, *addressed some of these disadvantages and advantages of student credit cards in his September 3, 2003, broadcast. While he directed his comments to parents, college students will benefit from the statistics and other information here.*

Starting Out...
Circle A if you agree with the statement, D if you disagree.

A D The average undergraduate leaves school with a debt of more than $15,000.

A D Students double their credit card debt between the time they arrive on campus and their graduation.

A D The average graduating senior has six credit cards in his or her name.

Words to Watch

ballooning: inflating, swelling

entice: tempt, persuade

grace period: the time in which a debt may be paid without being charged more interest

last resort: the final method to achieve an end

Nellie Mae: a company that provides a broad range of loans under federally and privately funded loan programs

potential: possible, likely

revolving credit: a type of credit card that gives the option of paying off the debt in whole or in payments, with interest being charged on the balance of the account

safety net: an idiom that means "something that will help if a problem arises"

shell out: an idiom that means "give" or "pay"

variable rate cards: credit cards with interest rates that change according to other interest rates, such as the prime rate or the Treasury Bill rate

---

Beware of Student Credit Cards
by Ray Martin

The average undergraduate leaves school with a debt of $18,900. That's up 66 percent from five years ago, according to a new study by loan provider Nellie Mae. A large part of this is, of course, student loans, which more and more students report needing these days, thanks to ballooning tuition bills.

However, a growing part of this debt is unnecessary; it's a result of four years of charging pizza and shoes and booze on new credit cards.

College students are prime targets for credit card companies, which set up tables on campus and entice students to sign up for new cards with promises of free T-shirts or other goodies. Unfortunately, many students eagerly apply for credit and use it unwisely.

Students **double** their credit card debt and **triple** the number of cards in their wallets between the time they arrive on campus and graduation, Nellie Mae found. Another scary finding: by the time college students reach their senior year, 31 percent carry a balance of $3,000 to $7,000.

So what's the message here? Don't allow your child to get a credit card? Sorry, Mom and Dad, once your kid turns 18, he or she can get a card without your permission. However, if the card is handled properly, your student will be glad to have a credit history upon graduation. The "Motley Fool" Web site—a financial education site—writes:

> Making the leap from college to the real world is going to be a whole lot tougher without a credit history. Without a credit card, you can't rent a car or get a good car insurance policy. You could get turned down for an apartment when a potential landlord checks your credit history and finds nothing there. Or you could be asked to shell out an enormous deposit before moving in. Once you graduate, getting a credit card will be more difficult. Let's say a pre-approved credit card offer does come your way. There's a good chance you'll be turned down. The reason? The lack of a revolving credit account on your credit report.

Martin suggests allowing your high school senior to sign up for a credit card so you can closely monitor how he uses it and be on hand to discuss managing credit.

Student Credit Cards

A college freshman is offered eight credit cards in his or her first semester. The average graduating senior has six cards in his or her name. Martin says that students only need one credit card. Yep, that's it, one.

Most students will receive offers for "student credit cards." These are simply cards that companies market specifically to students. The cards typically have lower credit lines—$500 to $1,000—and higher interest rates. Motley Fool found that the average rate on these cards ranges from 10 percent to 19.8 percent.

"Those rates are OK—not as good as adults with good credit, not as bad as people who have already mishandled credit. All of the ones at the low end of the scale are variable rate cards, so you can expect them to rise," the Web site reports.

Just as you would with any credit card, look for the lowest interest rate possible, a low or no fee card and a 25-day grace period. Keep the card limit low, even if offered a higher line of credit.

Prepaid Cards

Parents who are concerned about their college student falling into debt can consider giving their child a pre-paid card. This safety net allows parents to set a dollar amount on the card so nobody has to worry about the student driving up a large balance.

Never Co-sign on an Account

Whatever you do, however, never ever co-sign on a student's account. You don't want your student's financial mistakes appearing on your credit report.

Twenty-seven percent of students use a credit card to help finance their education. These students wind up with significantly more credit card debt when they graduate. The Nellie Mae study found that students who charged tuition and other related expenses left school with a credit card balance of $3,400. This is much higher than the average graduate's balance of $1,600.

Martin says paying for school with credit cards should be a last resort. Unlike student loans, you have to begin paying back credit cards immediately and you face a much higher interest rate.

The Impact of Debt

How does all of this debt impact your student? The biggest concern is how the debt and its management affect the credit report and the credit rating.

Nellie Mae found that over half of all graduates with debt feel burdened by that debt. And, for the first time, the study discovered "the probability of owning a home decreases by a small amount as debt levels increase. Family structure, age and income remain the most important determinants of home ownership, but an additional $5,000 of debt reduces the probability of owning a home by about one percent."

From Where I Stand... (Journal Responses)

1. I feel that I'm doing a good/poor (choose either "good" or "poor") job with using my credit cards because _____.
2. I think that a monthly credit card bill (for the total of all my credit cards) of _____ (state an amount) would be the highest I would feel comfortable with because _____.
3. If I were to graduate from college with a total debt of almost $19,000, I would feel _____ because _____.

JUST THE FACTS

1. The main idea of this selection is that a) too many companies send credit cards to students; b) there are many ways to reduce debt from credit cards; c) students have a legal right to get a credit card when they turn 18; d) the burden of credit card debt is felt by many college students and graduates.

2. According to the selection, if a student has a credit card debt of $1,000 when entering college, when he or she graduates the debt will be a) $1,200; b) $1,500; c) $2,000; d) $2,500.

3. According to the selection, students need a) only one credit card; b) one credit card for gasoline and one for all other expenses; c) one credit card for gasoline, one for food-related items, and one for all other expenses; d) three credit cards, to be used for any expenses.

4. The credit card balance of students who charged tuition and other related expenses is higher than the average student's credit card balance by a) $1,800; b) $2,800; c) $3,000; d) $3,500.

5. Martin says using credit cards should be a last resort because a) credit card companies will "hound you with additional offers"; b) credit cards can expire too quickly; c) you will feel better about yourself if you don't use credit cards; d) credit cards have a much higher interest rate than student loans.

EXPANDING HORIZONS

1. Read more about "Avoid Piling Up Credit Card Debt in College" at financialplan.about.com/od/moneyandcollegestudents/a/CollegeCredit.htm, and research answers to the following questions:

   You have a debt of $3,000 on your credit card and a 10 percent interest rate. You decide to pay off the bill by not charging anything else on it and by paying $100 each month. How long will it take for you to pay off the bill?

   The article advises that, unless you're sure you can resist the urge to use the credit card for anything but emergencies or items you can (and will) pay off at the end of every month, you should not do what?

   What does the article advise to get instead of a credit card? Why?

2. Kara Alaimo, of New York University, wrote "College Students Make the Grade with Credit" at www.youngmoney.com/credit_debt/credit_basics/050127. Answer the following questions from information in that article:

   In order to establish good credit and keep your interest rates down, what should you do?

   What did John Wooten, the senior at New York University, say was the result of missing one payment?

   When consumers amass debt with credit card companies, the companies often raise interest rates. Why?

   Consumers are advised to get a credit rating report every year. Why should you go to the trouble to do that?

3. Read "Your Legal Rights: Avoid Spring Break Scams," an article from the Office of Minnesota Attorney General Mike Hatch, at www.ag.state.mn.us/consumer/ylr/

ylr_College_04_Feb.htm. This article advises college students that they *should* use credit cards. From the article, answer these questions:

What is the worst case scenario of a spring break scam?

In what way can you check the reputation of a travel company you don't know?

What words or phrases should you be wary of in fine print? Why?

Why should you not deal with a company that wants its payment in advance?

Why should you consider using your credit card to pay for your trip?

4. Read "Credit Card Smarts" at www.collegeboard.com/article/0,3868,2-10-0-9139,00.html and look for answers to these questions:

What does the article cite as three good reasons to have a credit card?

The article says that credit cards are really _____ in disguise.

How high might the interest charge (finance charge) be each month on the unpaid portion of a credit card bill?

Cite at least three instances where a good credit report is valuable.

Why might a debit card be a better choice than a credit card?

WRITE ON!

1. Pretend you are the parent of a college freshman. Write a letter to your son or daughter, detailing both the advantages and disadvantages of using a credit card.

2. Write a letter to convince your parent or guardian to co-sign your credit card account.

3. Pretend you find a charge on your credit card for something that you did not buy. Write a letter of complaint to the credit card company. Since this is fictitious, you can conceive a charge for any item and for any amount; plus, you can state what steps you've already taken in order to get the issue resolved.

Personal finance guru **Michelle Singletary** *wears many hats—those of writer* (Spend Well, Live Rich: How to Live Well with the Money You Have), *radio host and correspondent* (NPR's Day to Day, BET's Real Business, *and* Howard University's Insight), *frequent television guest* (Nightline, Oprah, This Week in Business), *and syndicated columnist* ("The Color of Money"). *This article appeared on March 10, 2005, just as spring break was beginning for many American college students.*

Starting Out...

Circle A if you agree with the statement, D if you disagree.

A   D   Even though I have a student loan, I would probably go on a trip for spring break if I could come up with the money.

A   D   If I were taking a full load in college, my textbooks for the year will probably cost around $900.

A   D   If I have a student loan, any money that I have to spare should be applied to the loan.

Words to Watch

afflict: bother, trouble

all-inclusive: including everything (hotel, meals, and, sometimes, transportation) in a trip's price

four-star: of exceptional quality

maddening: frustrating, exasperating

rationalized: made excuses for ways of thinking or acting

compounded: calculated both the principal and interest of money

marginal: at a border or edge

NCAA: National Collegiate Athletic Association

scoff: make fun of, ridicule

vital: essential, necessary

On Spring Break, with Their Heads in the Sand

by Michelle Singletary

Typically when people talk about March Madness, they're referring to the NCAA basketball tournament.

But I want to discuss another March Madness. It's the madness that must afflict the thousands of college students who take spring break trips they can't afford.

I did a search on the Internet for spring vacation deals for college students and was floored by the places these young people are traveling to—Jamaica, the Bahamas, Cancun, Costa Rica, Miami, Las Vegas and South Padre Island, which is off the coast of Texas in the Gulf of Mexico.

I know two-income couples with full-time jobs who haven't been to some of these vacation spots. And yet college students with little or no savings, considerable student loan debt and perhaps unpaid credit card balances are taking off for fun in the sun.

National Lampoon Tours, a division of the company famed for "Animal House" and National Lampoon's "Vacation" movies, began this year offering all-inclusive trips to Las Vegas and Cabo San Lucas, Mexico. One spring break package included a four-night stay at a four-star hotel and airfare from Los Angeles to Cabo San Lucas. The cost: $860. Of course, that doesn't include spending money and maybe a roommate, but come on.

Rather than spend $860 for a four-day vacation, what could a college student do with that amount of money? Buy all his books for the year, perhaps? On average, students spent $898 for textbooks last year, according to the California Student Public Interest Research Group.

Unless all of these young people taking spring break trips are getting a free ride to college and won't have a financial worry in the world about paying for their books, fees, clothes and transportation to and from school, they ought to be vacationing at home.

Am I making too much of this March Madness?

Not when you look at the massive amount of debt that students (and their parents) are taking on to pay for a college education. Not when you look at survey after survey of the growing number of college students racking up a maddening amount of credit card debt.

Trust me when I say that young people flying or driving off to vacations they can't really afford are exhibiting behavior that will set them up for a lifetime of "I want what I want when I want it."

Here's what one freshman planning on vacationing in Miami said to me: "When exactly do you expect me to have fun? I am young and will only be this way for a little while longer. I have learned a lot about sacrificing and responsibility. I do understand that going to Miami may not be a wise decision, but I have rationalized the decision."

I couldn't get this young woman, who is funding her education largely with student loans, to see that her reasoning was flawed. She rationalized that because she had paid cash for the trip, she therefore could "afford" to take a break.

But it doesn't matter if you are paying cash for a luxury item if you have consumer (or in this case, student loan) debt. Any money you have to spare—say, for a vacation—should be applied to that debt or saved for necessities. Now *that's* sacrificing for your long-term financial well-being. That's the responsible thing to do whether you're young or old.

I'm not saying college students have to live like monks and deny themselves all worldly pleasures. But the time to party is when the bills are paid.

Let's suppose a college student who had $860 to spend on a vacation in Cabo San Lucas instead saved that amount every year for 10 years. At a rate of return of just 2 percent, compounded monthly and taxed at a marginal rate of 28 percent, he would end up with $10,178. That's a good chunk of change that could be used to buy a car or go toward the down payment on a home.

Now what if that student instead put that $860 spring break vacation on a credit card with an interest rate of 18 percent and made only the minimum payment of 2 percent? It would take him nearly 17 years to pay off that debt. In that time he would have paid more than $1,500 in interest. (Don't scoff, this happens all the time.)

I know college can be tough. Yes, many students work hard and could use some fun time. But they'd better learn now that they aren't entitled to that fun at the expense of handling their personal finances in a mature way. It's vital that they stop the madness (not just in March) and learn to spend wisely in their youth. As Tennessee Williams wrote in *Cat on a Hot Tin Roof*, "You can be young without money, but you can't be old without it."

From Where I Stand... (Journal Responses)

1. Students who have a student loan should/should not (choose either "should" or "should not") apply any extra money to paying off their loan because _____
   _____.

2. The most interesting part of this selection was _____ because
   _____.

3. If money were no object, for spring break I would prefer to go to _____
   (name a destination) _____ with _____ (name traveling companions)_____ because
   _____.

JUST THE FACTS

1. The main idea of this selection was a) students should not go into debt to pay for a vacation; b) credit card debt can be a burden for students and for graduates; c) some vacation sites are cheaper than others; d) some vacation sites are dangerous.

2. When she uses the term "March Madness," Singletary means a) the NCAA basketball tournament; b) both the college and state basketball tournaments; c) the feeling of apathy that overtakes some students and their studies; d) students who finance spring break trips with money that should be applied to loans.

3. Singletary says that, according to the California Student Public Interest Research Group, last year's students spent a) around $500 for textbooks; b) $663 for textbooks; c) $777 for textbooks; d) $898 for textbooks.
4. To rationalize going on her trip, the student from Miami said that a) her parents would pay for most of it; b) she would get a part-time job; c) her boyfriend had insisted that she join a group that was going; d) she would be young only once.
5. If a student put $860 on a credit card with an interest rate of 18 percent and made only the minimum payment of 2 percent, he or she would pay off the debt in a) 13 months; b) 5 years; c) 11 years; d) 17 years.

EXPANDING HORIZONS

1. Michelle Singletary received so many responses to this column that she wrote a follow-up just seventeen days later. Read that March 27, 2005, column at www.washingtonpost.com/wp-dyn/articles/A2622-2005Mar26.html and write a summary of what she said.
2. Use a link at www.washingtonpost.com/wp-dyn/business/columns/personalfinance/colorofmoney/ to read a recent "The Color of Money" column. Then write a summary of the article.
3. Singletary mentions National Lampoon Tours, which offers trips to Las Vegas and Cabo San Lucas. Visit the company's Web site at nationallampoontours.com/ and find the current rates for both of the destinations.

WRITE ON!

1. Explain Tennessee Williams's quote: "You can be young without money, but you can't be old without it."
2. I would feel uncomfortable if I were more than $_____ in debt because _____.
3. Defend or refute Michelle Singletary's position that students should use extra money to pay down their loans rather than go on a spring break trip.

Everybody can recognize a penny, nickel, dime, quarter, and various denominations of bills. But what is the history behind these coins and bills? What did Native Americans use as money? How has money changed over the years of U.S. history? These and other questions are answered in this selection about money in the United States

Starting Out...
Circle A if you agree with the statement below, D if you disagree:

A   D   Before the Revolutionary War, Native Americans had a difficult time adjusting to using pennies, nickels, dimes, and quarters.

A   D   The phrase "not worth a Continental" refers to money that proved to be worthless during the early days of the United States.

A   D   If you're carrying cash, it's probably in the form of Federal Reserve Notes.

Words to Watch

broken notes: money issued by banks that often went out of business

Continentals: money issued to fund the Revolutionary War (1775–1783)

Federal Reserve Notes: the only form of paper money currently being printed in the United States; issued in denominations from $1 to $100

greenbacks: paper money first issued to finance the Civil War (1861–1865), the name refers to the color of the money

legal tender: money a government says is acceptable to use to pay for debts

wildcat notes: money that was often worthless

virtually: almost, nearly

wampum: beads of shells strung in strands and used by American Indians as money

---

History of Money
from the NewsHour with Jim Lehrer *Web Site*

Way Before the Benjamins...
Money is a fact of life, it always has been. So as long as there has been an America, there have been many different kinds of currency.

Wampum
So you think carrying change in your pocket could be a pain? How about lugging around strings of beads made from the clam shells?

That is precisely what Native American tribes had to do. These beaded shells, called wampum, were the most common form of money in North America. By 1637, the Massachusetts Bay Colony declared wampum legal tender (ok to use as money).

Continentals

We're not talking about your grandparents' car here. What we are talking [about] are America's original "bucks." To finance the American Revolution-ary [War], Congress authorized the first printing of currency by the new repub-lic. But without the strong financial backing of gold or silver, the Continentals quickly devalued and were soon worthless—thus the expression "not worth a continental."

Wildcat and Broken Notes

Although these notes were actually issued by banks, they were as worthless as Monopoly money—maybe even less than that. With Monopoly money, you could at least put up a hotel on Park Place.

But back in the day when individual banks were allowed to print their own money, the so-called Free Banking Era, America was flooded with var-ious currency notes—many of which were redeemable in gold or silver, but some were worthless. Some banks would set up shop in remote mountain-ous regions, prompting people to comment that it was easier for a wildcat to redeem these notes than people—thus the name.

As for "broken" notes, the name refers to the frequency in which the banks that issued them went bust. Without the confidence that these notes could be redeemed, they were virtually worthless. By 1860, an estimated 8,000 different state banks were issuing "wildcat" or "broken" bank notes.

Greenbacks—United States Notes

Pressed to finance the Civil War, the US government resumed printing paper currency for the first time since it issued Continentals. The name itself, a ref-erence to its color, has become as much a part of Americana as apple pie. In addition to its new color, "greenbacks" incorporated a more complex design, including a Treasury Seal, fine-line engraving and various security measures.

Federal Reserve Notes

Open up your wallet—if you're carrying some cash on you, chances are it's a Federal Reserve Note. Following the Federal Reserve Act of 1913, these notes became the dominant form of paper currency in America. Over the years, these notes have changed very little—they have been reduced in size in 1929 and the words "In God We Trust" were added in 1955.

Currently, the $100 bill is the largest currency note in circulation. The largest bill ever circulated in the United States is the $10,000 bill, which features the face of Salmon P. Chase, who was Abe Lincoln's Secretary of the Treasury. If you have one, you can spend it, but most of them are in museums these days.

From Where I Stand... (Journal Responses)
1. The oldest/oddest (choose either "oldest" or "oddest") money that I have ever seen was _____.
2. If I could design a new dollar bill, here is how it would look: _____
   _____.
3. The part of this selection that I found the most interesting was _____
   _____ because
   _____.

JUST THE FACTS

1. The main idea of this selection is a) U.S. money has an interesting history; b) many forms of money have been used; c) Continentals were used as money; d) the United States issued money to finance wars.
2. The wampum that Native Americans used was a) beads made from clam shells; b) arrowheads and forms of pottery; c) fish and other products that could be eaten; d) building materials that were scarce in some areas.
3. Continentals were issued by Congress a) to help in the settlement of the West; b) to finance exploration in other countries; c) to finance the American Revolutionary War; d) so that taxes would not be raised.
4. Banks were allowed to print their own money during the a) Westward Ho! Movement; b) Vietnam War; c) the Civil Rights Era; d) the Free Banking Era.
5. The largest U.S. bill ever printed was for a) $500; b) $1,000; c) $5,000; d) $10,000.

EXPANDING HORIZONS

1. Wampum, used by many Native Americans, has a rich history. Read more about it and then summarize your findings. Online sites include these:
   www.nativetech.org/wampum/wamphist.htm
   www.wampumworks.com/history2.html
   www.kstrom.net/isk/art/beads/wampum.html
   web.syr.edu/~cfsmith/talks/cw97html/historicalwampum.html
2. Continental currency was first issued by the Continental Congress in 1775. Research more about this money from years ago. Online sites include these:
   www.frbsf.org/publications/federalreserve/annual/1995/history.html
   www.ishipress.com/colonial.htm
   www.moneyfactory.gov/newmoney/main.cfm/currency/history
   www.dailyreckoning.com/old%20site/oldWriters/King/Articles/MakingMoney.html
3. Look at the "Paper Money Glossary" site at www.littletoncoin.com/html/Paper_Glossary.htm and identify the following terms:

bank note	error note	grade
condition	face	great seal

micro-printing	press	security thread
national motto	printing plate	serial number

4. The selection cites "not worth a Continental," a phrase with an etymology (history) that comes from money. Look at these money-related phrases and define them.

ante up	have money to burn	pad the bill
be in the money	highway robbery	pass the buck
break the bank	in the hole	pay through the
bring home the	live high off the	nose
bacon	hog	pinch pennies
cash in your chips	money talks	quick buck
cheapskate	money to burn	red cent
chip in	nest egg	strapped for cash
Dutch treat	on a shoestring	tighten your belt
foot the bill	on the house	two bits

5. During the Free Banking Era, banks could print their own currency. Research more about this time and summarize your findings. Online sites to consult include these:

www.frbsf.org/currency/expansion/history/text2.html

en.wikipedia.org/wiki/History_of_Central_Banking_in_the_United_States#1837-1862:_Free_Banking_Era

www.kc.frb.org/pubaffrs/moneystory.htm

WRITE ON!

1. In 1956, President Eisenhower approved a Congressional resolution that declared "In God We Trust" to be the national motto of the U.S. State and defend your opinion about this: The phrase "In God We Trust" should/should not (choose either "should" or "should not") be printed on U.S. money because _____.

2. Recent controversy has surrounded the use of "under God" in the Pledge of Allegiance (the phrase was added in 1954). State and defend your opinion about the following: The phrase "under God" should/should not (choose either "should" or "should not") included in the Pledge of Allegiance because _____.

3. Write about a person whose face, in your opinion, should be on a coin or bill. Give detailed reasons for your choice.

Undergraduate Students and Credit Cards
from the Nellie Mae Web site

TABLE 5.1					
Credit card ownership by age	**18**	**19**	**20**	**21**	**>21**
Percentage who obtained first credit card	56%	21.4%	15.5%	4.8%	2.4%

Table 1: Percentage of students in 2004 reporting the age at which they obtained first credit card; source: self-reported survey data

1. More than half of students obtained their first credit card at what age?
2. Why do you think so many received a card at that age and not before?
3. What is the source of the information in the table above?

TABLE 5.2					
Credit card use by student's region of residence*	**NE**	**MW**	**S**	**W**	**Nation**
Percentage who have credit cards	71%	82%	78%	82%	76%
Average number of credit cards	3.90	4.76	4.06	3.90	4.09
Percentage who have four or more cards	40%	50%	42%	40%	43%
Average credit card debt	$1,850	$2,498	$2,373	$2,069	$2,169
Median credit card debt	$774	$1,207	$1,197	$890	$946
Percentage with balances between $3,000–$7,000	15%	20%	16%	16%	16%
Percentage with balances exceeding $7,000	5%	8%	8%	7%	7%

Table 2: Usage statistics in 2004 by region of the country; source: credit bureau data
*Regions as defined by the U.S. Census Bureau

Questions

According to the table above

1. Students with the highest percentage of credit card ownership live in what area of the country?
2. Students who live in what two areas of the country have a lower average credit card debt than the national average?
3. Students who live in what area of the country have the smallest average number of credit cards?
4. Students who live in what area of the country have the smallest percentage of credit cards with balances more than $7,000?

Answer the questions in Appendix A (pages 12–15) of Nellie Mae's "Undergraduate Students and Credit Cards," found at www.nelliemae.com/library/ccstudy_2005.pdf. Then compare your answers to those of others, which are reported on various graphs in the pages preceding the appendix.

*Some of the most persistent money problems today deal with identity theft—stealing information such as credit card numbers or driver's licenses to access the accounts of another person and commit a crime. The information below was gleaned from sites sponsored by the **Federal Trade Commission.***

Starting Out...

Read the statements below, and then circle A if you agree or D if you disagree.

A   D   When you open a new account, a good idea is to create an easy-to-remember password, like your mother's maiden name or the last four digits of your Social Security number.

A   D   Because you will often need it for identification, you should carry your Social Security card with you at all times.

A   D   When ordering new checks, you should pick them up from the bank instead of having them mailed to your home mailbox.

Words to Watch

amendment: a change or an alteration, as in a manuscript

consecutive: coming one right after the other in a logical sequence, as in "h-i-j" or "3-4-5"

flag: label, highlight

initiated: begun, started

opt out: to choose not to participate

precautions: safety measures, protections

scam: a deceitful business scheme, a swindle

thwart: stop, prevent

URL: uniform resource locator, the abbreviation for an Internet address

verify: confirm, make sure

About Identity Theft
by the Federal Trade Commission

Identity Theft Is a Serious Crime. How Does It Happen?

Identity theft occurs when someone uses your personal information without your permission to commit fraud or other crimes. While you can't entirely control whether you will become a victim, there are steps you can take to minimize your risk....

What should I do if my personal information has been lost or stolen?

If you've lost personal information or identification, or if it has been stolen from you, taking certain steps quickly can minimize the potential for identity theft.

Financial accounts: Close accounts, like credit cards and bank accounts, immediately. When you open new accounts, place passwords on them. Avoid using your mother's maiden name, your birth date, the last four digits of your Social Security number or your phone number, or a series of consecutive numbers.

Social Security number: Call the toll-free fraud number of any of the three nationwide consumer reporting companies and place an initial fraud alert on your credit reports. An alert can help stop someone from opening new credit accounts in your name....

Driver's license/other government issued identification: Contact the agency that issued the license or other identification document. Follow its procedures to cancel the document and to get a replacement. Ask the agency to flag your file so that no one else can get a license or any other identification document from them in your name.

Once you have taken these precautions, watch for signs that your information is being misused....

If your information has been misused, file a report about the theft with the police, and file a complaint with the Federal Trade Commission, as well. If another crime was committed—for example, if your purse or wallet was stolen or your house or car was broken into—report it to the police immediately.

How Can I Minimize My Risk?

When it comes to identity theft, you can't entirely control whether you will become a victim. But there are certain steps you can take to minimize your risk.

Order a copy of your credit report. An amendment to the federal Fair Credit Reporting Act requires each of the major nationwide consumer reporting companies to provide you with a free copy of your credit reports, at your request, once every 12 months....

Place passwords on your credit card, bank, and phone accounts. Avoid using easily available information like your mother's maiden name, your birth date, the last four digits of your Social Security number or your phone number, or a series of consecutive numbers. When opening new accounts, you may find that many businesses still have a line on their applications for your mother's maiden name. Ask if you can use a password instead.

Secure personal information in your home, especially if you have room-mates, employ outside help, or are having work done in your home.

Ask about information security procedures in your workplace or at businesses, doctor's offices or other institutions that collect your personal identifying information. Find out who has access to your personal informa-tion and verify that it is handled securely. Ask about the disposal proce-dures for those records as well. Find out if your information will be shared with anyone else. If so, ask how your information can be kept confidential.

Don't give out personal information on the phone, through the mail, or on the Internet unless you've initiated the contact or are sure you know who you're dealing with. Identity thieves are clever, and have posed as represen-tatives of banks, Internet Service Providers (ISPs), and even government agencies to get people to reveal their Social Security number, mother's maiden name, account numbers, and other identifying information. Before you share any personal information, confirm that you are dealing with a legitimate orga-nization. Check an organization's website by typing its URL in the address line, rather than cutting and pasting it. Many companies post scam alerts when their name is used improperly. Or call customer service using the num-ber listed on your account statement or in the telephone book....

Treat your mail and trash carefully.

Deposit your outgoing mail in post office collection boxes or at your local post office, rather than in an unsecured mailbox. Promptly remove mail from your mailbox. If you're planning to be away from home and can't pick up your mail, call the U.S. Postal Service at 1-800-275-8777 to request a vacation hold. The Postal Service will hold your mail at your local post office until you can pick it up or are home to receive it.

To thwart an identity thief who may pick through your trash or recy-cling bins to capture your personal information, tear or shred your charge receipts, copies of credit applications, insurance forms, physician statements, checks and bank statements, expired charge cards that you're discarding, and credit offers you get in the mail. To opt out of receiving offers of credit in the mail, call 1-888-5-OPTOUT (1-888-567-8688). The three nationwide consumer reporting companies use the same toll-free number to let consumers choose not to receive credit offers based on their lists. **Note:** You will be asked to provide your Social Security number, which the consumer reporting com-panies need to match you with your file.

Don't carry your Social Security number card; leave it in a secure place.

Give your Social Security number only when absolutely necessary, and ask to use other types of identifiers. If your state uses your Social Secu-rity number as your driver's license number, ask to substitute another number. Do the same if your health insurance company uses your Social Security number as your policy number.

Carry only the identification information and the credit and debit cards that you'll actually need when you go out.

Be cautious when responding to promotions. Identity thieves may create phony promotional offers to get you to give them your personal information.

Keep your purse or wallet in a safe place at work; do the same with copies of administrative forms that have your sensitive personal information.

When ordering new checks, pick them up from the bank instead of having them mailed to your home mailbox.

From Where I Stand... (Journal Responses)
1. After reading this selection, I think that I have been the most negligent about guarding _____
_____. I say this because
_____.
2. In order to guard my identity more closely, I will _____
because _____.
3. If I received a telephone call or an e-mail that asked for personal information, I would _____ because
_____.

JUST THE FACTS
1. The main idea of this selection is that a) identity theft can be a profitable business for an unscrupulous person; b) identity theft affects more than 50 percent of the population; c) an individual has ways to deal with and diminish the possibility of identity theft; d) identity theft has been exaggerated as a problem for online shoppers.
2. If you have lost your credit card, you should immediately a) cut up any other credit cards that you own; b) call the last place that you used the card; c) close the account; d) ask to be reimbursed for your last payment.
3. If your personal information has been stolen, you should a) file a complaint with the Federal Trade Commission; b) call the office of the Attorney General in your state; c) call all of your friends to alert them of the possibility that they will be contacted; d) ask that you be removed from future postal or electronic mailings.
4. You are entitled to a copy of your credit report a) three weeks after you report identity theft; b) every three months; c) six weeks after you report identity theft; d) once every year.
5. Concerning your mail and trash and Social Security card, the selection suggests all of the following except a) depositing your outgoing mail in a post office collection box; b) having a trusted neighbor pick up your mail when you are on vacation;

c) shredding charge receipts and other documents that may contain personal information; d) not carrying your Social Security card with you.

EXPANDING HORIZONS

1. The Federal Trade Commission has a great deal more information about identity theft. Go to the site www.consumer.gov/idtheft/con_about.htm#victim and choose one of the topics below to research further; then write a summary about what you learn:
   - How can someone steal my identity?
   - What are the effects of identity theft?
   - How can I tell if I'm a victim of identity theft?
   - What is "pretexting" and what does it have to do with identity theft?
   - How long can the effects of identity theft last?

2. Many places ask you to create a password for your account. Because it is usually easy to remember, one commonly used password is the maiden name of the person's mother. However, credit reports may carry this information about the mother's maiden name, and unscrupulous people can get copies of credit reports just by saying they are planning to rent property to a certain individual. Think of other passwords (words or combinations of words and numbers) that would be easy for a person to remember but would not be readily available for identity thieves to discover.

3. Additional information about identity theft and what a victim should do is available at www.consumer.gov/idtheft/. Read this and then summarize other hints that the selection gives.

4. The U.S. Department of Education has a site devoted to preventing the theft of students' identity. Read the information at www.ed.gov/about/offices/list/oig/misused/index.html and follow the links for additional information. Then summarize what you learn in these sites that you had not read in the selection "About Identity Theft" from the Federal Trade Commission.

5. A number of people have written online personal accounts about being victims of identity theft. Using Google or another search engine, read one of these accounts and then write your summary of the events in the victim's life before and after the theft.

WRITE ON!

1. Write a letter to a relative or a friend who is about to move into his or her own apartment. Warn this person about possible identity theft dangers.

2. Write from the point of view of someone who is the victim of identity theft. How do you feel? What kinds of problems have arisen because of the crime? What would you say to the person who stole your identity?

3. Now write a confession from the point of view of an identity thief. How did you feel when you committed the crime? How have you felt since then? What is making you confess? What would you say to the person whose identity you stole?

READ ON!

"1995 Annual Report: A Brief History of Our Nation's Paper Money." www.frbsf.org/publications/federalreserve/annual/1995/history.html.

"Anti-Phishing Working Group." www.antiphishing.org/.

Berger, Rose Marie, and Jodi Hochstedler. 2002. "Educated to Debt: College, Credit Cards, and Students: A Dangerous Mix." *Sojourners* Sept.–Oct.: 13.

Buia, Carole. 2002. "Extra Credit." *Time* Sept. 16: 88.

Dubner, Stephen J. and Steven D. Levitt. *Freakonomics: A Rogue Economist Explores the Hidden Side of Everything.* New York: HarperCollins, 2005."How to Commit Credit Card Fraud." www.identity-theft-help.us/identity-theft-how.htm.

Friedman, Milton and Anna Jacobson Schwartz. *Monetary History of the United States, 1867–1960.* Princeton: Princeton University Press, 1971.

"Identity Theft Prevention Help." www.identity-theft-help.us/identity-theft-prevention.htm.

MacDonald, Scott B. and Albert L. Gastmann. *A History of Credit and Power in the Western World.* New Brunswick, NJ: Transaction Publishers, 2001.

"MailFrontier Phishing IQ Test II." survey.mailfrontier.com/survey/quiztest.html.

Manning, Robert C. *Credit Card Nation: The Consequences of America's Addiction to Credit.* New York: Basic Books, 2000.

Newman, Eric P. *The Early Paper Money of America.* Racine, WI: Whitman Publishing Co., 1967.

Pinto, Mary Beth, et al. 2005. "Information Learned from Socialization Agents: Its Relationship to Credit Card Use." *Family and Consumer Sciences Research Journal.* June. 357.

"Remarks by Chairman Alan Greenspan on the History of Money." www.federal-reserve.gov/boarddocs/speeches/2002/200201163/default.htm.

"Student Credit Cards & Student Credit Card Education." www.schoolwork.org/astudent-credit-cards.html.

This "boss" looks as if he's enjoying his job. What job (paying or nonpaying) have you enjoyed the most? What made this job so special? Would you recommend this job to others? Why or why not? In contrast, what job have you had that has been the least pleasing? What aspects of it were particularly unpleasant? What could have been done to make the job better?

CHAPTER SIX

EMPLOYMENT

Problems and Solutions

Always be smarter than the people who hire you. —*Lena Horne*

Chose a job you love, and you will never have to work a day in your life. —*Confucius*

Getting fired is nature's way to telling you that you had the wrong job in the first place. —*Hal Lancaster*

If people knew how hard I worked to get my mastery, it wouldn't seem so wonderful at all. —*Michelangelo*

It is amazing what can be accomplished when nobody cares about who gets the credit.

—*Robert Yates*

Luck is a dividend of sweat. The more you sweat, the luckier you get. —*Ray Kroc*

People forget how fast you did a job—but they remember how well you did it. —*Howard Newton*

Pleasure in the job puts perfection in the work. —*Aristotle*

Real success is finding your lifework in the work that you love. —*David McCullough*

The harder you work, the harder it is to surrender. —*Vince Lombardi*

The more I want to get something done, the less I call it work. —*Richard Bach*

The phrase "working mother" is redundant. —*Jane Sellman*

The world is full of willing people; some willing to work, the rest willing to let them. —*Robert Frost*

We make a living by what we get but we make a life by what we give. —*Winston Churchill*

You know you are on the road to success if you would do your job, and not be paid for it. —*Oprah Winfrey*

Employment: Problems and Solutions

If you're like most students, you're enrolled in college with the goal of some-day finding a good—or better—job. While you may already be employed, your current job is probably not your dream job, nor is it paying you your dream salary. With so many candidates competing for so few good jobs today, how do you make sure a prospective employer appreciates your special skills? What can you do to put yourself at the head of the I-should-get-this-job pack?

The selections in this chapter can help as you prepare for that better job. Ellen Goodman's popular essay "Company Man" is a selection that will elicit a great deal of thought and discussion. Do you know someone who is a workaholic—or have you been accused of being one yourself? Just what does it mean to be a workaholic? What are the consequences of such a lifestyle—consequences for the worker, for his or her co-workers, and for the family?

Get ready to laugh when you read three of Max Messmer's "Resumania" columns, which point out actual mistakes that job applicants from all over the country have accidentally let slip by in their resumes. Studying these mistakes of others will be a good tool for learning what not to do when submitting your own application. After you've read this selection, you'll probably want to examine your resume for mistakes that you may have missed earlier.

Even if you have the perfect resume, you still face a highly competitive market. What will help you get your foot in the door for that job that you really want? What steps can you take now, while you're still a student, to make yourself stand out from the crowd when you're ready for a full-time position? "What I Did Last Summer" may give you just the idea you need to secure that high-paying job after you graduate.

Now that you have read the introduction to this chapter, go back and reread the quotations on p. 124. Then choose one of the quotations and write about whether you agree or disagree with it. Be sure to defend your opinion.

What happens when a workaholic dies? How does his or her life affect the family? How does it affect the coworkers? In this essay, first printed in 1979, readers discover insights about Phil, a man whose compulsive need to work led to his early death.

Starting Out...

Circle A if you agree with the statement or D if you disagree.

A   D   A person's good health is guaranteed if he or she doesn't smoke.

A   D   Working more than 40 hours a week is dangerous to a person's health.

A   D   A person should be promoted to a company's vacant position if he or she is the hardest worker.

Words to Watch

board: to receive meals or food and lodging

conceivably: possibly, believably

coronary thrombosis: an obstruction that often leads to destruction of the heart muscle

discreetly: subtly, inconspicuously, tactfully

extracurricular: outside of work

obituary: a published notice of a death, often with a brief biography of the deceased

stock options: rights to buy or sell specific securities or commodities at a stated price within a specified time

Type A: involving behavior marked by anxiety, impatience, and aggressiveness, often resulting in stress and possibly increasing the risk of heart attack

---

The Company Man
by Ellen Goodman

He worked himself to death, finally and precisely, at 3:00 A.M. Sunday morning.

The obituary didn't say that, of course. It said that he died of a coronary thrombosis—I think that was it—but everyone among his friends and acquaintances knew it instantly. He was a perfect Type A, a workaholic, a classic, they said to each other and shook their heads and thought for five or ten minutes about the way they lived.

This man who worked himself to death finally and precisely at 3:00 A.M. Sunday morning—on his day off—was fifty-one years old and a vice-president. He was, however, one of six vice-presidents, and one of three who might conceivably—if the president died or retired soon enough—have moved to the top spot. Phil knew that.

He worked six days a week, five of them until eight or nine at night, during a time when his own company had begun the four-day week for everyone but the executives. He worked like the Important People. He had no outside "extracurricular interests" unless, of course, you think about a monthly golf game that way. To Phil, it was work. He always ate egg salad sandwiches at his desk. He was, of course, overweight, by 20 or 25 pounds. He thought it was okay, though, because he didn't smoke.

On Saturdays, Phil wore a sports jacket to the office instead of a suit, because it was the weekend.

He had a lot of people working for him, maybe sixty, and most of them liked him most of the time. Three of them will be seriously considered for his job. The obituary didn't mention that.

But it did list his "survivors" quite accurately. He is survived by his wife, Helen, forty-eight years old, a good woman of no particular marketable skills, who worked in an office before marrying and mothering. She had, according to her daughter, given up trying to compete with his work years ago when the children were small. A company friend said, "I know how much you will miss him." And she answered, "I already have."

Missing him all these years, she must have given up part of her herself which had cared too much for the man. She would be "well taken care of."

His "dearly beloved" eldest of the "dearly beloved children" is a hard-working executive in a manufacturing firm down South. In the day and a half before the funeral, he went around the neighborhood researching his father, asking the neighbors what he was like. They were embarrassed.

His second child is a girl, who is twenty-four and newly married. She lives near her mother and they are close, but whenever she was alone with her father, in the car driving somewhere, they had nothing to say to each other.

The youngest is twenty, a boy, a high-school graduate who has spent the last couple of years, like a lot of his friends, doing enough odd jobs to stay in grass and food. He was the one who tried to grab at his father and tried to mean enough to him to keep the man at home. He was Phil's favorite. Over the last two years, Phil stayed up nights worrying about the boy.

The boy once said, "My father and I only board here."

At the funeral, the sixty-year-old company president told the forty-eight-year-old widow that the fifty-one-year-old deceased had meant much to the company and would be missed and hard to replace. The widow didn't look him in the eye. She was afraid he would read her bitterness and, after all, she would need him to straighten out the finances—the stock options and all that.

Phil was overweight and nervous and worked too hard. If he wasn't at the office, he was worried about it. Phil was a Type A, a heart attack natural. You could have picked him out in a minute from a lineup.

So when he finally worked himself to death, at precisely 3:00 A.M. Sunday morning, no one was really surprised.

By 5:00 P.M. the afternoon of the funeral, the company president had begun, discreetly of course, with care and taste, to make inquiries about his replacement. One of three men. He asked around: "Who's been working the hardest?"

From Where I Stand... (Journal Responses)

1. The most hours in one week that I have ever worked is _____; I worked this long because _____.
2. I think the wife in this essay should _____ because _____.
3. The saddest part of this essay is _____ because _____.

JUST THE FACTS

1. The main idea of this selection is that Phil a) was a hard worker; b) could easily be replaced; c) has children who are going to be just like him; d) had a lifestyle that led to his death.
2. Phil died a) while seated at his desk; b) at three o'clock on a Sunday morning; c) in the middle of a presentation to a major client; d) while attempting to get to an out-of-town meeting.
3. For Phil, casual dress was a) a sports jacket; b) jeans and an open-necked shirt; c) shorts and a T-shirt; d) not wearing a tie.
4. Phil was survived by a) no one; b) only his wife; c) only his two children; d) his wife and three children.
5. "Phil's favorite" was a) the current project at work; b) Phil's youngest child; c) the job he had recently been promoted to; d) his third wife.

EXPANDING HORIZONS

1. This type of essay is called a definition essay; in this case, Goodman defines what a company man is. Notice that she does this without giving a dictionary definition. Cite examples that Goodman uses to show the reader how a company man lives.
2. Irony is the difference between what happens and what is expected to happen. Explain what is ironic about Phil's time of death.
3. Phil had what is called a Type A personality. Research more about this and then summarize what you learn. Online sites to consult include these:

    www.hon.ch/News/HSN/510298.html

    www.jr2.ox.ac.uk/bandolier/booth/hliving/personHD.html

www.mindpub.com/art207.htm

heartandmindmatters.com/content/view/72/25/

4. Pulitzer Prize-winning Ellen Goodman is a prolific writer whose works have appeared in a number of places. Read another of her essays or columns and compare and contrast it to "Company Man." You can find many of her works at www.boston.com/news/globe/columns/ (click on "Ellen Goodman" for recent columns) and at www.postwritersgroup.com/goodman.htm#recentwork (click on "Recent Columns" on the right-hand side).

5. One of the phrases that Goodman deliberately repeats throughout the essay is that Phil "worked himself to death, finally and precisely at 3:00 A.M. Sunday morning." What effect does this repetition have?

WRITE ON!

1. This essay defined Phil, a company man who was, as the reader saw through details, not a family man. Using this essay as a model, write a definition essay about a family man (or woman).

2. Write a short character sketch (a description of someone) about someone whom you would call a workaholic. You might include a physical description of the person as well as details about his or her work and personal life.

3. Use your imagination and describe Helen's life five years in the future. Will she remarry? Will she be wealthy? What kind of relationship will she have with her children? Will she be happier than she is in this essay?

Max Messmer is chairman and chief executive officer (CEO) of Robert Half International Inc., the world's first and largest specialized staffing firm. He is the author of several books, including Fifty Ways to Get Hired. *Messmer's syndicated column "Resumania," which takes a look at mistakes that job applicants have made in résumés sent to companies located all over the country, appears in a number of newspapers. Below are three of his columns.*

Starting Out...

Circle the answer that best applies to you.

When I write a résumé, I use spell-checking software because it will find mistakes I make.

    Always   Sometimes   Never

I make sure that I have current addresses for those people I list as references.

    Always   Sometimes   Never

On a résumé, I am specific in listing past job duties and responsibilities.

    Always   Sometimes   Never

Words to Watch

alignment: arrangement, configuration

attachment: a file that can be opened in an e-mail message

Bates Motel: an allusion to the motel in the movie *Psycho*

bloopers: mistakes

detail-oriented: looking for fine points

dialogue: conversation

fastidious: picky, choosy, fussy

feat: achievement, accomplishment

gratitude: appreciation, thankfulness

instigator: ringleader, mastermind

password-protection: a computer feature that prevents someone from entering a site without typing in a particular code

prospective: potential, possible

rapport: relationship, bond

redundancy: repetition, replication, repeating

virtually: nearly, almost

Resumania

by Harold M. "Max" Messmer Jr.

Have Someone Else Check Your Resume

"DUTIES: Restocking bens."

Must have "bin" hard work.

This simple error would not have been picked up by spell-checking software, which is why it's always a good idea to have someone else review your resume before you send it to a prospective employer. In fact, it should be a requirement.

Here are some additional bloopers that might have been caught by a careful proofreader:

"I am at a lose to find another job."

Admittedly not a winner.

"POSITION: Sales rep. Satisfying customers and making sure customers are satisfied."

From the "department of redundancy department."

"HOBBIES: Painting by the numbers and fixing slot machines."

Fixing them to do what?

"EDUCATION: Curses in liberal arts, computer science and accounting."

Shame on you!

"LANGUAGES SPOKEN: English, French, Germany."

Do you speak Spain, too?

Here's an item from a cover letter that probably doesn't say what the writer intended.

"I wear many hats as a writer; I wear many hats as an administrator. In fact, I am never hatless."

Haven't we all sat behind this person at the movies?

"I have no adversion to hard work. I am responsible and reliable and will more than fullfill your quest for the best candidate. My attitude and ambition seperates me from the pack."

I'm afraid your spelling also sets you apart.

Here's a Resumania item from a candidate who is not ashamed to sing her own praises: She writes, "I don't usually toot my own horn, but in this case I will toot away."

Good for you.

More job seekers should describe their talents with confidence. Everyone brings something unique to the position, and as an applicant, your role is to get noticed. In a competitive market, telling a hiring manager why you're the perfect fit for the job can make all the difference.

Proofread Your E-Resume

The Internet has changed the way we do many things, including submitting resumes to prospective employers. In fact, in a survey commissioned by Robert Half International, executives said their preferred way of receiving resumes is electronically. But beware; the relatively casual nature of e-mail dialogue can be deceptive. While a friendly exchange of back-and-forth messages with a hiring manager can help you build a rapport, if you get too comfortable you might forget all of your communication is ultimately being evaluated. No matter how well you and your contact at the company seem to click, this is business. And your business is to land the job.

When you're sending your resume online, be just as fastidious as you would if you were sending it by regular mail. You may even want to print it and review the hard copy to make sure you didn't overlook anything. These next bloopers are a case in point:

"I am a gratitude in psychology."

But, thankfully, not English.

"EDUCATION: Universalcity graduate."

And on your left is the famous Bates Motel...

Another key piece of advice if you're sending your resume online is to be sure the employer can open it. One recent job-seeker learned this the hard way. He e-mailed his resume to various companies but neglected to change his password-protection setting. When it came time to open the resume attachment, employers were "locked out."

Here are some additional entries to the Resumania files.

"I am applying for this position to offer the perfect environment to demonstrate my many different talents."

We can't wait to see the atmosphere you bring with you.

"Looking forward to hearing from you thanks sincerely..."

A little punctuation might have been in order.

I enjoyed this next Resumania item from a cover letter in which the candidate included references.

"REFERENCES: Bill, Tom, Eric. But I don't know their phone numbers."

Do you know where they hang out?

Finally, from another cover letter: "Your time is valuable, and so is mine. My hat is tossed into the ring. How soon can we meet?"

Nothing like a little pressure...

Don't Put Your Worst Foot Forward

"QUALIFICATIONS: Have an intimate knowledge of insurance and documents involved with insurance. Took 40-hour class. Have failed state insurance test twice, but am sitting through class again and expect to see improvement in the future."

This might be called "putting your worst foot forward."

"REASON FOR LEAVING PREVIOUS JOB: Was fired for turdyness."

The unfortunate misspelling aside, there's no need to indicate on a resume reasons for leaving previous employment. Save this topic for the interview, if the hiring manager asks.

Being specific in listing past job duties and responsibilities on a resume is well advised. Carrying it to an extreme, on the other hand, will frustrate a busy hiring manager who may be reviewing dozens of resumes for a given job opening. This next resume writer took more than a page describing what he did for his last employer. Here's a sample:

"DUTIES: Opened store in morning. Unlocked door, and made sure that 'Open' sign was displayed. Checked and set thermostat to proper temperature. If something isn't working, responsible for calling appropriate repair person in time before customers arrive, take messages from answering machine and write down each message, including names of the callers, telephone numbers or things they want or need...."

On and on it went, right through a typical day, every task mentioned, virtually every minute accounted for. While the job seeker might have shown how detail-oriented he is, the prospective employer most likely lost interest back on Page 1.

Many mistakes on resumes result from knowing what we want to say, but not being sure of exactly how to phrase it.

"Maintained a 4.0 average while juggling a full-time mom at home."

That's no small feat.

"PERSONAL: I can describe myself in three words: Dedicated, Hardworking and very strategic thinking."

But a tad shaky on counting words.

And, finally:

"EDUCATION: Suspected to graduate early next year."

Sounds suspicious to me, too.

Easily Fixed Resume Mistakes

"OBJECTIVE: I'm very good on the phone and have patient's to work with difficult customers." Those patients are getting more than they bargained for...

Here's another item, this time from a cover letter:

"Attached you'll find my resume highlighting my porject management experience."

We'll let you know when our next "porject" gets off the ground.

SPECIAL SKILLS: "Music writter."

Spelling errors are the easiest mistakes to fix on a resume, yet they remain the most common examples of Resumania. At the very least, job seekers should take advantage of their computer's spell-check function. At best, they should have several people review their application materials before they're submitted.

This next example emphasizes the importance of not relying entirely on spell-checking software. Many words sound the same but are spelled differently and obviously carry an entirely different meeting. For example, this from a Florida job seeker, who said of her current job, "Duties include taking care of the male."

Or this example:

OBJECTIVE: "Gainful employment witch best utilizes my abilities."

Will you be using your powers for good?
Here are a few more spelling bloopers:

"PREVIOUS RANK: Senior instigator."

Could be trouble.

SKILLS SUMMARY: "More than 25 years' experience as manger."

A fixture at the annual Christmas pageant.

Poor spelling isn't the only avoidable mistake on resumes. Be careful with alignment of columns, or you could end up with something similar to this next candidate's effort. She mixed up the positions held with reasons for leaving, with unfortunate results.

Position	Reason for Leaving
Nurse's Aide	Summer ended
Lifeguard	Patient died.

"REFERENCES: Appliances upon request."

We could use a new coffee maker and microwave.

This job seeker from New York wrote, "To my other positive traits please ad attention to detail."

Only if you promise to ad an extra D.

From Where I Stand... (Journal Responses)

1. My favorite example of a mistake in this selection was _____

   because _____;

   to correct the mistake, the applicant should have _____.

2. In reading these examples from real résumés, I realize that _____

   _____.

3. If I were to submit a résumé that I later realized had spelling, grammar, or usage errors, I would _____

   because _____.

JUST THE FACTS

1. The main idea of this selection is that a) people can make themselves look foolish; b) candidates for a job usually can't spell well; c) candidates for jobs should submit résumés that are without flaws; d) different companies require different information on résumés.

2. Messmer says that a) it's always a good idea to have someone else review your résumé before you send it in; b) it is considered unethical for another person to review your résumé; c) your résumé will be returned with corrections on it if you have many spelling mistakes; d) many companies will overlook simple spelling mistakes.

3. Messmer says that, when you're sending your résumé online, a) you can expect a more prompt reply from the director of hiring; b) you need to be just as fastidious as if you were sending it by regular mail; c) you can assume that your résumé will be read by several people; d) you risk having the e-mail deleted by someone thinking you've sent junk mail.

4. In the selection, one writer was asked to give references; he made a mistake when he a) wrote only first names and no phone numbers; b) as a reference, used the ex-husband of the company president's current wife; c) forgot to fill in any names or other contact information; d) gave only phone numbers but no names associated with them.

5. One applicant made a mistake when she a) mixed up her positions held with her reasons for leaving; b) sent the résumé to a branch office instead of the main office; c) addressed the résumé to the wrong person; d) said that she would "demand a salary of at least $75,000."

EXPANDING HORIZONS

1. Messmer cautions against mistakes involving homophones (words that sound the same but are spelled differently and carry different meetings). His example was this: "Duties include taking care of the male." The writer obviously meant "mail" instead of "male," but the mistake made for a humorous blooper. Below are some homophones that are commonly used incorrectly. Decide which usage below contains the correct spelling:

   Charlie and Marlene decided to (build, billed) a lemonade stand.

   (Two, To, Too) many people came into the restaurant.

   The instructor refused to (accept, except) the late assignment.

   Visit the company's Web (cite, sight, site) for further information.

When I have a cold, I like to drink a variety of (teas, tease, tees).

Can you (sew, so, sow) a new skirt?

There was (undo, undue) influence placed on the defendant.

Even though it was March, the high temperatures made it feel (summary, summery).

The boat at the local (peer, pier) suddenly sank.

Two of the (miners, minors) came out of the shaft alive.

"Give (peace, piece) a chance," sang Joey and Micah.

The jury was not (holey, holy, wholly) convinced of the woman's guilt.

Can you (ensure, insure) that I will get a good grade if I study the chapter?

Because Sue was (lacks, lax) in her studies, she didn't pass the course.

2. While these articles from "Resumania" address some of the problems that have arisen on various résumés, a number of other mistakes are common. Take a look at the following Web sites and summarize the mistakes that they detail:

"Avoid the Top Ten Résumé Mistakes," www.careerbuilder.com/JobSeeker/Career-Bytes/0501avoidtopten.htm

"Most Frequent Résumé Mistakes," www.career.vt.edu/JOBSEARC/Resumes/mistakes.htm

"Avoid These 10 Résumé Mistakes," www.quintcareers.com/resume_mistakes.html

"Avoid the Top Résumé Mistakes," content.monstertrak.monster.com/resources/archive/jobhunt/resumemistakes/

"Nine Worst Résumé Mistakes," www.forbes.com/2001/11/01/1101resume.html

3. The most common format for a résumé is one written in reverse chronological order. With this format, you begin with your latest job and then go backward. Compose your own résumé in this format. You can see examples by clicking on "chronological résumé" at www.resume-resource.com/exrevchron.html.

4. Another résumé format is the combination, which uses parts of the reverse chronological style and the functional style (which organizes the professional experience you have according to particular skills or occupations). Write your résumé in this format. You can see examples by clicking on samples at www.epistemelinks.com/Edge/Resume/Center_5.asp (click at the bottom).

5. If you need help finding the right words to use to describe your skills, take a look at the verbs listed at "Résumé Writing and Résumé Samples" on the site www.ujobbank.com/resume/resumesamples.shtml; then update your resume to include the appropriate verbs.

Write On!

1. Write about what you would look for on an employee's résumé. Include what, in your opinion, would set one candidate for a job apart from another.

2. Write a letter to a candidate for a job, giving him or her the news that another person had been selected for the job. Think about how much information you should include about why the candidate was not selected.

3. Write about a time that you felt you were perfect for a job that you did not get. Why do you think that you were denied the job? How would your life be different if you had gotten the job?

"Very impressive educational background...now let's discuss WHO you know."
www.cartoonstock.com. Reprinted by permission.

Questions
1. What is implied in this cartoon?
2. Do you agree that sometimes it's not what you know but rather whom you know that gets you a job? Support your opinion.
3. Do you know of anyone who's gotten a job because of his or her connections with someone in a company or business? How has this person worked out as an employee?
4. Under what circumstances, if any, should a person be given a job because he or she has connections with someone in a company or business?

In a competitive job market, you need to examine all the possibilities that can help you get an advantage in your future career. Pursuing an internship while still in college is one of those options. In this article, first published in the IEEE (Institute of Electrical and Electronics Engineers) publication Spectrum, *contributing editor* **Scott Kariya** *relates how internships can work for you.*

Starting Out...
Take time to think about and discuss these questions:
- If you were an employer, would you give more weight to the résumé from a student who had worked an internship in your line of work than from one who had not? Why or why not?
- Should interns, who are employed for only a short period of time before they return to college, be put on high-priority projects? Why or why not?
- When you have begun a new job, how long did it take before you felt comfortable at what you were doing? Why did it take that length of time?

Words to Watch

automated test suites: devices that allow time to build test procedures to verify necessary functions a product should perform

carrots we have to dangle in front: an idiom that means "what we promise as a reward"

device drivers: software that controls devices that are connected to, or part of, a computer

EE-to-be: someone who will become an electrical engineer

employment landscape: outlook for jobs

Ethernet: a type of networking technology for local area networks

eye-opening: an idiom meaning "showing truths that had not been evident"

GB/s: gigabytes (units of computer memory or data storage) per second

leg up: an idiom meaning "a position of advantage"

long-term investment: a deal extending over a relatively lengthy time period

MERL 3-D: works in three dimensions sponsored by Mitsubishi Electric Research Laboratories

real-time: relating to computer systems that update information at the same rate they receive information

right fit: an idiom meaning "a good match for someone's qualifications"

synchronization: a relation that exists when things occur at the same time

x: times

What I Did Last Summer
by Scott Kariya

An internship gives you a leg up in the job market,
But be sure you make the most of it.

Ben Weatherman is under the gun. Customers of National Instruments, an Austin, Texas, maker of PC- and network-based testing and automation systems, have been demanding a clock synchronization feature for the company's new real-time measuring products. The Ethernet-based solution that Ben is developing must overcome interfering network signal traffic and pesky timing delays that cause tiny but significant miscues—no mean feat. But Ben is confident he can finish the project in three months. He has to—his summer internship ends in August.

Internships like Ben's offer engineering students a unique window into the real-world workplace and can help students make better career decisions. In the current employment landscape, that on-the-job experience can also prove invaluable. The National Association for Colleges and Employers (NACE, Bethlehem, Pa.) reports a 36.4 percent drop in hiring of recent college grads, who in many cases are competing for fewer openings with more experienced unemployed workers. But accomplishments like Ben's can make all the difference when prospective employers are sifting through endless resumes in search of qualified candidates.

Different Companies, Different Goals

Commercial firms typically use internships to evaluate prospective employees, a kind of try-before-you-buy arrangement. National Instruments' goal is to hire 25 percent of its interns after they graduate, while IBM Corp. generally hires a third of its interns. In NACE's job Outlook 2002 survey, employers rated their internship programs more effective at recruiting new hires than on-campus hiring or even their own Web site.

There may also be a more immediate objective: interns can be a cheap way to get work done. "We're not looking for a long-term investment—we're looking for a short-term return," is how Joe Marks puts it. Marks is head of Cambridge Research Labs (Cambridge, Mass.), owned by Mitsubishi Electric Co. Interns with specific academic or lab experience are typically assigned to high-priority projects, creating a temporary team to tackle immediate and specific technical problems. Choice internships slots can also be a reward that firms hand out to the academic partners with whom they collaborate on research projects. "It's one of the carrots we have to dangle in front of them," says Marks.

Not all internships for engineers are strictly technical in nature. Each summer the Washington Internship for Students of Engineering (WISE), of which the IEEE is a sponsor, brings 16 promising engineering students to Washington, D.C., to investigate how government officials decide complex technology issues. In this largely unstructured program, students choose their own topics, like third-generation wireless technologies or rural broadband access, then interview relevant legislators, and bureaucrats, and finally write a public policy paper.

The biggest lesson is typically the triumph of politics over technology, an eye-opening experience for many interns. Erin File, an electrical engineering intern from Ohio, was surprised to learn firsthand that legislators "made decisions based on what their constituents or (political) party wanted. The technical issues didn't seem to be a factor."

Find the Right Fit

Making the most of an internship starts, and ends, with initiative. Researching available internships can be done on the Internet, in a library, or through career placement centers. Savvy students also query professors and fellow students. Some of the choicest positions are not advertised anywhere; instead, intern recruiters ask professors they know to recommend their top students. "We receive a lot of unsolicited resumes but very rarely take people from that list," confides the head of one corporate-sponsored research facility.

A tip from her advisor clued Olga Karpenko, a computer science Ph.D. candidate at Brown University, into Cambridge Research Labs and the labs' pioneering work in three-dimensional computer graphics. She contacted researchers there directly, and her resume caught the eye of Ramesh Raskar, who hired her for an internship last summer.

When assessing internships, consider fall, spring, or multi-term programs. Although not as plentiful as their summer counterparts, non-summer programs are less competitive, so you may actually have more choices. Moreover, an extended non-summer internship often allows more complex and satisfying work.

Rick Cordaro, an electrical engineering major at Iowa State University, doesn't regret having worked at IBM's optical engineering facilities last fall, even though it means he'll be graduating a semester late. His work on testing and evaluating 10-GB/s optical Ethernet transceivers let him work with "highly technical people from the best schools," he says. A summer internship wouldn't have been long enough. "It probably took me three months just to become proficient at what I was doing, let alone get good at it."

Ready to Work

In a short, work-packed internship, a bit of advance preparation shortens the learning curve. Olga Karpenko, the MERL 3-D graphic intern, met with her manager several weeks before her start date. "He gave me a couple of papers to read so I could get a better idea of the projects," she said. "I wanted to get a head start." It paid off. Her summer research led to her coauthoring a research paper that will be published in the Eurographic 2002 proceedings.

Once you've started working, don't let your initiative stop. Seek out and introduce yourself to co-workers and managers. Advice from experienced workers in your intended field can be valuable not just in completing the tasks at hand, but also in setting your career directions.

Make sure that you know specifically what is required of you, then do your best to do more. Well-managed companies rate employees' performance with grades: typically the lowest acceptable rating is "meets requirements." Top workers earn a rating of "consistently exceeds requirements," and outstanding interns will do likewise. Shawn Liu, a manager at National Instruments and himself a former intern, recalled how one intern made a lasting impression. Assigned to speed up the reading and writing of data to disk drives, the intern took it further, Liu recalls: "We wanted a 15x performance increase, and he took it to thousands. He also added more features, more file caching."

Take This Internship And...

But what if your internship doesn't live up to your expectations? Harried managers often assign their most boring thankless tasks to neophyte interns. Or there's the problem of no work. "I've heard about other interns who went to companies that couldn't keep them busy," says EE-to-be Cordaro. "They'd sit at their desks for five hours playing solitaire." And most interns, new, unsure, and eager, are loath to gripe.

If you're handed a lousy assignment, experts suggest first trying to understand the work, how it came about, and how it fits into the overall business environment. Testing, for example, may seem monotonous, but knowing how undetected flaws can unseat a whole product may give it new relevance. Designers of the Hubble Space Telescope suffered tremendous embarrassment when it was discovered to have a flawed main mirror, later fixed by Space Shuttle astronauts making an orbital house call.

Treat the assignment as a problem and approach it with different strategies. Maybe you can discover a new way to complete the assignment that will become the new standard for others. And don't be afraid to ask your supervisor for additional or different duties. He or she may have no idea you're unhappy.

Here, your approach is critical. "Be assertive but not obnoxious," advises Samer Hannadeh, coauthor of *The Internship Bible* and cofounder of the careers Web site Vault.com. Arrange for a one-on-one meeting; explain how you've tried to address the problem, and offer alternatives that can satisfy both your objectives and the company's. Remember that internships frequently lead to permanent employment. Here's a chance for you and the company to see how the other solves problems and decide if a permanent working relationship is a good thing to pursue.

Back to Ben Weatherman, the National Instruments intern. When he graduates from Iowa State next spring, his resume will boast the clock-synchronization project, along with several earlier projects building device drivers and automated test suites. To potential employers, these real-world accomplishments demonstrate that his 3.9 grade-point average in computer engineering isn't just book smarts. Ben predicts he will return to National Instruments after graduation. "With this economy, he says, it's a very comforting thing."

An Intern Checklist

Find the right fit. Do your research through the Internet, college career center, and library. No matter what your interest or objective, you'll likely find a program that suits your goals.

Try word of mouth. Ask professors and fellow students about desirable programs—sometimes that's the only way in.

Take the all-season approach—internships in the fall or spring can be less competitive and more interesting due to the longer schedule.

Go above and beyond. Do more than just the expected, and get to know people throughout the organization.

Fix what's broken. If you don't like the assigned project, speak with your supervisor and offer solutions.

From Where I Stand... (Journal Responses)

1. If I had a job that was so boring that I could play solitaire instead of doing real work, I would _____
because _____.

2. If I were looking for a job, the first thing I would do is _____
_____.

3. An incident when I felt I worked harder than a coworker (but was not rewarded for my work) was when _____
_____.

JUST THE FACTS

1. The main point of this selection is that a) internships can be boring if a worker isn't given a good project; b) a number of interns in the field of education and sociology have decided to switch fields; c) internships can be a good way of finding permanent employment; d) interns in California and New York typically find more job openings than interns in other parts of the country.

2. Intern Ben Weatherman worked during the summer for a firm that dealt with a) agricultural equipment; b) computer-related systems; c) sports equipment and performance; d) home-based appliances.

3. The author states that the biggest lesson the interns in Washington, D.C., learn is that a) sometimes the interns put in longer hours than the politicians; b) frustration

sets in when the politicians are in their home states and the interns cannot contact them; c) "the triumph of politics over technology"; d) how much devotion politicians have to the projects the interns work on.

4. Some of the best positions for internships a) are advertised on the Internet; b) are found in journals and trade magazines for specific job groups; c) come as a result of unsolicited résumés being sent to companies; d) come from recommendations from professors.

5. The selection states that interns who have a problem with their assignment should a) approach the problem with different strategies; b) send an e-mail to supervisors telling of the problem; c) ask their professors for guidance in how to approach the problem; d) immediately begin to look for other work.

EXPANDING HORIZONS

1. Interview someone in the career placement center on your campus, and then compile a report about your findings. Some questions to consider are these:
   * what services the center provides
   * who can take advantage of these services
   * which companies usually ask for help through the center

2. Visit the job board at Vault.com and see what jobs are listed for your state or your area of interest. Click on at least three of the jobs to see what they offer. Then write a short paper to compare and contrast the three job offerings. If you were offered all three jobs, which would you choose? Why?

3. Conduct an interview with someone in the human resources department of a local company, asking
   * what the company looks for in an employee
   * if the company is currently hiring
   * if the company hires interns, and if so, under what time period and what conditions
   * what is the best way to get a job in the company

4. The article states that intern Erin File "was surprised to learn firsthand that legislators 'made decisions based on what their constituents or (political) party wanted. The technical issues didn't seem to be a factor.'" Write an essay defending or criticizing the legislators' actions. Be sure to include why you think they acted correctly or wrongly.

WRITE ON!

1. You find out that one of your instructors has contacts with a company for which you would like to intern. Write a letter to your instructor, asking him or her to recommend you to the company. Be sure to point out your qualifications and to emphasize why you think you would be a good intern.

2. You're a summer intern with a firm that you hope hires you after graduation. You put in long hours doing your assignment and you feel as if you're doing a good job with it. You notice, however, that the intern who sits close to you—and who gets the

same paycheck as you—does practically nothing except play games on the computer. Write about how you should approach this problem.

3. If you had the time to be able to work as an intern for any company in the world, what company would you choose? Why?

READ ON!

"Are You a Workaholic?" www.careerjournal.com/myc/killers/20041130-raudsepp.html.

Bermont, Todd. *10 Insider Secrets to Job Hunting Success!* Chicago: 10 Step Publications, 2002.

Block, Jay A. and Michael Betrus. *101 Best .Com Resumes and Cover Letters*. New York: McGraw-Hill, 2001.

———. *101 Best Resumes for Grads*. New York: McGraw-Hill, 2003.

Criscito, Pat. *E-Résumés: A Guide to Successful Online Job Hunting*. Hauppauge, NY: Barron's, 2005.

"Grammar Checker." www.grammarstation.com/GC.html.

"Grammar: Rules, Rules, Rules?" www.forumeducation.net/servlet/pages/vi/mat/gram.htm.

"How to Rein in Your Inner workaholic." www.af.mil/news/story.asp?storyID=123004645.

Internship-USA. internship-usa.com/.

Kaplan, Robbie Miller. *How to Say It in Your Job Search*. Paramus, NJ: Prentice Hall Press, 2002.

Maciejko, James J. *The ABC's of Coronary Heart Disease*. Chelsea, MI: Sleeping Bear Press, 2001.

Maltz, Susan. A *Fork in the Road: A Career Planning Guide for Young Adults*. Manassas Park, VA: Impact Publications, 2003.

"Personality Type." www.yourhealthstyle.com/macdill/perstype.html.

Philipson, Ilene J. *Married to the Job: Why We Live to Work and What We Can Do About It*. New York: Free Press, 2002.

Powers, Paul. *Winning Job Interviews: Reduce Interview Anxiety, Outprepare the Other Candidates, Land the Job You Love*. Franklin Lakes, NJ: Career Press, 2005.

"Search for Internships." www.findtuition.com.

"A Spelling Test." www.sentex.net/~mmcadams/spelling.html.

"To Be *B* or Not to Be *B*—Is That the Question?" www.pubmedcentral.nih.gov/articlerender.fcgi?artid=101259.

"Workaholism: A Socially Acceptable Addiction." www.expressitpeople.com/20040517/management1.shtml.

Think about the lack of simplicity shown in this picture. What practical advice could you give to this person to make her life simpler? Do you follow this advice in your own life? If so, how? If not, why not?

Think about some complicated part of your life—maybe your school schedule, your family schedule, or your work schedule. Write about at what point you would say that "enough is enough" and make changes. In other words, how much more complicated would your life have to get in order for you to demand some simplicity?

CHAPTER SEVEN

SIMPLICITY
Is It Too Complicated?

A truly great man never puts away the simplicity of a child.   *—Chinese proverb*

I adore simple pleasures. They are the last refuge of the complex.   *—Oscar Wilde*

Be content with what you have; rejoice in the way things are. When you realize there is nothing lacking, the whole world belongs to you.   *—Lao Tzu*

It is simplicity that makes the uneducated more effective than the educated when addressing popular audiences.   *—Aristotle*

It is the sweet, simple things of life which are the real ones after all.   *—Laura Ingalls Wilder*

Learn to get in touch with the silence within yourself and know that everything in this life has a purpose.   *—Elizabeth Kübler-Ross*

Life is really simple, but we insist on making it complicated.   *—Confucius*

Live simply that others might simply live.   *—Elizabeth Seaton*

Normal is getting dressed in clothes that you buy for work and driving through traffic in a car that you are still paying for—in order to get to the job you need to pay for the clothes and the car, and the house you leave vacant all day so you can afford to live in it.   *—Ellen Goodman*

Nothing is as simple as we hope it will be.   *—Jim Horning*

Perhaps too much of everything is as bad as too little.   *—Edna Ferber*

Simplicity is making the journey of this life with just baggage enough.   *—Charles Dudley Warner*

Simplicity is the peak of civilization.   *—Jessie Sampter*

The main purpose of science is simplicity and as we understand more things, everything is becoming simpler.   *—Edward Teller*

Who is rich? He who rejoices in his portion.   *—The Talmud*

Go confidently in the direction of your dreams!
Live the life you've imagined.
As you simplify your life,
the laws of the universe will be simpler.   *—Henry David Thoreau*

Simplicity: Is It Too Complicated?

If you're like the majority of students, you're juggling work time and family time with your studies—with maybe a little leisure-time thrown in to help you keep your sanity. Since you began college, life has probably become more frenzied than you ever imagined, and you may sometimes feel as if you're being swallowed up by your responsibilities. Wouldn't it be nice, in the words of Henry David Thoreau, to "simplify, simplify" as many parts of your life as you can?

Easier said than done, you say? Maybe not. This chapter is devoted to helping you find simplicity, both in your everyday life and in your academic life. The first two selections in this chapter suggest ways of simpler living; the second two address simplification in writing, something from which all college students—actually, all writers—can benefit.

In "Followup/Distraction" Paul Ford relates how he realized that his work was suffering from major interruptions because of new technology. To remedy the situation, he voluntarily turned away from the speed-of-lightning advances of his computer and returned to a slower way of working he'd experienced ten years before. He notes that he was vulnerable to two different types of distractions, and in reverting to an older, simpler method of working he became a more focused worker.

"Simple Solutions: Suggestions for Simplifying Your Life" begins with examples of people who found their lives filled with materialism and commercialism, and outpacing their needs. After they realized their unhappiness, they took concrete steps to change and gain contentment. The selection also offers a number of specific recommendations to help simplify your life, creating more time and also saving more money.

The second half of the chapter takes a different approach to simplicity; these selections focus on simplicity in writing. At this stage of your college career, you're probably enrolled in a writing class or you have classes that emphasize writing skills. In "Complex Language. It Can Cloud People's Minds," Jack Trout and Steve Rivkin stress the importance of writing in clear and easily understandable language. They offer two types of examples: the first illustrates how simple language benefits both the writer and the reader, and the second points out that some writing may sound intellectual to the writer but only puzzles the reader.

Now that you have read the introduction to this chapter, go back and reread the quotations on p. 146. Then choose one of the quotations and write about whether you agree or disagree with it. Be sure to defend your opinion.

Do you, like most of us, sometimes get overwhelmed with all the modern conveniences that are available and wish for a time when you didn't have as many choices? In this selection, writer **Paul Ford** *tells about feeling weighed down by the many options offered on the Internet, options that often led to distractions for him. His solution may surprise you.*

Starting Out...

Circle A if you agree with the statement or D if you disagree.

A   D   I don't find getting spam e-mails to be irritating.

A   D   I enjoy reading programming manuals about computer material.

A   D   When I'm working on a project, I'm not easily distracted.

Words to Watch

aflutter: excited, agitated

Ahab doesn't just chase the whale: an allusion to the ship's captain in *Moby Dick*, a man obsessed with capturing a great white whale

ARPANET: <u>A</u>dvanced <u>R</u>esearch <u>P</u>rojects <u>A</u>gency <u>NET</u>work, the forerunner of the Internet, created by the U.S. military during the Cold War

bland: boring, unappealing

blog: a blend of "Web" and "log," a Web site that includes posts by one or more individuals

buzzword: a stylish or trendy word or phrase

fathom: understand

latent: something is inactive and may become active in the future

Metafilter: a community Web log to share and discuss interesting links

paradigms: patterns or models

peak oil: a controversial theory regarding how long the world can keep producing oil

rapacious: aggressive, avaricious

the rose has lost its bloom: an idiom meaning "what once seemed appealing no longer is"

Web 2.0: a term applied to a possible change of the World Wide Web from a collection of Web sites to more advanced applications

Wikipedia: an Internet encyclopedia written by volunteers

WordPerfect for DOS: a word processing program, popular in the late 1980s and early 1990s, that ran on DOS (a <u>d</u>isc <u>o</u>perating <u>s</u>ystem), a group of similar operating systems

Followup/Distraction
by Paul Ford

There are two kinds of distraction, at least.

I'm getting so much spam. Hundreds of messages a day trying to seduce me by appealing to my darkest lusts and my greed. So I've gone back to basics. I stopped using my fancy word processor and installed WordPerfect for DOS, which was last updated about a decade ago, and which lets me type in gray letters on a blue screen without using any windows and without the need of a mouse. It never crashes. I also bought a little device called an AlphaSmart Neo, which is mostly sold to schools. The Neo is just a keyboard that stores text as you type it. It does nothing else. It doesn't tell the time or let me play games. It runs off of double-A batteries, and the batteries last for hundreds of hours. Using the AlphaSmart and WordPerfect, I've started to enjoy computing again. There is no Wikipedia, no email, no constantly changing the MP3s I'm listening to, no downloading going on. The spam still piles up but I'm not aware of it because my email program is shut down until I want to send a message.

Right now there's a new buzzword out there: Web 2.0. No one is quite sure what it means, but the basic idea is that by some clever programming you can bring forward some of the latent abilities of a web browser; you can make applications that are more dynamic and more interactive than regular web pages. Pages that update dynamically and reward interaction. Google is the pioneer here, with its clickable Google Maps and zippy Google Mail. Being the geek that I am, I have looked closely at the blog posts and articles about Web 2.0 and I understand what's going on, the new paradigms. I enjoy seeing all of the creativity going into these new dynamic to-do lists and calendars and forums. But I don't feel much like participating. I'm still programming at work, doing my job, but the rose has lost its bloom. I can't convince myself to stay up nights reading programming manuals.

It's not because I'm nostalgic for the old days of Web 1.0. They came and went and it was fun to be part of something so exciting as the early blossoming of the Internet, when everything seemed possible and young people could become rich just by willing it. But more and more I want my computer to do less and less. I don't want more information, more feeds, more sources. When I write, when I think, the Internet is just too much for me to fathom. It's a wonderful tool for research, a good way to kill a few hours. I grew up with computers, started hacking away when I was twelve. I always thought that the Internet would make me more productive, more aware of the world around me, but instead I'm using technology that was laughable in 1995 and getting much more done. I feel more in command of my own mind, more reliant on my own thoughts, when I work in this stripped-down fashion.

I figure there are two different kinds of distractions: the wide kind and the narrow kind. The Internet is the widest possible distraction because it lets you wander so far afield that getting work done—if you are, like me, the distractable sort of person—getting work done is almost impossible. I'm not the sort of person who can read a book with footnotes and ignore the footnotes. I have to read every footnote. I often prefer the footnotes because they point in so many directions. But when wide distractions are available I avoid the narrow distractions, and those are the useful distractions. Let's say you're thinking hard about a concept—say, kittens. Kittens are young cats. They have paws and they are sometimes friendly. Your stepmother, you remember, didn't let you have a kitten. Why was that? Was she allergic, or did she really just hate you? Now, that's something worth thinking about. A concept worth exploring. That's a narrow distraction, a good distraction.

But with a wide distraction you think about kittens and all of a sudden your email pops up and you're thinking about Viagra, and about how horrible the world is and how it's filled with rapacious greedy spammers. You're not able to think about kittens any more, so you check out the news to find out that China has a manned space program. Click. And that peak oil is a real problem and we might be living in an age where electricity becomes prohibitively expensive. Click. And that Apple just released a new iPod again, and everyone is all aflutter. There's really no way to bring all of that back to kittens. You've been broadly distracted. You might as well play some solitaire and go to bed.

Distraction is necessary. Minds need to wander to get anything done. But the Internet is sort of the mental equivalent of the snack aisle at a convenience store, filled with satisfying fatty chips and tasty cream-filled cakes. God knows I've spent enough time with both the Internet and cream-filled cakes to see the similarities. And I now know that what I want, mentally, is a well-cooked meal. A book gives me that, a well-written, carefully-edited book. Even though your average book is filled with distractions—I mean, Ahab doesn't just chase the whale. There's all sorts of stuff in *Moby Dick* besides that. Otherwise it probably wouldn't be that good of a book. But the distractions are useful. They get us from one point to another. Sailing wide seas of opinion in a million does not do the same thing. This is not to condemn blogs. They are often great. But there are so many of them, and I will be dead for a long, long time. And on my deathbed do I want to say, I sipped mightily of Metafilter, and saw many video clips that made fun of Rosie O'Donnell, and I am richer for it? Or should I try to make contact with the culture that existed before 1992? The Internet makes it so easy to think that nothing of importance ever took place before the ARPANET was created.

It is a wonder of the world, the Web. I have facts at hand by the thousands about everything from the different kinds of government to the names of the stars of television shows I've never even seen. I'm smarter, then, with my computer on, but not much deeper. I worry that my knowledge of the world is actually growing shallower, in fact, because for every idea there are a dozen articles and Wikipedia entries to read that allow me to avoid thinking for myself. And it's not like any of that is going away, nor will I be staying away from it. Just putting it aside for a few hours a day so that I can think without the world humming in my ear, sitting in front of my blue screen with gray text, or stretched in bed with my little portable keyboard, a working setup so bland it's actually inspiring.

From Where I Stand... (Journal Responses)

1. The type of spam that I dislike the most is _____

   _____

   because _____.

2. When I'm on the Internet, what annoys me the most is _____

   _____ because

   _____.

3. Something that I used to benefit from/get pleasure from (choose either "benefit from" or "get pleasure from") was _____

   _____,

   but I no longer enjoy it because _____.

JUST THE FACTS

1. The main idea of this selection is the author a) is tired of reading blogs that try to explain computer advances; b) likes the way that Wikipedia and other online sources help his research; c) has turned to a simpler way of working on the Internet; d) wishes that he had more knowledge of how to use the Internet.

2. The author reveals that he has installed a) some of the latest software and is quite pleased with most of it; b) a certain brand of popular software but is quite unhappy with it; c) a word processor that is at least 10 years old; d) several brands of encyclopedias that he recently purchased.

3. The new buzzword that the author cites is a) Web 2.0; b) paradigms; c) creative intellect; d) Google.
4. The author points out that he a) is employed by a major software firm; b) has recently learned how to use a computer; c) teaches computer classes; d) started hacking with computers when he was 12.
5. The author says that the Internet a) has been used for "evil and unseemly deeds"; b) has reached its height of creativity; c) is the widest possible distraction; d) helped him solve a difficult health problem.

EXPANDING HORIZONS

1. Ford relates that he has purchased and now uses an AlphaSmart Neo, a keyboard that stores text as it is typed. Research more about this product and write a review from what you learn.
2. Wikipedia, an online encyclopedia, is written collaboratively by people from all over the world. Anyone can add or edit an entry in Wikipedia by a simple click. Go to en.wikipedia.org/wiki/Main_Page and read "Today's Featured Article." Read at least three of the links in the article, and then write a summary of what you learn.
3. Buzzwords (trendy words or phrases) are often used by those in a specialized field to try to impress others. Pick five of these buzzwords and define them:

best practice	going forward	quantum leap
challenge	knowledge base	seamless integration
corporate culture	lifelong learning	thought leader
customer-centric	next generation	touch base
diversity	paradigm	wellness
due diligence	proactive	

4. Google maps are handy resources. Go to maps.google.com/ and create a map of your town (type in the city and state in the box at the top). Then get directions from your current location to a site at least three states away (type in, for instance, Los Angeles, California, to Dallas, Texas).
5. Ford uses a metaphor (a direct comparison between two seemingly unrelated subjects) in the sentence "...the Internet is sort of the mental equivalent of the snack aisle at a convenience store...." In this case, the Internet is compared to a snack aisle. Take a look at these sentences and find the metaphor in them:

All the world's a stage.

The mother inspected the inflammation with an eagle's eye.

After a few hours in the desert, my parched throat became a sponge when I found a canteen of water.

One movie star's silken hair shone in the camera's lights; the other star's hair was a limp dishrag.

When the sale began, one man in particular was an octopus, grabbing products left and right.

WRITE ON!

1. Ford writes, "I'm smarter...with my computer on, but not much deeper. I worry that my knowledge of the world is actually growing shallower, in fact, because for every idea there are a dozen articles and Wikipedia entries to read that allow me to avoid thinking for myself." Do you find that to be true of yourself or not? Defend your answer.

2. Think about something that you used to enjoy or some item that you used a few years ago but that is not part of your life now. Describe why you liked this activity or item, and then relate the reasons why it is no longer something you participate in or use.

3. Ford says he has "gone back to basics." What in your life could you do in a more complicated or modern way, but you prefer to do in a basic way? What are the advantages and disadvantages in doing it your way?

*For many people, life has become far too hectic. Materialism and commercialism have overtaken what should be important. In this article, from Aerobics and Fitness Association of America, **Victor M. Parachin**, a freelance writer from Oklahoma, looks at how some people have intentionally changed their lives; he then gives a number of ideas to reduce the stress of your own life.*

Starting Out...

Circle the answer that best applies to your own life:

I think that I work too many hours.

Never Sometimes Often Always

I sometimes buy things I don't need.

Never Sometimes Often Always

I trade vehicles more often than I need to.

Never Sometimes Often Always

Words to Watch

the American Dream: an American ideal of a happy and successful life that all may hope for

consequently: as a result

Easter: the Christian holiday that celebrates the resurrection of Jesus

ensuing: following, subsequent

evolutionary: a gradual process in which something changes into a different form

greenhouse effect: a phenomenon in which the earth's atmosphere traps solar radiation

Hanukkah: an eight-day Jewish holiday that commemorates the rededication of the Temple of Jerusalem

Kwanzaa: an African-American cultural festival, celebrated from December 26 to January 1

mystics: those who are interested in religious mysteries or occult rites and practices

budget buster: a made-up term meaning "something that breaks the financial plan"

ozone layer: a region of the upper atmosphere containing a relatively high concentration of ozone that absorbs solar ultraviolet radiation

perks: short for "perquisites," payments or benefits received in addition to a regular wage or salary

psyche: spirit or soul

shoestring: a small sum of money

Simple Solutions: Suggestions for Simplifying Your Life
by Victor M. Parachin

"For the past three years, I worked 70 to 90 hours each week," says Kenneth Hobbs, a former financial executive. "Although I complained about it, I secretly enjoyed it. Working long, hard hours—often until midnight—showed I was an important person. People were impressed that I worked so hard." Whenever Hobbs had some free time he would never admit it. "I would just tell people, 'I have a lot of control over my schedule right now.' I thought if I told people I wasn't busy, it would erode their confidence in me."

Materially, Hobbs' hard work paid off. He and his family lived in the most affluent section of the city. Their home had a three-car garage filled with luxury vehicles, a sports court in the back and a swimming pool. However, in spite of material success, Hobbs was uneasy and unhappy with his life. "Over the last year or so I noticed that except for work, I had little else in my life—few friends, no contact with the city in which I lived, and no community involvement. Worse, I would become furious if I was kept waiting by store clerks, delivery people or work colleagues."

After a period of evaluation, Hobbs made a profound and drastic decision. He quit his job, and his family relocated to the small town where he grew up. He sold the cars for a used but reliable utility vehicle. He then found a less stressful position that gives him plenty of time for himself and his family.

An increasing number of people are like Hobbs. A major survey recently released by the nonprofit Merck Family Fund found that a majority of Americans, alarmed by materialism and greed, rank nonmaterial things like more family time and less job stress among their deepest aspirations. More and more people are coming to the conclusion that the American Dream is not simply about a larger house, expensive cars and exotic vacations. It's also about peace of mind and being part of a community. They recognize the wisdom of Henry David Thoreau's declaration, "Life is frittered away by detail...simplify, simplify."

Here are some suggestions for living more simply.

- Don't buy what you don't need.

    Although this sounds relatively easy to do, most of us have a habit of cluttering up our homes with unnecessary things. Before making your next purchase, ask yourself some important questions: Is this an item I will regularly use? Have I had some need in the past for this item? Will this purchase enhance my life now? "You always find people buying fancy kitchen gadgets like a Mr. CrepeMaker, even though they're never need[ed] to make a crepe in their lives," says Aaron Ahuvia, Ph.D., assistant professor of marketing at the University of Michigan, Ann Arbor. Likewise, many people purchase expensive exercise equipment, hoping it will motivate them from a sedentary lifestyle to one that is more active. "But if they never managed to even take a 15-minute walk in the past, there's no reason to believe they will use some fancy equipment now," says Ahuvia. "Many home gyms are currently being used as coat hangers."

- Keep your car parked.

  Make the conscious decision to use your car less and less. Hop on a bus, train or subway. Using public transportation is less stressful than driving and you can use the time to read, meditate or just daydream. By driving less, you will also cut down on your car expenses as well as help improve the environment. The exhaust that puffs out of the nation's estimated 190 million automobiles contributes to smog, ozone layer depletion and the greenhouse effect. Also, consider biking or walking to do some errands. This will give you additional exercise and allow you an opportunity to enjoy scenery often missed while driving.

- Stop chasing the almighty dollar.

  "The steady pressure to consume and absorb involves a cruelty to intestines, blood pressure and psyche unparalleled in history," notes author Herbert Gold. Distance yourself from the rat race by living with less to enjoy life more. A bigger house, a newer car, more possessions and the latest fashionable clothing create tremendous stress to generate a larger income but do not lead to happiness and fulfillment. Mystics, philosophers and sages have uniformly warned about the dangers of materialism. Benjamin Franklin wrote, "Money never made a man happy yet, nor will it. There is nothing in its nature to produce happiness. The more a man has, the more he wants. Instead of it filling a vacuum, it makes one. If it satisfies one want, it doubles and triples that want another way."

- Follow your calling.

  Life is too short to waste doing work that does not bring you satisfaction and fulfillment. Many people in highly paid careers are fundamentally unhappy with their work and, consequently, their living. The solution is to make a change and follow your calling. Ask yourself what the ideal life and work would be for you. Then examine ways to make that dream a reality. "It's never easy to leave a career in which you've spent much of your lifetime," says Michael Dainard, author of *Breaking Free From Corporate Bondage*. "It's even harder if you've reached a high level of success and are locked in by the golden handcuffs of a large salary, benefits, expense accounts, perks and prestige."

Dainard speaks from personal experience. He was director of marketing for CBS-TV stations but left his lucrative work to follow his heart. "I wanted to be a writer, my dream since I was a child," he explains. "I'm now creating a path to realize that dream. I've already published two books and 14 screenplays, and I'm working daily on writing projects. My family life is considerably richer. I've never worked harder. However, it no longer seems like work because I really enjoy what I'm doing."

- Get rid of clutter.

  "People tend to underestimate how clutter contributes to their stress," says Jann Jasper, a professional organizing consultant in Jersey City, New Jersey. Today, her job is to help others make homes more simple and serene. Only a few years ago, she was a veteran buyer of flea market treasures. Jasper accumulated so many possessions that eventually she had no place to display or store them. Unwilling to part with her goods, she piled them in her living room with just enough space for a path. "It felt lousy to live that way," she recalls. "Just looking around at all my stuff made me feel stressed." After she got rid of the clutter, the pleasure of being in her home returned.

- Favor frugal food.

  "Instead of going out to dinner, we eat at home and then the whole family slips out for dessert," says Joan Marie, an Illinois teacher and mother of two teens. "Also, we order food in rather than eat at a restaurant. We tend to order less because we can supplement with a large vegetable or fruit salad from our own refrigerator. This provides us with healthier meals at less cost."

- Keep the car you own.

  "Cars are the largest expense over a family's lifetime," declares Larry Burkett, author of *Debt Free Living*. He notes people spend more on cars than they do on a house because car interest rates are higher than home interest rates and they are replaced more often. Burkett recommends driving your present vehicle longer rather than trading it in on a newer model. "It's always cheaper to drive the car you already own," he says. "It may not be as popular or as much fun, but it's always cheaper to fix the car you own than to buy another one."

- Vacation on a shoestring.

  Whether your vacation is a week or a weekend, it does not need to be a budget buster. With some careful planning and a little creativity, you can enjoy a memorable vacation without assuming huge expenses. Kevin Hanson and his wife like to vacation at a ski resort off-season. "Many ski resorts offer summer activities with discounted lodging prices," says Hanson. "We hike and bike through the hills and mountains." Other ways to cut expenses include flying at off-peak times such as weekends or late nights, riding the rails (often children under age 2 can ride free, and children up to age 12 can get half-price fares when accompanied by an adult) or driving to a vacation spot. Using your car is not only the most economical way to travel, but it offers the greatest flexibility and best scenery.

- Celebrate holidays in thrifty ways.

  Don't let a major or minor holiday slip by without thinking about ways to observe it in more thrifty ways. Here is an example from one Pennsylvania family who found a creative way to simplify Christmas. "My husband and our four children began to question the commercialism and materialism connected to this time of year," explains Cindy Richards. "So we came up with the idea of buying one small gift for each person, which is given on Christmas day. Then, we hit the after-Christmas sales and buy gifts at up to 75% off. Our family gathers again during the first week of January for a second festive party when we exchange presents again. This is something we've done for three years. We find we enjoy a more peaceful Christmas by avoiding holiday shopping crowds and cutting down on expenses. The money we save is given to a local charity." Whether it be Hanukkah, Kwanzaa, Easter, a birthday or wedding celebration, think about creative but thrifty ways to enjoy a holiday.

- Designate a "poor" month.

  Pick a month and designate it as your "poor" month. During those 30 days, buy only the absolute basics and do not use charge cards. Keep all transactions cash only. This tightening of your financial belt accomplishes three goals. First, you will see how easy it is to simplify. Second, you will save money which can be banked, applied to other debts or donated to a worthwhile charity. Third, you will notice how freely and carelessly money is spent. After living through one "poor" month, you will be more financially cautious in ensuing months.

  As you try to cultivate an easier lifestyle, don't become discouraged. Remember that developing a simple-living mindset doesn't happen overnight. For most people, it is an evolutionary process. It's done one step at a time. As you take each step, you gain more confidence and discover new ways of doing things.

From Where I Stand... (Journal Responses)

1. The area in my town or county where I would prefer to live is _____ _____ because _____.

2. In an ideal job, I would work about _____ hours a week because _____.

3. If I had extra money to donate to a charity, I would donate it to _____ _____ because _____.

JUST THE FACTS

1. The main idea of this selection is a) simplifying your life is easier said than done; b) people are too materialistic; c) many things can be done to live more simply; d) sometimes people are surprised at how expensive living simply is.

2. To simplify his life, Kenneth Hobbs a) obtained permission from his boss to work from home; b) did not apply for a promotion that he was sure he would get; c) asked his wife to help him more; d) relocated to the small town where he had grown up.

3. One of the advantages for keeping your car parked not cited in the selection is a) cutting down on car expenses; b) helping to improve the environment; c) getting additional exercise; d) reducing calls from car insurance salespersons.

4. According to the selection, the largest expense over a family's lifetime is the money spent on a) education; b) clothing; c) cars; d) homes.

5. One of the money-saving examples of vacationing on a shoestring that is not included in the selection is a) vacationing off season; b) booking hotels through Internet sites; c) flying at off-peak times; d) driving to the destination.

EXPANDING HORIZONS

1. The suggestions that Parachin offers for simplifying your life are these:

Don't buy what you don't need.

Keep your car parked.

Stop chasing the almighty dollar.

Follow your calling.

Get rid of clutter.

Favor frugal food.

Keep the car you own.

Vacation on a shoestring.

Celebrate holidays in thrifty ways.

Designate a "poor" month.

Now choose which is the best suggestion for yourself and write about why it is a good suggestion.

2. When looking for a job, many people consider not only the salary but also the "perks," the extra payments or benefits a company offers. Suppose you are offered essentially the same job in two different businesses or companies. Write about what perks might lure you to choose one place of employment over the other.

3. The article cites that a survey by the Merck Family Fund found that a majority of Americans rank nonmaterial things like more family time and less job stress among their deepest aspirations. Read more about this survey at hackvan.com/pub/stig/articles/yes-magazine-money-issue/yol/b1arts/yfb.html and then write a summary-and-response to the information on the site.

WRITE ON!

1. Take one of the suggestions from the article and apply it to your own life. Do you think your life would be better? Why or why not?

2. Write about a time that you had to simplify your lifestyle, whether you wanted to or not.

3. Look at the suggestions that Parachin gives, and then choose which you think you would be least likely to apply to your life. Then write about why it wouldn't work for you.

In this article, a chapter from their book The Power of Simplicity: A Management Guide to Cutting Through the Nonsense and Doing Things Right, *business strategist **Jack Trout** and communications consultant **Steve Rivkin** look at the power of simplicity in writing, stressing the importance of using clear and understandable terms. They offer examples of writing that is simple and direct and also examples that serve only to confuse the reader and make the writer sound self-important. While the book is aimed at businesspeople, the message is appropriate for all writers. "Complex Language. It Can Cloud People's Minds" comes from* The Power of Simplicity, *by J. Trout, with Steve Rivkin. Copyright © 1999 Reprinted with permission of The McGraw-Hill Companies.*

Starting Out...

Take a look at these sentences and see if you can write them in clearer terms:

- You would be unwise to calculate the number of Gallus domesticus in your ownership in advance of the time of their emergence from their reproductive bodies consisting of an ovum or embryo together with nutritive and protective envelopes.
- Homo sapiens residing in abodes constructed of brittle and transparent materials made by silicates fusing with boric oxide, aluminum oxide, or phosphorus pentoxide would be injudicious to propel concreted earthy or mineral matter through the air with a hand or arm motion.
- Your organ of light sensitivity exceeded the size of the enlarged, saclike portion of your alimentary canal

---

Words to Watch

accelerating profit curves: trends of making more money

bryophitic: having to do with chiefly terrestrial, nonvascular plants

buzzword: a stylish or trendy word or phrase

conglomerates: composite rocks made up of particles of varying size

core competency: a made-up phrase meaning "what we do well"

cross-functional expertise: people from different departments

cutaneous: pertaining to the skin

Fortune 500: published by *Fortune* Magazine, an annual list of the 500 largest companies in the U.S., based on the most recent figures for revenue

futurist: one who believes that the meaning of life and one's personal fulfillment lie in the future and not in the present or past

incentivization: a made-up word meaning "something that induces action or motivates effort"

John Maynard Keynes: a noted British economist (1883–1946)

modality: a tendency to conform to a general pattern or belong to a particular group or category

nouveau: fashionably new and different

post-capitalism: referring to a wide picture of global forms of economic organization

theory of relativity: a scientific theory in physics formulated by Albert Einstein

---

Complex Language. It Can Cloud People's Minds

by Jack Trout, with Steve Rivkin

> I notice that you use plain, simple language, short words,
> and brief sentences. That is the way to write English. It is
> the modern way and the best way. Stick to it.
> —Mark Twain, in a letter to a young friend.

When Shakespeare wrote *Hamlet,* he had 20,000 words with which to work. When Lincoln scribbled the Gettysburg Address on the back of an envelope there were about 114,000 words at his disposal. Today there are more than 600,000 words in *Webster's Dictionary.* Tom Clancy appears to have used all of them in his last thousand-page novel.

Language is getting more complicated. As a result, people have to fight off the tendency to try out some of these new and rarely used words.

What if some famous adages had been written with a heavier hand and some fancier words? Here's a sampling of some simple ideas made complex:

- Pulchritude possesses profundity of a merely cutaneous nature. (*Beauty is only skin deep.*)

- It is not efficacious to indoctrinate a superannuated canine with innovative maneuvers. (*You can't teach an old dog new tricks.*)

- Visible vapors that issue from carbonaceous materials are a harbinger of imminent conflagration. (*Where there's smoke, there's fire.*)

- A revolving mass of lithic conglomerates does not accumulate a congery of small green bryophitic plants. (*A rolling stone gathers no moss.*)

You get the point. Good writing and speech can't be confusing. They have to be clear and understandable, and the shorter the better.

Television journalist Bill Moyers had this advice for good writing: "Empty your knapsack of all adjectives, adverbs and clauses that slow your stride and weaken your pace. Travel light. Remember the most memorable sentences in the English language are also the shortest: 'The King is dead' and 'Jesus wept.'"

If all these new words aren't bad enough, business people are busy inventing their own language. Here is a direct quote from one futurist and management guru: "Managers have come to understand that there are multiple modes of change. One is what I call 'paradigm enhancement,' which the total-quality, continuous-improvement message has been all about. The other is radical change—or paradigm-shift change—which is unlike any other kind of change that you must deal with."

Fortune[4] magazine reported that Better Communications, a firm in Lexington, Massachusetts, that teaches writing skills to employers, clipped these management speak phrases from what it described as "memos from hell" circulating at Fortune 500 companies.

- Top leaders helicoptered this vision. (*The bosses are looking beyond next week.*)
- Added value is the keystone to exponentially accelerating profit curves. (*Let's grow sales and profits by offering more of what customers want.*)
- We utilized a concert of cross-functional expertise. (*People from different departments talked to each other.*)
- Don't impact employee incentivization programs. (*Don't screw around with people's pay.*)
- Your job, for the time being, has been designated as "retained." (*You're not fired yet.*)

Why do businesspeople talk so mysteriously about things like core competency (*what we do well*) or empowerment (*delegating*) or paradigms (*how we do things*)? It's gotten so bad that in a book entitled *Fad Surfing in the Boardroom*, the author had to publish a dictionary on nouveau business words and the *Wall Street Journal* (June 8, 1998) has uncovered a new sport called "buzzword bingo." Employees tally points in meetings by tracking the jargon and clichés their bosses spout. ("Deliverables," "net net" and "impactfulness" all score points.)

We sense that businesspeople feel that by using these pompous words they will look as smart, complicated, and significant as possible. But all it really does is make them unintelligible.

Jack Welch, the highly successful chairman of General Electric, put it well when he said in an interview in the *Harvard Business Review:*

> Insecure managers create complexity. Frightened, nervous managers use thick, convoluted planning books and busy slides filled with everything they've known since childhood. Real leaders don't need clutter. People must have the self-confidence to be clear, precise, to be sure that every person in their organization—highest to lowest—understands what the business is trying to achieve. But it's not easy. You can't believe how hard it is for people to be simple, how much they fear being simple. They worry that if they're simple, people will think they're simple-minded. In reality, of course, it's just the reverse. Clear, tough-minded people are the most simple.[5]

All that said, what's a manager to do to fight off complexity? Help is available.

Dr. Rudolph Flesch staged a one-person crusade against pomposity and murkiness in writing. (Among his books is *The Art of Plain Talk.*) He was one of the first to suggest that people in business who write like they talk will write better.

Flesch's approach would work like this in responding to a letter: "Thanks for your suggestion, Jack. I'll think about it and get back to you as soon as I can." The opposite of his approach would be: "Your suggestion has been received this date, and after due and careful deliberations, we shall report our findings to you."

Others have discovered that you can actually measure simplicity in writing. In the 1950s, Robert Gunning created the *Gunning Fog Index*, which shows how easy something is to read in terms of the number of words and their difficulty, the number of complete thoughts, and the average sentence length in a piece of copy.

You can win the fight against fog by adhering to 10 principles of clear writing.

1. Keep sentences short.
2. Pick the simple word over the complex word.
3. Choose the familiar word.
4. Avoid unnecessary words.
5. Put action in your verbs.
6. Write like you talk.
7. Use terms your readers can picture.
8. Tie in with your reader's experience. (*The essence of positioning.*)
9. Make full use of variety.
10. Write to express, not impress.

You have to encourage simple, direct language and ban business buzzwords not only in writing but also in talking.

But more than that, you have to encourage simplicity as the way to better listening. Overwhelmed by the incessant babble of the modern world, the skill of listening has fallen on hard times. Studies show that people recall only 20 percent of what they heard in the past few days.

In a July 10, 1997, article, the *Wall Street Journal* reported that we've become a nation of blabbermouths who aren't listening at all. We're just waiting for our chance to talk.

And if all this weren't bad enough, the newspaper reports, biology also works against attentive listening. Most people speak at a rate of 120 to 150 words a minute, but the human brain can easily process 500 words a minute leaving plenty of time for mental fidgeting. If a speaker is the least bit complex and confusing, it takes a heroic effort to stay tuned in instead of faking it.

Meetings and presentations that aren't simple and to the point are a waste of time and money. Little will be communicated as people simply dial out. This can be very costly.

Many years ago, an associate and I were leaving a two-hour meeting where a design firm had presented its recommendations in a multimillion-dollar logo design project. As usually, the presenters used terms such as "modality" and "paradigms" and threw in vague references to "color preference." It was a presentation loaded with obscure and complex concepts. Because of my low rank, I admitted to my fellow worker that I was quite confused by what was said and was asking for his overview. He suddenly smiled and looked quite relieved. He then went on to admit that he hadn't understood a word that was said but was afraid to admit it so as to appear stupid.

That company wasted millions of dollars changing a perfectly good logo because no one in the meeting had the courage to ask the presenters to explain their recommendations in simple, understandable language. If they had, they and their logos would have been laughed out of the room.

The moral of this story is that you should never let a confusing word or concept go unchallenged. If you do, some expensive mistakes can be made. Tell presenters to translate their complex terms into simple language. Never be afraid to say, "I don't get it." You have to be intolerant of intellectual arrogance.

Don't be suspicious of your first impressions. Your first impressions are often the most accurate.

Don't fight the feeling of looking foolish. In some ways the most naïve-sounding questions can turn out to be the most profound.

Let's give Peter Drucker the last words on simple language.

One of the most degenerative tendencies of the last forty years is the belief that if you are understandable, you are vulgar. When I was growing up, it was taken for granted that economists, physicists, psychologists—leaders in any discipline—would make themselves understood. Einstein spent years with three different collaborators to make his theory of relativity accessible to the layman. Even John Maynard Keynes tried hard to make his economics accessible.

But just the other day, I heard a senior scholar seriously reject a younger colleague's work because more than five people could understand what he's doing. Literally.

We cannot afford such arrogance. Knowledge is power, which is why people who had it in the past often tried to make a secret of it. In post-capitalism, power comes from transmitting information to make it productive, not from hiding it.

A Simple Summation

Big ideas almost always come in small words.

[4]"Jargon Watch," *Fortune*, February 3, 1997, p. 120.

[5]Noel Tichy and Ram Charan, "Speed, Simplicity, Self-Confidence: An Interview with Jack Welch," *Harvard Business Review*, September–October 1989, p. 114.

From Where I Stand... (Journal Responses)

1. When I'm at work or in a social situation and I hear people using words or phrases that I don't understand, I _____ because _____.

2. When I'm in a class and I hear the instructor using words or phrases that I don't understand, I _____ because _____.

3. One time when my first impression of someone turned out to be accurate was when _____.

JUST THE FACTS

1. The main idea of this selection is a) language has evolved and our vocabulary should evolve as well; b) language should be kept simple; c) businesspeople must use certain business-related terms if they are to be successful; d) new and rarely used words can help a writer be more precise.

2. According to Trout and Rivkin, if businesspeople use pompous words, they feel they will look a) smart; b) as if they went to a good school; c) silly; d) pompous.

3. Dr. Rudolph Flesch's suggestion for businesspeople to write better is to a) use a thesaurus whenever possible; b) find a new word every day and put it to use; c) have a number of people on the staff proofread their material; d) write like they talk.

4. One of the ten principles of clear writing listed in the selection is not a) keep sentences short; b) put action in your verbs; c) tie in with your reader's experience; d) use the "ten dollar words."

5. According to the selection, if you are confused by a word or concept you should a) immediately ask for an explanation; b) consult a dictionary; c) fire the people who are being so difficult to understand; d) go back to the context.

EXPANDING HORIZONS

1. This article uses footnotes, which are located at the bottom of a page of a book and give references about specific parts of the text. In "Simplicity: Why People Fear It So Much," you will see "*Fortune*[4]" and "Clear, tough-minded people are the most simple.[5]" The numbers written above the text (called *superscript*) indicate to readers that they can find out where information in that section came from by looking at footnotes

with the same numbers. For instance, at the end of the article the footnote for *Fortune*[4] reads this way:

[4]"Jargon Watch," *Fortune*, February 3, 1997, p. 120.

This tells the reader that the material used came from an article titled "Jargon Watch," which appeared on page 120 of the February 3, 1997, issue of *Fortune* magazine. (No author for this article was given in the magazine, so no author is mentioned in the footnote.)

The fifth footnote says:

[5]Noel Tichy and Ram Charan, "Speed, Simplicity, Self-Confidence: An Interview with Jack Welch," *Harvard Business Review*, September–October 1989, p. 114.

In seeing this, the reader knows that the information came from "Speed, Simplicity, Self-Confidence: An Interview with Jack Welch," an article written by Noel Tichy and Ram Charan, on page 114 of the September–October 1989 issue of *Harvard Business Review*.

Now take a look at these footnotes and tell what information they are passing on to the reader:

    a. "What's the World Coming To," *Good News Digest*, April 25, 2006, p. 93.

    b. Paula Fowler and Leslie Abbott, "I'm Beginning to Sound Just Like My Mother," *Mother-Daughter Review*, June 23, 2005, p. 98.

2. One of the ten principles of clear writing that the authors cite is this: Put action in your verbs. Below you will find a number of sentences with dull verbs. Change the verb to one that conveys a better picture for your reader. For instance, if you had "The man came down the road," you could change the dull verb *came* to *jogged, ambled, rushed, sauntered,* or many other verbs to better depict what you want to convey.

    The horse went around the racetrack.

    Three police cruisers were going down the highway.

    The telephone awakened me.

    Buddy came in the house late last night.

    I looked at the clock in the classroom, hoping that the time would pass.

3. Another of the ten principles of clear writing is to avoid unnecessary words. Use fewer words to get the same meaning in the phrases below:

    There are a number of _____

    Find us located adjacent to _____

    Several employees are in receipt of _____

    As regards your inquiry _____

    We had no need at that point in time _____

    At the same time we were speaking _____

    Please be aware of the fact that _____

    Your cost is in the neighborhood of _____

    I called during the time that the trade show _____

    Our premier product exhibits the ability to _____

In the event that our supplies decrease _____

Do you have a requirement for _____

You have got to reply _____

We are in close proximity to the your facility _____

Our warehouse has in excess of _____

4. Clichés are worn-out expressions—ones you've heard many times before. They're so overused that there's no zest left in them. Because of this, as a general rule you should avoid clichés. Look at the underlined clichés below and rewrite the sentence to eliminate them.

Increases in taxes will be a problem <u>till the end of time</u>.

My failing grades, thank goodness, have been <u>few and far between</u>.

The book details the <u>trials and tribulations</u> of a young couple.

If <u>the powers that be</u> give their approval, we can see changes in our organization.

Kim and Jose both knew it was <u>the end of the line</u> for their relationship.

My mom has <u>always been there for me</u>.

<u>In no way, shape, or form</u> will I ever set foot in that restaurant again.

Jim's criticizing Patsy's gossiping is <u>like the pot calling the kettle black</u>.

Our new products are <u>selling like hotcakes</u>.

I was so hungry I <u>could eat a horse</u>.

<u>Time flies</u> when you're having fun.

Pat is calling clients <u>like there's no tomorrow</u>.

You can ask <u>till the cows come home</u>, but I won't postpone the test.

Her apologies were a case of <u>too little too late</u>.

Was Mr. Thompson just <u>passing the buck</u> or was he really innocent?

WRITE ON!

1. Write about a time when you felt inadequate in some way. How did you react? Would you react the same way today?

2. Without using real names, write a letter to someone who (in your opinion) acted as if he or she were better than you. Describe the situation and how you felt.

3. Write about a time that you saw someone being treated unfairly. How did you react? Would you react the same way today?

In order to win the latest reality show, you have to spend at least two weeks alone on this desert island. Talk about simplicity in life! The creators of the show will send you with enough food to last for that time, and you may bring four changes of clothes and one item of sleepwear. But apart from those things, you have decisions to make.

Questions

1. You must bring one book, so which one will it be? Explain your reasoning.
2. You must bring one CD or tape, so what will it be? Explain your reasoning.
3. For the last three days of your time on the island, you can have one guest. If you have the option of bringing anyone—a real or fictional person, someone living or deceased—whom would you elect to bring? Explain your reasoning.
4. You may bring ten extra items. What do you choose to bring, and why would you choose those items?
5. Now think about what you have chosen not to bring. Of the items that you normally are used to having, what do you think you would miss the most? Why?

When I Heard the Learn'd Astronomer
by Walt Whitman

When I heard the learn'd astronomer,
When the proofs, the figures, were ranged in columns before me,
When I was shown the charts and diagrams, to add, divide, and measure them,
When I sitting heard the astronomer where he lectured with much applause in
    the lecture-room,
How soon unaccountable I became tired and sick,
Till rising and gliding out I wander'd off by myself,
In the mystical moist night-air, and from time to time,
Look'd up in perfect silence at the stars.

Questions

1. In this short poem, the poet is listening to an accomplished astronomer give a highly detailed lecture about the stars. The poet, however, "grew tired and sick" of the lecture and went out to the "mystical moist night-air" to find own beauty of the heavens. In applying this poem to aspects of your everyday life, what else can you think of that you can appreciate better by doing rather than hearing about it?
2. The word "learn'd" is a contraction for "learned" (pronounced with the accent on the last syllable, learnED). Do you think this word has a positive or negative connotation in this poem? Or is it ambiguous?
3. What other poems by Walt Whitman do you know? What do you think makes Whitman's poetry so important? Read another short poem by Whitman, such as "The Noiseless, Patient Spider," and then write a paragraph in which you compare the ideas found in the two poems.

READ ON!

Carlson, Richard. *Don't Sweat the Small Stuff and It's All Small Stuff: Simple Ways to Keep the Little Things from Taking Over Your Life.* New York: Hyperion, 1997.
———. *Easier Than You Think… Because Life Doesn't Have to Be So Hard: The Small Changes That Add Up to a World of Difference.* San Francisco: HarperSanFrancisco, 2005.
"Cliché Finder." www.westegg.com/cliche/.
"Doublespeak." en.wikipedia.org/wiki/Doublespeak.
Gribbin, John R. *Deep Simplicity: Bringing Order to Chaos and Complexity.* New York: Random House, 2004.
Grigsby, Mary. *Buying Time and Getting By: The Voluntary Simplicity Movement.* Albany: State University of New York Press, 2004.
Holder, R. W. *How Not to Say What You Mean: A Dictionary of Euphemisms.* New York: Oxford University Press, 2002.
"Jargon Finder Dictionary." www.emcf.org/pub/jargon/words/index.htm.
"Living a Better Life." www.betterbudgeting.com/frugalliving.htm.
"Living Lightly in Breadth and Depth." www.scn.org/earth/lightly/vslinks.htm.
"Plain English." www.deccanherald.com/deccanherald/aug10/at12.asp.
Rogers, James T. *The Dictionary of Clichés.* New York: Barnes & Noble Books, 2001.
"The Simple Living Network." www.simpleliving.net/.
"Simple Living/Money Savers." members.tripod.com/~SJEWELRYS/simple.html.
"Simplicity in Writing." www.iup.edu/lec/PADE/selectproceed13.htm.
"'Tis a Gift to be Simple: The Power of Simplicity in Corporate Communications." www.joannebrown.com/article04.html.
Twigg, Nancy. *Celebrate Simply: Your Guide to Simpler, More Meaningful Holidays and Special Occasions.* Knoxville, TN: Counting the Cost Publications, 2003.
Zinsser, William Knowlton. *On Writing Well: The Classic Guide to Writing Nonfiction.* New York: HarperCollins, 1998.

Take a close look at this photograph, and picture yourself as one person in it. First, write about the circumstances behind why this picture was taken and why it is important to you. Then choose another person in the picture, someone from a different generation, and write that person's opinion about why this picture is important.

CHAPTER EIGHT

FRIENDS, FAMILIES, AND PARENTHOOD

Between men and women there is no friendship possible. There is passion, enmity, worship, love, but no friendship.   —*Oscar Wilde*

Family faces are magic mirrors. Looking at people who belong to us, we see the past, present, and future.   —*Gail Lumet Buckley*

Family is a mixed blessing. You're glad to have one, but it's also like receiving a life sentence for a crime you didn't commit.   —*Richard Pryor*

Friendship doubles our joy and divides our grief.   —*Swedish proverb*

I can get up in the morning and look myself in the mirror and my family can look at me too and that's all that matters.   —*Lance Armstrong*

If you can give your son or daughter only one gift, let it be enthusiasm.   —*Bruce Barton*

If you cannot get rid of the family skeleton, you may as well make it dance.   —*George Bernard Shaw*

If you don't know [your family's] history, then you don't know anything. You are a leaf that doesn't know it is part of a tree.   —*Michael Crichton*

In the end, we will remember not the words of our enemies, but the silence of our friends.
—*Martin Luther King, Jr.*

It's the ones you can call up at 4:00 a.m. that really matter.   —*Marlene Dietrich*

My mother had a great deal of trouble with me, but I think she enjoyed it.   —*Mark Twain*

No person is your friend who demands your silence, or denies your right to grow.   —*Alice Walker*

"Stay" is a charming word in a friend's vocabulary.   —*Louisa May Alcott*

The family you come from isn't as important as the family you're going to have.   —*Ring Lardner*

We usually meet all our relatives only at funerals where someone always observes, "Too bad we can't get together more often."   —*Sam Levenson*

Friends, Families, and Parenthood

Are you familiar with the old saying "People are more interesting than anybody"? On the surface, it seems to be a remark that indicates the obvious, but it makes a good point if you think about it in terms of the many and varied relationships that we all have.

Take just a minute to mentally list all the people that you've ever had some kind of connection with.

It's really a pretty long list because people can be connected in many different ways. Most of you have family members that you connect to, but your age often is an indication of how many of your family members are still living. For instance, if you're still in your teens, you're likely to have younger brothers and sisters as well as living parents, grandparents, or even great-grandparents, and some of you may even have children yourselves. On the other hand, if you're a nontraditional college student, you may be the "older generation" in your families, having lost elder relatives but being of an age to have children and perhaps grandchildren.

While you are probably tightly connected with your families, other connections can, over time, become just as important as some familial links. Students often quickly bond with those with whom they share college classes, or associate with at work, or live close to.

On a more individual level, sometimes you may become close to another person just because of a kindness that someone does for you, or vice versa. The bond may begin with a small gesture, but then its glue seems to stick as time goes by.

And of course you are connected to your spouse or another person with whom you share romantic feelings. In fact, this connection may be the strongest—or the most frustrating—of all.

In this chapter, the selections look at various ways that relationships can affect students. Judy Brady's "I Want a Wife," a satirical view of gender roles, gives a number of reasons why the author is interested in someone who will do all the "wifely" things that are expected of married females.

"Three Credits and a Baby" relates one student's experiences as a full-time student and a full-time single mom—and she gives a number of hints about how to be successful at both.

Have you ever found yourself to be the recipient of sexist remarks? Have you ever reacted to a situation and, in retrospect, wished that you'd taken a different stance? Professor Bill Gary's "Reactionary" looks at how he has dealt with being a single dad, and how his response to the reaction of others has changed over time.

Finally, do you think there can be humor in parenthood? Even people who are not fathers will laugh at the wittiness—combined with the truth—in Tom Bodett's "Symptoms of Fatherhood." This reading details some of the thoughts a man has and the emotions he goes through as a new parent—even though in the past he swore he'd never behave in the way he describes.

Now that you have read the introduction to this chapter, go back and reread the quotations on p. 172. Then choose one of the quotations and write about whether you agree or disagree with it. Be sure to defend your opinion.

What is your definition of a "wife"? Is she defined by the chores or obligations that she performs? In this famous essay, first published in the premiere issue of Ms. *magazine in the early 1970s, author **Judy Brady** explains why she wants a wife herself.*

Starting Out...
Circle A if you agree with the statement or D if you disagree.

A   D   A wife should work to send her husband to school.

A   D   A wife should keep the house clean.

A   D   After the husband is employed, a wife should stay at home and take care of the couple's children.

Words to Watch
attendant: one who waits on another
hors d'oeuvres: appetizers served before a meal
incidentally: apart from the main subject, parenthetically
replenished: refilled, stocked up
monogamy: the practice or condition of having a single sexual partner during a period of time
peers: people who have equal standing with another or others, as in rank, class, or age

---

I Want a Wife
by Judy Brady

I belong to that classification of people known as wives. I am A Wife.

And, not altogether incidentally, I am a mother. Not too long ago a male friend of mine appeared on the scene fresh from a recent divorce. He had one child, who is, of course, with his ex-wife. He is looking for another wife. As I thought about him while I was ironing one evening, it suddenly occurred to me that I, too, would like to have a wife. Why do I want a wife?

I would like to go back to school so that I can become economically independent, support myself, and if need be, support those dependent upon me. I want a wife who will work and send me to school. And while I am going to school I want a wife to take care of my children. I want a wife to keep track of the children's doctor and dentist appointments. And to keep track of mine, too. I want a wife to make sure my children eat properly and are kept clean. I want a wife who will wash the children's clothes and keep them mended. I want a wife who is a good nurturing attendant to my children, who arranges for their schooling, makes sure that they have an adequate social life with their peers, takes them to the park, the zoo, etc. I want a wife who takes care of the children when they are sick, a wife who arranges to be around when the children need special care, because, of course, I cannot miss classes at school. My wife must arrange to lose time at work and not lose the job. It may mean a small cut in my wife's income from time to time, but I guess I can tolerate that. Needless to say, my wife will arrange and pay for the care of the children while my wife is working.

I want a wife who will take care of my physical needs. I want a wife who will keep my house clean. A wife who will pick up after my children, a wife who will pick up after me. I want a wife who will keep my clothes clean, ironed, mended, replaced when need be, and who will see to it that my personal things are kept in their proper place so that I can find what I need the minute I need it. I want a wife who cooks the meals, a wife who is a good cook. I want a wife who will plan the menus, do the necessary grocery shopping, prepare the meals, serve them pleasantly, and then do the cleaning up while I do my studying. I want a wife who will care for me when I am sick and sympathize with my pain and loss of time from school. I want a wife to go along when our family takes a vacation so that someone can continue to care for me and my children when I need a rest and change of scene. I want a wife who will not bother me with rambling complaints about a wife's duties. But I want a wife who will listen to me when I feel the need to explain a rather difficult point I have come across in my course of studies. And I want a wife who will type my papers for me when I have written them.

I want a wife who will take care of the details of my social life. When my wife and I are invited out by my friends, I want a wife who takes care of the baby-sitting arrangements. When I meet people at school that I like and want to entertain, I want a wife who will have the house clean, will prepare a special meal, serve it to me and my friends, and not interrupt when I talk about things that interest me and my friends. I want a wife who will have arranged that the children are fed and ready for bed before my guests arrive so that the children do not bother us. I want a wife who takes care of the needs of my guests so that they feel comfortable, who makes sure that they have an ashtray, that they are passed the hors d'oeuvres, that they are offered a second helping of the food, that their wine glasses are replenished when necessary, that their coffee is served to them as they like it. And I want a wife who knows that sometimes I need a night out by myself.

I want a wife who is sensitive to my sexual needs, a wife who makes love passionately and eagerly when I feel like it, a wife who makes sure that I am satisfied. And, of course, I want a wife who will not demand sexual attention when I am not in the mood for it. I want a wife who assumes the complete responsibility for birth control, because I do not want more children. I want a wife who will remain sexually faithful to me so that I do not have to clutter up my intellectual life with jealousies. And I want a wife who understands that my sexual needs may entail more than strict adherence to monogamy. I must, after all, be able to relate to people as fully as possible.

If, by chance, I find another person more suitable as a wife than the wife I already have, I want the liberty to replace my present wife with another one. Naturally, I will expect a fresh, new life; my wife will take the children and be solely responsible for them so that I am left free.

When I am through with school and have a job, I want my wife to quit working and remain at home so that my wife can more fully and completely take care of a wife's duties.

My God, who *wouldn't* want a wife?

From Where I Stand... (Journal Responses)
1. A wife's obligations should include _____
   because _____.
2. A husband's obligations should include _____
   because _____.
3. The part of this selection that I agree/disagree (choose either "agree" or "disagree") with most is _____
   because _____.

JUST THE FACTS

1. The main idea of this selection is a) the author has discovered that she has feelings for a woman; b) the author's mother was mistreated as a wife; c) the author really wants a divorce but hasn't told her husband; d) the author wishes that someone would do for her what a wife is expected to do.
2. The author says that she would like to a) go back to school and become economically independent; b) have enough money to stay home and not worry about financial obligations; c) quit school at this point in her life; d) know why everyone thinks she must have a degree in order to have a better life.
3. The author says that she wants a wife who will a) take care of the children; b) be available for "anytime" meals; c) agree to take out the garbage; d) willingly work different shifts if her employer asks her to.
4. The author says that she wants a wife who will a) drop everything if a business trip is necessary; b) be willing to send the children to their grandparents' house if the parents need to entertain; c) take care of the details of the social life; d) "know her place" when in the presence of employers.
5. The author says that she wants the liberty to a) come home when she thinks that she can contribute in a meaningful way; b) freely visit with family members who have caused problems in the past; c) "walk through the door and smell a good dinner in the oven"; d) replace the present wife with another one.

EXPANDING HORIZONS

1. This interview was first published in 1971. Interview someone who was married at that time or before, and ask that person how he or she thinks the role of women has changed—if at all. Be sure to ask the person's reasons for his or her opinion.

2. Create a timeline of the women's movement in the United States. Online sites to consult include these:

   feminism.eserver.org/theory/feminist/Womens-Movement.html

   www.legacy98.org/move-hist.html

   www.amazoncastle.com/feminism/sufftime.shtml

3. This selection is in a genre of literature called "satire," a piece of literature designed to ridicule the subject of the work. Read other satiric essays and write your opinion of them. Online essays include these:

   "How to Poison the Earth," 72.14.207.104/search?q=cache:eGrUhh0pGxQJ: mail.esdnl.ca/~craig_janes/0000B118-011EDDAE.9/How%2520to%2520 Poison%2520The%2520Eart1.doc+%22satiric+essay%22+-swift&hl=en

   Versions of Mark Twain's attempt at spelling reform, victorian.fortunecity.com/ vangogh/555/Spell/twain-cadmus.html

4. This Brady selection was originally published in the first issue of *Ms.* magazine. Read an article from a current issue of *Ms.* and write a summary of it. You may use an issue in hard copy, or you may access the magazine online at www.msmagazine.com/.

5. This selection is a definition essay, a type of writing that explains what a term means. Write your own definition essay of one of the following topics (or one that is approved by your instructor):

love	unhappiness
compassion	attraction
honesty	peace
education	ignorance

WRITE ON!

1. Think about people you know who seem happily married, and write your opinion about what makes their marriage successful.

2. Take the opposite point of view and write a piece similar to this one, but titled "I Want a Husband."

3. Interview someone from another country and find out if men and women from that country have defined roles in marriage. If so, what are they? If not, what is the norm for the roles of husbands and wives?

Attending college as a single parent poses many problems, as mom/student **Jennifer Merritt** *well knows, and she details some of the predicaments below. This article, which Merritt wrote when she was a student intern and a senior public relations major at Florida A&M University in Tallahassee, Florida, appears on the RealWorld University Web site.*

Starting Out...
Circle A if you agree with the statement or D if you disagree.

A   D   Generally speaking, single parents who are college students have an easy time because they have help from their own parents.

A   D   You should turn only to people whom you know well for help while you are in college.

A   D   A child who can respond to *Barney and Friends* is not too young to understand what is going on in his or her parent's life.

Words to Watch

$700⁺ : the plus sign (⁺) means "or more" or "or higher," so this means "seven hundred dollars or more"

equivalent: equal

FAMU: the abbreviation for Florida A & M University

FAMU Rattler: the rattler is mascot for Florida A & M University

inquisitive: curious, inquiring

reimbursements: compensations, payments

support network: a group of people to count on for assistance and encouragement

testimony: proof, evidence

vouchers: coupons or tickets for payment

Three Credits and a Baby
by Jennifer Merritt

I remember the day so vividly. Here I was...my high school band's drum major...an advanced-placement student...and the "Most Likely to Succeed" candidate...standing in the middle of the doctor's office. It occurred to me the summer before my senior year in high school that I was about to experience one of the most difficult problems facing more than 512,000 teenagers a year. No, I'm not talking about what college to attend; I'm talking about how was I going to survive as a teenage mother?

When I first started writing this article, I didn't think of myself as a success, but I now realize that success is the achievement of something desired or attempted. My goal was to graduate from college so I could provide a life equivalent to or better than mine for my child's sake. Here I am in my senior year of college, and I have successfully managed to take care of an inquisitive four-year-old girl name Gabrielle.

Even though I thought I would die or either my parents were going to kill me, some way or another, I managed to make it this far. Here I am, a living testimony that you can succeed in college as a single parent. If you think being a typical college student alone requires a lot of responsibility, imagine getting up two hours before your class to prepare your child for school just so you can make it on time to school yourself.

That's just the beginning. Imagine leaving straight from class and swinging by the day care center to pick up your child, then going home to prepare dinner, do homework, run a bath, do homework, read bedtime stories, and do more homework… every day.

Also, don't forget about the occasional sick nights that may run into the start of your first class the next morning. From these experiences and more, I devised a short list of successful strategies you can use as a single parent in college:

1. Surround yourself with a support network.
2. Talk to your child or children.
3. Save money.
4. Take advantage of single parent programs.

1. Surround yourself with a support network.

I think this strategy is the most important of all the strategies. Have you ever heard the saying, "It doesn't just take a family, but it takes a whole village to raise a child"? I discovered that letting people know about my situation also gave them permission to help. You would be shocked to find out how many people are willing to help you when you're trying to help yourself.

Never be ashamed to talk about being a single parent. Sometimes your support network is made up of people you don't even realize are there. Your network can involve church members, close friends, and even professors. I never knew that one of the best day care directors in the city was a member of my church. I kind of felt stupid when I went to her day care and realized that she was a member of my church. If I had mentioned my need for a day care provider to any of the members in my church, my search for a day care would have been easier.

2. Talk to your child.

If your child can respond to *Barney and Friends*, then your child is not too young to understand what is going on. At an early age, I taught Gabrielle what we were doing. When you tell children your goals, it makes it that much easier for them to adjust.

For example, when I first decided for Gabrielle to come to college with me, it took a long summer of preparation. At least every other day I reminded her what was going to happen soon. I would say, "Gabrielle, we're going to Tallahassee where Mommy can go to school at FAMU, and we'll come back to visit Grandma and Grandpa soon."

Going to school in Tallahassee became so routine to Gabrielle that people were amazed that a two-year-old knew how to pronounce the word "Tallahassee" so well. Children can understand a lot more than we give them credit for. When I heard Gabrielle repeat this [Tallahassee] for the first time, it really shocked me.

3. Save money.

Saving money can be a lot easier than you think. You have to be creative about it. Because I have such a large network of friends and associates, people are always coming over to my apartment to visit. As you enter my apartment, one of the first things you'll see is a piggy bank with the words "Help Gabrielle become a FAMU Rattler" on it. Now most people think this is cute, but sometimes it offends people who are not Rattler fans. Whenever the pig gets full, I put the money in the bank for an emergency fund for Gabrielle.

Also, instead of buying McDonald's all the time, tell your child that he or she can help you make dinner. That is a way for the two of you to spend quality time together before ending another busy day.

4. Take advantage of single parent programs.

There are various programs available to assist parents who are students. One that I'm very familiar with is called Project Independent. This program offers day care tuition reimbursements for students that work at least 20 hours a week. The program even gives gas vouchers to help the parent get from school to work. These programs vary from state to state, but almost every state offers a program of this type. Go to the local Health Department or Children and Families Department to find out every thing that's available. Personally, not having to worry about full day care expenses (ranging from as low as $300 to as high as $700+ per month) was a load off my shoulders.

From Where I Stand... (Journal Responses)

1. The most difficult decision I've had to face was _____
_____.

2. So far, the highest achievement I've accomplished has been _____
_____.

3. A hectic day in my life goes like this: _____
_____.

JUST THE FACTS

1. The main idea of this selection is a) students can be single parents and also be successful at college; b) the author regrets having a child before she graduated; c) the author realized too late that she would be in debt because of her child; d) colleges need to provide more support for single parents.
2. The author became pregnant when she was a a) college senior; b) college junior; c) college freshman; d) high school senior.
3. The author stresses the importance of surrounding oneself with a) lots of books for school and for the child; b) a support network; c) a cozy place for study inside the house or apartment; d) music.
4. Gabrielle is the author's a) baby-sitter; b) best friend; c) child; d) person she turns to when she needs to cry.
5. The author states one way to save money is to a) ask friends to come to a pot luck dinner; b) take the bus rather than drive the car; c) have your child help make dinner; d) use books from the library rather than purchase them.

EXPANDING HORIZONS

1. Interview someone in the financial aid department of your school to find out what different types of financial aid are available and how students determine whether they are qualified for this aid. Summarize your findings in a short paper.
2. Merritt writes, "My goal was to graduate from college so I could provide a life equivalent to or better than mine for my child's sake." Write about what, at this point in your life, is one of your goals.
3. Merritt quotes the African proverb "It takes a whole village to raise a child." A proverb is a short, concise saying in frequent and widespread use that expresses a basic truth or practical principle. Choose one of the proverbs below, explain what it means, and state whether or not you agree with it. Cite reasons for your opinion.
   - A bird in the hand is worth two in a bush. —English Proverb
   - Better give a penny then lend twenty. —Italian Proverb
   - Children should be seen and not heard. —Proverb of unknown origin
   - Darkness reigns at the foot of the lighthouse. —Japanese Proverb
   - Even a small thorn causes festering. —Irish Proverb
   - Feather by feather the goose can be plucked. —French Proverb
   - Give a man a fish, and he'll eat for a day. Teach him how to fish and he'll eat forever. —Chinese Proverb
   - He that is rich will not be called a fool. —Spanish Proverb
   - If all pulled in one direction, the world would keel over. —Yiddish Proverb
   - Kill not the goose that lays the golden eggs. —English Proverb
   - Love enters a man through his eyes, woman through her ears. —Polish Proverb
   - Make hay while the sun shines. —English Proverb
   - Never marry for money. Ye'll borrow it cheaper. —Scottish Proverb
   - One of these day is none of these days. —English Proverb

- Praise the young and they will blossom. —Irish Proverb
- Rats desert a sinking ship. —French Proverb
- Small children give you headache; big children heartache. —Russian Proverb
- The darkest hour is that before the dawn. —English Proverb
- We'll never know the worth of water till the well go dry. —Scottish Proverb
- You cannot make a silk purse out of a sow's ear. —Irish Proverb

WRITE ON!

1. Merritt gives credit to her support network for help. Who are the people in your support network? Specifically, what do they do to support you?
2. Merritt says that saving money can be easier than you think. Write about one way you could or do save money.
3. Which two aspects of this article did you find to be the most informative or useful? Why?

*Professor **Bill Gary**, father to son Isaac, teaches English at Henderson (Kentucky) Community College. In this selection, he writes about some of the problems he has encountered in being a conscientious, devoted dad and how his response to single-parenting problems has changed over time.*

Starting Out...
Read the statements below and then circle A if you agree or D if you disagree:

A   D   I've put my foot in my mouth and regretted something that I said to a stranger.

A   D   Some ads are sexist.

A   D   I have felt insulted by something someone has said to me.

Words to Watch
accolades: compliments, honors
boo-boo: a slang term for a minor cut on a child
boycotting: refusing to purchase
contentions: arguments, debates
featurette: a short film
hypersensitive: overly tender, easily hurt
ilk: kind, type
pigeonholing: classifying, categorizing
reactionary: an opponent of change, an extreme conservative
self-absorbed: egotistical, thinking only of oneself
sexist: showing bias based on gender
stereotyping: giving qualities of a few to an entire group
tripped about her words: an idiom meaning "stammered" or "didn't know what to say"
wearing my feelings on my sleeves: an idiom meaning "not hiding my emotions"
whiling: spending in an idle or pleasant way

Reactionary
by Bill Gary

Every morning I watch a local news show as I prepare my son and myself for our day. A feature of the early newscast is a three-minute featurette by Dr. James Dobson, founder of Focus on the Family. I remember the first time I reacted positively to something that Dr. Dobson had to say. I was ironing my shirt for work while my then four-year-old son, Isaac, sat on the sofa playing with the cat. "Divorce is something that is all too common today," Dr. Dobson said. He then quickly listed a few causes of divorce, including fathers who work too much and fathers who are hands off when it comes to raising the kids. Then, Dr. Dobson listed the further dangers of the absent dad after divorce.

I looked from my wrinkled shirt to my happy son and back to Dr. Dobson, whose shirt was already starched and pressed. I smiled.

Had this been six years earlier, I probably would have pressed a hole through my starched shirt and mumbled something ugly about Dr. D. Before, whenever the good doctor leveled such contentions, I balked. *What about the dads who are present and involved? What about me?* I would ask the TV screen. He never answered and he never mentioned me or the other male parents of my ilk. Why did he never mention me?

But this day was different. This day was the beginning of my realization. Yes, I thought, I had finally climbed out of my hypersensitive, self-absorbed phase of single parenting.

I am not sure exactly when that period in my life ended, but I am glad it did. I had been numb for a long time, numb to what was really going on around me and easily offended to what wasn't. If it wasn't someone on television, then it was someone in the real world pigeonholing me where I did not belong.

When Isaac was seven months old, I took him to Florida for a visit with my parents. We had a layover in Nashville, so I spread out his play blanket, out of the way from the others waiting on our flight, and he and I lolled on the floor, playing with a few stuffed animals and a board book, *Animals from A to Z.* We were happily whiling away the hours when a woman who had evidently been watching us attempted to strike up a conversation:

"He's adorable. How old is he?"

I smiled. "Seven months."

"What's his name?"

"Isaac," I said.

"Well, he's just the cutest thing. And you do so well with him. Where's Mommy?"

I was insulted. "I'm sure I don't know," I snapped, turning my attention back to Isaac and his toys.

Now, I do not know what the woman thought after she left us, but I am sure it was one of two things—she either felt bad about herself and wondered why or she felt bad about me and no doubt knew why.

Once, when going through the checkout line at the grocery store where I've shopped for over a decade now, I snapped at another most likely kindhearted person. Isaac was two months old at the time. He was in his Graco infant carrier, securely fastened to the grocery cart. With my right hand on him, I removed the goods from the cart with my left and began placing them on the belt.

The checker smiled and said, "So, you're babysitting today."

I glared back at her. "If that's what you want to call it. I call it raising my child." She apologized and tripped about her words for awhile, trying to explain, commending me, and letting me know that she just doesn't see too many daddies with infants out shopping.

Now, almost eight years later, I am finally finding the ability to look at her again without feeling ashamed of my reaction.

I began boycotting products that were hyped by sexist commercials. I wrote letters to certain product manufacturers. From television and magazine ads alone, I began noticing that only moms could heal a boo-boo with a medicinal first aid spray; only moms could make Jell-O; only moms could bring down a fever; and only moms could select baby furniture while dads worried about the cost. I decided then that if it's chosen by *choosy moms*, then this dad wouldn't buy it.

Data presented on www.deltabravo.net, the web site for SPARC (Separated Parenting Access & Resource Center) says that 71% of all high school dropouts come from fatherless homes. These children's fathers are who Dr. Dobson was speaking to, not me. He is speaking to the absent father whose children make up 70% of juveniles in state operated institutions; he was speaking to the absent fathers whose children are 5 times more likely to commit suicide; 32 times more likely to run away; 10 times more likely to abuse chemical substances; and 20 times more likely to end up in prison than those whose fathers are a part of their lives.

No matter their stereotyping or their restricted views of my son and me, these people were, in their own way, reaching out in what was meant to be a positive way. Whether they were telling me my son was cute or well-behaved, telling me "You are very good with him," or even asking "Where's Mommy?" none of these people meant any harm. In truth, their intentions were entirely good. They were offering accolades for Isaac and me. And I couldn't see that.

From Where I Stand... (Journal Responses)

1. The most interesting part of "Reactionary" was _____

_____

because _____.

2. One time when I said something that I later realized was inappropriate was

_____

_____.

3. If I could ask the author of this selection two questions, I would ask _____

_____ and

_____ because

_____.

Just the Facts

1. The main idea of this selection is that a) sometimes people should keep their opinions to themselves; b) most people think that a single father doesn't parent as well as a single mother; c) sometimes a compliment is mistaken for something rude or ignorant; d) many people find giving a polite response to be difficult.
2. In the beginning of the selection, Gary was watching a newscast by a) Matt Lauer; b) Dr. James Dobson; c) the local news team; d) Diane Sawyer.
3. Gary recounts an incident that took place a) at his son's preschool playground; b) when he was taking his son to get a haircut; c) at the Nashville airport; d) while he was making breakfast.
4. Gary recounts another incident that took place a) when a woman asked if Gary's son had any siblings; b) while he was attempting to find a baby-sitter; c) when a woman voiced disapproval about candy; d) in the line at the grocery.
5. In the end, Gary says that he realized that a) he could never win the "single father battle"; b) his son would grow up to be "a fine fellow"; c) people had been "offering accolades" for his son and himself; d) the best solution was to politely say that he was just trying "to be a good dad."

Expanding Horizons

1. Note the title that Gary uses for this piece: "Reactionary." While the dictionary definition of a reactionary is "a person who is extremely conservative," Gary uses the title as a play on the word "reaction." Explain why he did this.
2. Visit the Web site Etiquette Hell at www.etiquettehell.com/content/eh_main/gen/eh_index.shtml. Click on a category (on the left) and then read several of the letters in that category. Choose the letter that you think is the most interesting, or most amusing, or most outrageous, and write a response to it.
3. Gary cites data from SPARC, the Separated Parenting Access & Resource Center. This organization says that its goal is "to ensure that children of divorce continue to have meaningful relationships with both parents, regardless of marital status." Visit the SPARC Web site at www.deltabravo.net. Click on the article index and choose an article to read. Then write a summary-and-response of the article.
4. Of the incident in the airport, Gary writes, "Now, I do not know what the woman thought after she left us, but I am sure it was one of two things—she either felt bad about herself and wondered why or she felt bad about me and no doubt knew why." Explain what he means by that statement.

Write On!

1. Pretend you are the advice columnist for your school newspaper and you receive a letter from "Pat," who wants to know what to do in response to having been insulted by a fellow student (you may decide what the insult was). Write your response to Pat.
2. When parents divorce, what criteria should be used to determine with whom their child or children live? Defend your answer.
3. Gary writes that he "wrote letters to certain product manufacturers" of products with ads that he found sexist. Think of an ad that offends you, and write a letter to the manufacturer. Include why you are offended by the ad and what the manufacturer could do to improve.

Annabel Lee
by Edgar Allan Poe

Edgar Allan Poe, one of the most well-known American writers, composed this poem after the death of his young wife, who was presumably the inspiration for it. As you read it, take note of the poem's setting and the mood.

Words to Watch
maiden: unmarried woman
winged seraphs: angels
coveted: envied
highborn kinsman: angels
sepulchre: the former spelling of *sepulcher,* a tomb
dissever: separate, divide

It was many and many a year ago,
In a kingdom by the sea,
That a maiden there lived whom you may know
By the name of Annabel Lee;
And this maiden she lived with no other thought
Than to love and be loved by me.

I was a child and she was a child,
In this kingdom by the sea;
But we loved with a love that was more than love—
I and my Annabel Lee;
With a love that the winged seraphs of heaven
Coveted her and me.

And this was the reason that, long ago,
In this kingdom by the sea,
A wind blew out of a cloud, chilling
My beautiful Annabel Lee;
So that her highborn kinsman came
And bore her away from me,
To shut her up in a sepulchre
In this kingdom by the sea.

The angels, not half so happy in heaven,
Went envying her and me—
Yes!—that was the reason (as all men know,
In this kingdom by the sea)
That the wind came out of the cloud by night,
Chilling and killing my Annabel Lee.

But our love it was stronger by far than the love
Of those who were older than we—
Of many far wiser than we—
And neither the angels in heaven above,
Nor the demons down under the sea,
Can ever dissever my soul from the soul
Of the beautiful Annabel Lee.

For the moon never beams without bringing me dreams
Of the beautiful Annabel Lee;
And the stars never rise but I feel the bright eyes
Of the beautiful Annabel Lee;
And so, all the night-tide, I lie down by the side
Of my darling—my darling—my life and my bride,
In the sepulchre there by the sea,
In her tomb by the sounding sea.

Questions

1. What is the setting of this poem?
2. How does the speaker let readers know that the relationship between himself and Annabel Lee was more than just friendship?
3. Poe chose particular words to add to this poem's mood (the feeling a reader is supposed to have when reading the poem). What is the mood, and which words contribute to it?
4. What was the one thought that Annabel Lee had?
5. Why did the angels take Annabel Lee away?
6. Where does the speaker spend all of his evenings?

Funnyman Tom Bodett's first newspaper piece about withdrawing from smoking—cold turkey—brought him so much acclaim that he soon became a regular on National Public Radio. One collection of his commentaries, Small Comforts: More Comments and Comic Pieces, *was published in 1987 and contains this view of fatherhood.*

Starting Out...

Circle the response that best describes yourself:

I use "baby talk" when I'm around a baby.

    Always   Sometimes   Never

I get bored when I hear people talk about their children.

    Always   Sometimes   Never

If a child is in my care, I'm more aware of potential dangers than when I'm alone.

    Always   Sometimes   Never

Words to Watch

adversely: negatively, unfavorably

ambivalent: uncertain, indecisive

anomaly: abnormality, irregularity

articulate: characterized by the use of clear, expressive language

attune: adjust, regulate

couplet: two lines that rhyme

enzyme: a protein produced by living organisms

gastric: relating to the stomach

guttural incantation: sounds coming from the throat and repeated without thought or aptness

loin fruit: offspring, child

nuances: subtle or slight degree meanings, feelings, or tones

prefigures: predicts, foreshadows

uncannily: so insightful as to seem extraordinary or supernatural

watering holes: a slang term for bars or saloons

yours truly: the person writing or speaking

Symptoms of Fatherhood
by Tom Bodett

I used to swear I'd never be one of those guys who talk about their kids. (Of course, before that I swore I'd never be one of those guys who even have kids. So you can see how I am about swearing.) I've found, however, that something happens to a man when his own child is born, something rich and inexplicable and, so the experts tell me, chemical.

There has always been lots of talk about the hormonal imbalances and emotional trauma a mother experiences before and immediately after the birth of a child, but lately attention is turning to the effect of childbirth on the male glandular system. It's really quite astounding once you examine it. For instance, it's been proven that the male brain secretes an enzyme into the optic nerve shortly after the onset of fatherhood that allows a man for the first time in his life to see things in store windows like colored blocks and "Li'l Slugger" baseball jammies. It also enables him to tell a cloth diaper from a dipstick rag and a stuffed teddy from a mounted duck.

Another brain fluid, probably a mild sedative, is let loose in the hearing canal. Upon reaching the inner ear, this solution makes a man's head spin when he receives a smile or coo from his own loin fruit. More important, it also serves as a flap-damper against children screeching in public places or infants whining on airplanes. Sounds that once would make a man's fillings ache or compel him to tear an airline magazine in two now only leave him to stare dumbly at their source with an appreciative smile.

An ambivalent chemical, this same stuff that serves to dampen the sounds of everyone else's children can also actually attune a man's ear to those of his own. His hearing can become so sensitive that he'll bolt upright from a dead sleep should his child so much as gurgle in its crib downstairs through two closed doors.

Another biochemical, probably from a gastric gland, enters into a father's abdominal cavity in the postnatal period. This natural body fluid, technically known as *Papa-Bismol*, is, of course, a stomach relaxer. Foul and foreign substances, such as those to be found in a child's diapers, no longer trigger his gag reflex. It may even allow for closer inspections of them in times of illness or moments of simple paternal curiosity. Other infant malfunctions such as oral ejections (spit-up) or nasal discharges (snot) can be greeted with equal reserved under the influence of Papa-Bismol.

Quite frankly, some effects of childbirth on the male of our species are of totally known origin. One of these affects his sense of time and direction. Time appears to move at an accelerated rate as the child matures, and all roads lead home. Neighborhood watering holes lose their appeal, and dads are uncannily on time for supper for the first time in their married careers. It's entirely possible that this disorientation in space and time is responsible for the quirks which appear in a new father's speaking habits.

Normally articulate and well-spoken young men can be found leaning into cradles and bassinets repeating a string of guttural incantations. The ability to interpret language is simultaneously impaired. It's not unusual to have a new father claiming to have heard the word "daddy" from a child who's only utterance to date was that of passing stomach gas.

This stage quickly passes and is replaced by another speech anomaly, the Couplet Stutter. This causes the male parent to double words which previously served him well solo. Some examples: "no-no," "yum-yum," "bye-bye." In cases where a word cannot be doubled up and still make sense, the Couplet Stutter gives way to the *Aiee Syndrome*. For instance, the sentence "Junior sees the dog-dog" is meaningless, but "Junior sees the doggie" makes perfect sense to everyone but the kid, who can't understand why Dad has to *Aiee* every noun in the dictionary when he points it out.

These very speech afflictions may be responsible for other, yet-to-be-explained new-father nuances. Men who could not have given a hoot how *Babar Gets to Candyland* in prenatal years can be found engrossed in that particular narrative long after the child has given up for the evening. The story of the Three Little Pigs can lead to mild depression in fathers who don't get a chance to huff and puff the doors down before the kid nods off.

Renewed interest in ogres, trolls, fairies, and pirates generally prefigures the disintegration of formal education. This just might be what is behind such irrational social behavior as pulling out wallet-sized baby photos in airport lounges or suggesting a petting zoo as an interesting night on the town.

Overall, as you can see from this definitive study, the male is much more likely than previously thought to be adversely affected by biological changes due to childbirth. Of course none of these symptoms of fatherhood has arisen in yours truly, and the only reason I'm aware of them at all is that I'm a voracious reader and get all my information from books.

In fact I'm in the middle of one particularly riveting volume at the moment. It seems there were these three men, and this tub. In an interesting blend of careers there was a butcher, a baker, a… hold on a minute. I think I hear something downstairs in the baby's room.

From Where I Stand... (Journal Responses)

1. The most humorous part of this selection was _____

   _____

   because _____.

2. When I hear adults using baby talk, I feel _____

   _____

   because _____.

3. The youngest person I have a special relationship to is _____

   _____;

   I feel close to this person because _____

   _____.

JUST THE FACTS

1. The main idea of this selection is a) fatherhood can be both a blessing and a curse; b) men who are about to become fathers should get together to discuss their families; c) sometimes men change after they become fathers; d) a man who becomes a father often bores others when talking about his children.

2. The author says that the male brain secrets an enzyme that allows a man for the first time to see a) an inner beauty in the mother of his child; b) what his future might hold; c) things in store windows; d) the wisdom in some of the things his own parents told him.

3. The author says that the male brain secrets a fluid in the hearing canal that a) makes his head spin when he receives a smile or coo from his own child; b) helps him hear strange noises; c) helps him better distinguish sounds when he is at work; d) becomes a danger when it reaches the inner ear.

4. According to the selection, "Papa-Bismol" is a) the name that the author's son uses for his grandfather; b) what the author takes when he is nervous; c) a stomach relaxer; d) what the author gives his child when the child is ill.

5. According to the selection, one effect of childbirth on men is the loss of a) private time with the mother of the child; b) extra income; c) time playing sports; d) the appeal of "neighborhood watering holes."

EXPANDING HORIZONS

1. Read more about the life of author Tom Bodett at www.bodett.com/bio.htm, and then write a summary of what you learn.

2. Interview at least three parents and ask them about the changes in their lives when they first had children. Collect your findings and write about what you learn.

3. This selection comes from Bodett's book *Small Comforts: More Comments and Comic Pieces*. Read another selection from this book and then write a summary of it.

4. Read other selections about becoming a parent and then write a summary of one of them. Online sites include these:

www.creativeparents.com/daddying.html

www.theonion.com/content/node/38396

www.babycenter.com/dilemma/pregnancy/pregnancysex/1398665.html

parenting.ivillage.com/newborn/nmomcare/0,,bxlh,00.html

5. *The Best American Humorous Short Stories* is available free via the site at www.gutenberg.org/etext/10947. Go to the site, select an author, and then select and read one of his or her short stories. Answer the following questions about the story:

What was the general plot of the story?

What was the setting (the time and place) of the story?

Who were the main characters and what happened to them?

Did you find the story humorous? Why or why not?

WRITE ON!

1. Write a letter to someone who has just become a father or mother for the first time, telling what you think parenthood will be like and how it will change his or her life.

2. Write about the qualities an ideal father or mother should have.

3. Write about at least two times that you have witnessed a father or mother doing something that did not show good judgment toward his or her child. How should the parent have reacted?

READ ON!

"Are Wives Obsolete?" www.sfgate.com/cgi-bin/article.cgi?f=/chronicle/archive/2001/08/19/IN215102.DTL.

Beere, Carole A. *Gender Roles: A Handbook of Tests and Measures.* New York: Greenwood Press, 1990.

Bombeck, Erma. *Just Wait Until You Have Children of Your Own.* New York: Ballantine Books, 1971.

Cosby, Bill. *Fatherhood.* New York: Berkley Publishers, 1987.

"Daddy on Board." www.daddyonboard.com/weblog.php.

"Discussion Forum 'Why I Want a Wife.'" forums.lbcc.cc.ca.us/eng1olkr_wk3/forum.asp?M=252&P=219&T=219.

Halberstam, David. *The Teammates.* New York: Hyperion, 2003.

Noel, Brook and Arthur C. Klein. *The Single Parent Resource.* Belgium, WI: Champion Press, Ltd., 1998.

Pease, Barbara and Allan Pease. *Why Men Don't Listen & Women Can't Read Maps: How We're Different and What to Do About It.* New York: Broadway Books, 2001.

Rosanoff, Nancy. *Knowing When It's Right: An Intuitive Approach to Improving Relationships.* Naperville, IL: Sourcebooks, 2002.

Scudder, John R., Jr. and Anne H. Bishop. *Beyond Friendship and Eros: Unrecognized Relationships Between Men and Women*. Albany: State University of New York Press, 2001.

"Society Establishes Gender Roles for Us." mentalhelp.net/psyhelp/chap9/chap9p.htm.

"Taking Charge of Your Life—Can Men and Women Be Friends?" www.brandy-winecenter.com/TC11-04-01.htm.

Taylor, Barbara A. 2004. "Lending Single-Parent Students a Helping Hand." *Community College Week* July 19:4.

"To Be Friends or Not… That is the Question?" femail-secure.vendercom.com/friendsfeature.htm.

Whitaker, Mark. 1993. "Getting Tough at Last." *Newsweek* May 10: 22.

"With More Equity, More Sweat." www.washingtonpost.com/wp-srv/national/longterm/gender/gender22a.htm.

Would you ever stand in front of a tank for a cause you believe in? The man in the famous photograph above did so, and he became an international symbol of extraordinary ethical fortitude.

This photograph was taken during the Tiananmen Square uprising in Beijing, China, in 1989. A series of student-initiated demonstrations in support of democracy had begun in mid-April. China's communist officials took a dim view of the protests, and after seven weeks the government sent tanks and soldiers to suppress the protests. As the tanks drove through Beijing's streets, random shots were fired and hundreds of people were killed.

In the midst of the protests the man in the picture took a firm position, standing in the middle of the road (ironically named "Pathway of Everlasting Peace") as he tried to stop a line of advancing tanks.

Can you think of an issue that you believe in so passionately that you'd risk your life for it? Why is this cause so important to you?

CHAPTER NINE

ETHICS, OR "DO THE RIGHT THING"

Action indeed is the sole medium of expression for ethics. —*Jane Addams*

All my growth and development led me to believe that if you really do the right thing, and if you play by the rules, and if you've got good enough, solid judgment and common sense, that you're going to be able to do whatever you want to do with your life. —*Barbara Jordan*

Always do right—this will gratify some and astonish the rest. —*Mark Twain*

Do not do unto others as you would they should do unto you. Their tastes may not be the same.
—*George Bernard Shaw*

Good people do not need laws to tell them to act responsibly, while bad people will find a way around the laws. —*Plato*

Honor is better than honors. —*Abraham Lincoln*

Never let your sense of morals get in the way of doing what's right. —*Isaac Asimov*

Such is the brutalization of commercial ethics in this country that no one can feel anything more delicate than the velvet touch of a soft buck. —*Raymond Chandler*

The cosmos is neither moral or immoral; only people are. He who would move the world must first move himself. —*Edward Ericson*

The power of choosing good and evil is within the reach of all. —*Origen*

To care for anyone else enough to make their problems one's own is ever the beginning of one's real ethical development. —*Felix Adler*

We can discover this meaning in life in three different ways: (1) by doing a deed; (2) by experiencing a value; and (3) by suffering. —*Victor Frankl*

When I do good, I feel good; when I do bad, I feel bad. That's my religion. —*Abraham Lincoln*

Conventionality is not morality. —*Charlotte Bronte*

You cannot make yourself feel something you do not feel, but you can make yourself do right in spite of your feelings. —*Pearl S. Buck*

Ethics, or "Do the Right Thing"

If you pick up any newspaper or news magazine, turn on the television to any news channel, even if you listen to random conversations long enough, you're sure to hear a story about some kind of ethical problem. Every media outlet reports these stories with relish, and the pubic seems never to get enough of the coverage.

Prison abuse scandals, accusations about lies told during elections, businesses charged with unscrupulous practices, disputed procedures or games in sports, dubious methods of medical practice, plagiarism by both students and authors—all of these questions and more dominate the news and are parts of the issue of ethics in our world today. This chapter looks at ethics in three specific areas (education, business, and medicine) and one general area (telling white lies).

In a series of columns for the independent newspaper at her college, student Jennifer Marie Bear addressed the common problem of cheating in "Why Students Cheat." Bear interviewed both students and faculty to find the answer to her questions, and she discovered that the reasons behind cheating are many and varied—and they may surprise you.

"Ethics in Business" is a compilation of material posted on the Web site of the George S. May International Company, an organization known worldwide for helping businesses improve their operations. This selection examines what "little things" employees may do that cause ethical problems—little things such as taking credit for someone else's work, writing or speaking in an inappropriate way, using office supplies at home, or conducting personal business while on company time. The selection also includes a checklist to evaluate your own ethics in the workplace, as well as suggestions for becoming a more ethical employee.

Medical ethics comes into question in "Of Headless Mice...and Men." This selection, which originally appeared in *Time* magazine, looks at the ethics of cloning both animals and humans. When the article was written in 1998, news about the laboratory creation of headless mice and headless tadpoles had just been released, and other news about possible experiments to achieve human cloning had been announced. The author looks at the medical reasons behind the successful creation of the modified mice and tadpoles and the ethical implications of creating humans in the same way.

The final selection is "White Lies," an excerpt from Sissela Bok's highly influential book *Lying: Moral Choice in Public and Private Life*. Telling white lies, part of what Bok calls "harmless lying" is, according to the author, the most common form of dishonesty. Bok raises ethical questions about why people often tell white lies, whether a kind of lying not meant to harm anyone actually exists, and whether some lies that are considered to be "white lies" are, in actuality, harmful to others.

Now that you have read the introduction to this chapter, go back and reread the quotations on p. 197. Then choose one of the quotations and write about whether you agree or disagree with it. Be sure to defend your opinion.

*Plagiarism is a widespread problem on campuses all over the country. Below are two installments of a five-part series written by student **Jennifer Marie Bear** for the* Oregon Daily Emerald, *an independent campus newspaper at the University of Oregon.*

Starting Out...
All of the following are forms of plagiarizing. Rate these from 1 (no big deal) to 5 (really big deal) to indicate how serious you think that they are.

   1 2 3 4 5   Buying a paper online and turning it in as your own

   1 2 3 4 5   Not putting quotation marks around a citation in a paper

   1 2 3 4 5   Putting a test answer sheet in a position so another student can see your answers

---

Words to Watch

cardinal sin: a wrongdoing of the highest order

cavalier: marked by a disregard of what is important

cutting corners: an idiom meaning "doing something in the easiest or least expensive way"

GPA: an acronym for "grade point average," a measure of academic achievement based the number of credits and grade points earned per course

internship: short, supervised work for which a student receives college credit

mentor: a wise and trusted counselor or advisor

mindset: outlook, way of thinking

pegs: categorizes, classifies

pressure cooker: an idiom meaning "a situation of difficulty or stress"

succumbed: gave in, surrendered

susceptible: at risk, vulnerable

TEP: an acronym for Teaching Effectiveness Program

transgressions: wrongdoings, offences

writhed: thrashed about, struggled

Why Students Cheat
by Jennifer Marie Bear

The whys of cheating are plentiful—there are almost as many reasons for cheating as there are students who do it. And according to national statistics, there are a lot of students doing it.

In 1999, Donald McCabe of Rutgers University, one of the nation's leading researchers on academic integrity, directed a national survey of 2,100 students on 21 different college campuses to determine the extent of cheating. More than 75 percent of student respondents admitted to cheating in some form.

According to Director of Student Judicial Affairs Chris Loschiavo, the University has not participated in any of the recent studies on academic integrity, but it did engage in one of McCabe's earlier studies in 1992 and 1993. Loschiavo said the past survey found that about 80 percent of students at the University admitted to cheating.

However, the number of students who own up to cheating in surveys is in sharp contrast with the number of academic dishonesty cases that are processed through the Office of Judicial Affairs.

From 2002 to 2003, there were 202 academic dishonesty cases at the University, while enrollment totaled 18,421. That means 1.1 percent of the student population was caught cheating.

Regardless of how many students cheat and get away with it, most students know cheating is a cardinal sin in the academic community. So what factors motivate students to do something they know is wrong?

Teaching Effectiveness Program Director Georgeanne Cooper said students may cheat for a variety of reasons.

"Some do it just to see if they can get away with it, some do it because they feel pressure to do well, maybe even people cheat to gain some illusion of self-worth or avoid the shame of failure," Cooper said.

Cooper added that she has dealt with academic dishonesty both as a teacher and as a parent. She specifically recalled one instance where she suspected her daughter of cheating on a math test.

"When I asked her about it, her answer was pretty cavalier: 'Mom, it's just a math test,'" Cooper said.

TEP Faculty Consultant Laurie Jones Neighbors also deals extensively with the issues surrounding academic dishonesty. She said students are motivated to cheat during extreme conditions, such as when their computer crashes the night before a paper is due and the student has to make a choice between not turning in the assignment and turning in something they didn't write.

"It's not like students are 'Ha, ha, ha, I'm cheating,'" Neighbors said. "Students I find who do intentional cheating are in desperate circumstances."

But perhaps the biggest factor pushing students to cheat is the pressure cooker known as college life.

"Between trying to fit in all the credits, and trying to make sure you get a good internship or job, and dealing with your parents—there's a million stresses," sophomore Allie Major said.

According to the University Counseling and Testing Center's 2002–03 report, stress is a big part of students' lives. In fact, 42.4 percent of the students who turned to the counseling center for aid did so in part because they "don't handle anxiety well."

Counseling Center Senior Staff Psychologist Ron Miyaguchi said the temptation to cheat doesn't really come up in his sessions with students, but many students he sees have scrambled priorities, which could result in them choosing to cheat.

"Students are typically in the mindset of short-term goals—for example, my goal is to get an 'A' in this class," he said.

Academic Learning Services Instructor Amy Nuetzman also said students focus too much on the short term and fail to recognize how demanding college classes are. They're fine for the first few weeks of the term, but when homework deadlines, paper deadlines and test deadlines start piling up, many students think the only way to dig themselves out is by cutting corners, Nuetzman said.

"A lot of students have told me that they are short on time actually writing the paper and they feel like they just have to whip it out," Nuetzman said.

But the final part of the equation explaining why students cheat is the fact that many students don't realize they're cheating.

"A lot of students don't understand the standards the University holds them to," said Hilary Berkman, director of the Office of Student Advocacy.

She added that some instances of cheating are clearly intentional, such as purchasing a paper off the Internet, but other academic transgressions, such as failing to cite a paper properly, are often unintended.

"Academic dishonesty isn't black and white," she said. "The cases we see can be very complicated in that maybe the student hasn't done everything correctly, but that isn't necessarily an act of dishonesty."

Profile of a Cheater

Contrary to the myth that only lazy or stupid students resort to plagiarizing a paper or peeking at a neighbor's exam, anyone can be a cheater. A high GPA and strenuous study habits are no protection against the temptation to cheat.

In fact, students who are academically ambitious can sometimes be even more susceptible to the promise of a guaranteed A than a regular student.

University graduate student Casey Wood knew she was close to receiving A's in her summer term classes. She was the kind of student who spent 15 to 20 hours a week studying. But when an opportunity to cheat on one of her final exams presented itself, she succumbed to the temptation.

"I wanted to make sure I would get an A," Wood said.

Another student in her class on special education research methods had received an advance copy of the final exam and e-mailed it to Wood. They tackled the questions together, and since the professor allowed students to bring a page of notes to the final, Wood had an easy way to cheat.

"My plan was to just go in with the final all completed with all the answers," she said.

But feelings of guilt writhed in the back of her mind as the date of the final exam approached.

"I kind of convinced myself that I didn't do anything wrong, but underneath it all I think I knew that I did something against my morals and values," Wood said.

So she did something most cheaters wouldn't dream of doing.

"I didn't get caught for cheating—I turned myself in," she said.

According to Student Judicial Affairs Director Chris Loschiavo, this is a very rare occurrence. Only one or two students in the last four years have come forward on their own and admitted to cheating.

Wood's mentor, Daniel Close, director of the Family and Human Services program at the College of Education, was also surprised by Wood's open admission of wrongdoing.

"We've never seen this before," Close said. "We're still baffled. We don't have experience with this."

But besides the surprise of Wood turning herself in, Close was also surprised that she had cheated at all.

"It just didn't make sense," Close said. "It was sad for me that she allowed herself to be put in that position. I've had her in four classes; she's been a paper grader for me, I know she's an honest person."

Unlike many other students who resort to cheating, Wood wasn't under any extreme circumstances and it wasn't a cheat-or-fail situation. She had studied extensively for the final exam and she said the material it covered wasn't difficult to master, but she was still worried about failing to achieve perfect grades.

"It was my first term in graduate school and I really wanted to do well," Wood said. "I put more pressure on myself than anyone else to get good grades. It's almost like I had to prove to myself I'm just as smart as anyone else."

Wood actually ended up earning an A in the class, but after the investigation it was changed to an F. And as part of her punishment, she had to complete an academic integrity seminar, retake a class that counts for research credits and write a letter of apology to her professor.

"That was probably one of the more difficult consequences, having to face him and admit what I did wrong," Wood said.

Although Wood pegs herself as an honest person, this wasn't the first time she cheated on a test. When she was a senior undergraduate she looked at another student's paper during a test, but just like she did in the other case, she confessed to her professor. The consequences for her transgression were less harsh, however, and she only got an F for the quiz, not the whole class.

Wood said she is very open about her mistakes and has confided in several of her professors, but she hasn't confessed the incident to her parents yet.

"I don't want them to think I've always cheated," she said. "I don't want them to be disappointed in me."

Twice she's cheated, twice she's turned herself in and now Wood said she has definitely learned her lesson and will never cheat again.

"One thing I've learned is grades aren't the most important thing," she said. "When I look back in five years I might remember my GPA but I won't remember what grade I received in a class."

From Where I Stand... (Journal Responses)
1. In the list of all the problems that students face, cheating is high/low (choose either "high" or "low") on the list because _____.
2. If I were an instructor in a class and I clearly saw a student cheating, I would _____ because _____.
3. If I saw a student cheating, I would/would not (choose either "would" or "would not") report the incident to the instructor because _____ _____.

JUST THE FACTS
1. The main idea of this selection is students cheat a) because of peer pressure; b) when they feel stress from family; c) for a variety of reasons; d) to build up their self-esteem.
2. In Donald McCabe's national survey, the percentage of students who admitted to cheating in some form was a) 10 percent; b) 25 percent; c) 50 percent; d) 75 percent.
3. Reasons for cheating listed by Georgeanne Cooper did *not* include that students a) just want to see if they can get away with it; b) feel pressure to do well; c) feel a need to help others; d) gain some illusion of self-worth.
4. An example of an unintentional "academic transgression" (example of cheating) named in the article was a) failing to cite a paper properly; b) buying a paper from the Internet; c) writing a section of another student's paper; d) supplying test questions or answers for students in another class.
5. Undergraduate student Casey Wood a) was unaware that her actions were considered to be cheating; b) turned herself in for cheating; c) confessed that she wondered whether her conscience was being tested; d) asked for help from both the university and several members of her class.

EXPANDING HORIZONS
1. Find a copy of your college or university's policy on academic honesty. If you were a college administrator speaking to incoming freshmen, what particular points of the policy would you emphasize? Why? What points would you add to or delete from the policy?

2. Either write about or discuss in class the most common method of cheating that you have witnessed. How might this problem be solved? What could college or university officials do to prevent cheating?

3. In the article, instructor Amy Nuetzman said that "students focus too much on the short term and fail to recognize how demanding college classes are. They're fine for the first few weeks of the term, but when homework deadlines, paper deadlines and test deadlines start piling up, many students think the only way to dig themselves out is by cutting corners...." In a personal narrative, write about how you have dealt with deadlines in the past (giving at least three examples) and what, if anything, you have learned about deadlines since being in college.

4. Casey Wood confessed that she had cheated. Write an editorial for your school newspaper, defending the punishment that she received or telling why you disagree with it and what penalty you think that she should have received instead.

WRITE ON!

1. Interview a student or college representative and get that person's opinion about why students cheat; then write a short summary of your findings. (If you quote the person you interview, remember to use quotation marks around his or her exact words.) What new insights did you find? What conclusions can you come to as a result of your survey?

2. Suppose this article were required reading for everyone in your college or university. Write about what you see as a possible outcome of so many people reading "Why Students Cheat."

3. What moral obligation, if any, does a student have if he or she witnesses cheating? Defend your answer.

*The **George S. May International Company,** a consulting firm dedicated to help-ing businesses improve their operations and efficiency, posts on its Web site a number of articles about business ethics. The selection below contains excerpts from some of those articles.*

Starting Out...

The following behaviors are considered to be examples of unethical business prac-tices, but you may consider some more serious than others. Rate them from 1 (no big deal) to 5 (really big deal) to indicate how wrong you think they are.

    1   2   3   4   5   Calling in sick when not really sick

    1   2   3   4   5   Using an ethnically derogative term when referring to another person

    1   2   3   4   5   "Fudging" on a time sheet, billing sheet, estimate, or report

---

Words to Watch

billing sheets: reports that show how much a company is owed

breached: broken, violated

compliance: observance, conformity

component: part, factor

confidentiality: privacy, discretion

cornerstone: foundation, basis

cues: signals, signs

derogative: expressive of a low opinion

expense reports: statements that show how much money an employee should be reimbursed for conducting company business

fudged: slang for "faked" or "falsified"

gratuity: tip, freebie

manipulate: rig, fake, falsify

scores: multiples of twenty

time sheets: reports that show how much work time an employee has put in

---

Ethics in Business

from the George S. May International Company Web site

"Little Things" Mean a Lot

Business ethics involves a lot more than compliance with company policies, laws and financial regulations. These are major concerns with high visibil-ity. It makes headlines when these are not obeyed. For those reasons, most organizations do not have problems with these issues. Instead, it's the "lit-tle things" that cause problems.

For most business people, it is the day-to-day, seemingly insignificant actions and behaviors by individuals that represent the largest area for ethics problems—and the greatest opportunity for ethics improvement.

The little things that we do every day are often forgotten by us. However, they can make a significant impact on people who see a certain behavior. Remember, your behavior sets an example. Even if you are not the boss, there is always someone else who watches you for cues on how to act in certain situations—for good and bad. These observers may be your fellow workers, neighbors, your spouse, or your children. What messages are you "sending" by your actions, words, and attitudes?

To help you examine your personal ethics and see where you stand and where you need to improve consider the following...

- "Little white lies" you don't (or do) tell;
- Jokes you share with others;
- Ways you treat and talk about co-workers;
- Things you say to make a sale;
- E-mails you write and forward to others;
- Ways you handle customer complaints (including the number of people they get passed to);
- What you put on your billing sheets, time sheets, and expense reports;
- Office supplies you don't (or do) take home;
- Commitments you make and keep (or don't keep);
- Personal business you don't (or do) conduct at work;
- "Unimportant" work rules you follow (or break);
- Things you reproduce on the copy machine;
- Standards you set for yourself;
- Level of quality you put into whatever you do;
- Credit you appropriately share (or don't share) with others.

These, and scores of behaviors like them, reflect who you are and what you stand for. When it comes to ethics and integrity, everything is important—including (and especially) "the small stuff."

Check Yourself Out

Self-evaluation is a critical component of business ethics. People should spend as much time looking in the mirror as they do watching and judging the behavior of others. Periodically examine and reflect on your own behaviors to ensure you are staying on the ethical track.

Use the following ethics self-assessment as a guide to identifying your integrity strengths and the areas you need to work on.

Ethics Self-Assessment

In the previous several months, have I...

- Conducted personal business on company time?
- Used or taken company resources for personal purposes?
- Called-in sick when I really wasn't?
- Used an ethnically derogative term when referring to another person?
- Told or passed along an ethnically or sexually oriented joke?
- Engaged in negative gossip, or spread rumors about someone?
- "Bad mouthed" the company or management to co-workers?
- "Snooped" into a co-worker's conversations or private affairs?
- Passed along information that was shared with me in confidence?
- Knowingly ignored (violated) an organizational rule or procedure?
- Failed to follow through on something I said I would do?
- Withheld information that others needed?
- "Fudged" on a time sheet, billing sheet, estimate, or report?
- Knowingly delivered a poor quality (or defective) good...or service?
- Been less than honest (lied or manipulated the truth) to make a sale?
- Accepted an inappropriate gift or gratuity?
- Taken or accepted credit for something that someone else did?
- Failed to admit to or correct a mistake I made?
- Knowingly let someone screw up and get into trouble?

5 Ways to Ethically Consider Situations

Embrace Racial, Cultural, and Creative Diversity

Many of the benefits society enjoys have come from a very diverse group of people from throughout the world. For an example, we all enjoy technological advances were developed by weird creative types who also were different. Diversity is something to be embraced. It is a great strength and competitive business advantage.

Don't Take What Isn't Yours ... Don't Accept What You Haven't Earned

This is self-explanatory. It applies to everything from office supplies to "the credit" for work done by others.

Maintain Confidentiality

If you agree to confidentiality, honor your agreement. If you can't or won't agree to keeping a confidence, make that clear before you accept the information.

Spread the "Straight Scoop"

Don't try to BS your way through an explanation or a sale. The short-term hassle you might save by doing that can come back to bite both you and your organization. And it's just plain unfair to the people you deal with. Don't know an answer? Tell the person you'll get back with them. Then, do the necessary research. Pride yourself on being able to say that every answer you give is as correct as it can be. Ethics is about being and doing right, not sounding right.

"Means" Are Just as Important as "Ends"

Be extremely cautious of the old "The end justifies the means" argument. Don't work through a task only to find that the result has been tainted by the less-than-ethical way you chose to get there. Means are as important as ends and need to be treated as such.

From Where I Stand… (Journal Responses)

Choose one of the following quotations and write a response to it. Do you agree or disagree with the quotation? Defend your position.

1. "To know what is right and not do it is the worst cowardice."—Confucius
2. "Honesty is the cornerstone of all success, without which confidence and ability to perform cease to exist."—Mary Kay Ash
3. "It is not who is right, but what is right, that is of importance."—Thomas H. Huxley

---

JUST THE FACTS

1. The main idea of this selection is a) the day-to-day insignificant actions and behaviors by individuals represent the largest area of ethics problems; b) almost all companies are guilty of poor ethics at some time; c) e-mails from company executives often provide clues about business ethics; d) a company's leadership is responsible for the ethics of all its employees.

2. The ethics self-assessment checklist included all of the following *except* a) have I conducted personal business on company time?; b) have I used or taken company resources for personal purposes?; c) have I called in sick when I really wasn't? d) have I asked for a raise when I really didn't deserve one?

3. The example the author cites for embracing creative diversity is a) knowing that a "geek" can help if your computer crashes; b) everyone enjoys technological advances that were developed by weird creative types; c) creative people rarely advance in a company, so your chances for a promotion are better; d) creative people are usually well off financially and they contribute more than their share to the company parties.

4. According to the author, if employees do not know an answer they should a) give the kind of answer that they think is expected; b) call the person who should know the answer; c) tell the person asking the question that they will get back, and then do the necessary research to give as correct an answer as possible; d) make it well known who should have been the person responsible for the answer.

5. According to the author, "the end justifies the means" argument a) usually has a place in business ethics; b) is the best way to address most business problems; c) is something to be extremely cautious of; d) is the least likely way to get good results.

EXPANDING HORIZONS

1. The George S. May International Company has produced several more articles dealing with business ethics, which can be found at the Web site ethics.georgesmay.com/. Read one more of these articles and write a summary of it.

2. In January 2005, the Vermont Teddy Bear Company began marketing a stuffed animal called the "Crazy for You" bear, and the supply immediately sold out. However, a number of mental health advocates and others were outraged that the bear came in a straitjacket and had "commitment papers." Read about the controversy concerning the sales and decide if you think the company is being ethical in selling this product. Then write an editorial supporting your decision. Online sites to find information include these:

    www.signonsandiego.com/news/nation/20050217-1114-crazybear.html
    sfgate.com/cgi-bin/article.cgi?f=/g/a/2005/01/13/teddyjacket.DT
    www.msnbc.msn.com/id/6989224/

3. In the last few years, high-ranking officials from a number of well-known companies have been accused of unethical business practices. Research
    - the charges behind some of these individuals and/or companies.
    - the current state of the lawsuits.
    - possible repercussions if individuals are found guilty (or what has happened to those who have already been found guilty).
    - the effects on the company's stock after charges were filed.

4. Pretend you're the owner of a company and write a code of ethics for your organization. Use the links on www.ethicsweb.ca/codes/ to find ideas about what to include in your code and how to word it.

5. The Business Ethics Timeline at www.ethics.org/be_timeline_chart.html looks at the ethical climate, major ethical dilemmas, and business ethics developments in the decades 1960s, 1970s, 1980s, 1990s, and 2000s. For instance, in the 1960s, one of the developments cited was the birth of the social responsibility movement. Choose one decade and then one aspect of that decade; then research more about that feature. Write a summary about your findings.

WRITE ON!

1. Write a letter to the editor detailing your feelings about unethical business practices. You may address concerns about a local or national company or about ethics in general.

2. Write about what you would do if you saw a coworker taking credit for a project that he or she did not work on. Defend your actions.

3. Give an example of bad business ethics that you have witnessed. What was done in this situation? What should have been done to make the situation right?

In this selection, which originally appeared in Time *magazine in 1998, Pulitzer Prize-winning columnist* **Charles Krauthammer** *takes a look at the field of genetic cloning and warns about the potential problems that might be associated with the cloning of human beings.*

Starting Out...

Circle A if you agree with the statement or D if you disagree.

A   D   Creating animals that cannot breathe has ethical merit if the reason behind the creation is to enhance medical science.

A   D   If it were possible to produce headless humans and use their organs for keeping the "original" human alive, doing so would be ethical.

A   D   If you create a real clone, you can't transfer your consciousness into it to extend your life span past that of your existing physical body's life span.

Words to Watch

abyss: deep hole, void

acquiesce: accept, agree to

as per: according to, like in the work of

Brave New World: a reference to a 1932 book by Aldous Huxley that forecast developments in reproductive technology

breached: broken, violated

disemboweling: surgically removing an important part or substance

draconian: cruel, severe

flinch: shy away from, cringe

fore-brain: the front part of the brain

Frankenstein: a reference to the creator of a monster

incubating: keeping alive, nurturing

narcissism: vanity, egotism

plundering: stealing, looting

quasi: in some sense or degree

skeptical: doubtful, disbelieving

Of Headless Mice...and Men
by Charles Krauthammer

Last year Dolly the cloned sheep was received with wonder, titters, and some vague apprehension. Last week the announcement by a Chicago physicist that he is assembling a team to produce the first human clone occasioned yet another wave of Brave New World anxiety. But the scariest news of all—and largely overlooked—comes from two obscure labs, at the University of Texas and at the University of Bath. During the past four years, one group created headless mice; the other, headless tadpoles.

For sheer Frankenstein wattage, the purposeful creation of these animal monsters has no equal. Take the mice. Researchers found the gene that tells the embryo to produce the head. They deleted it. They did this in a thousand mice embryos, four of which were born. I use the term loosely. Having no way to breathe, the mice died instantly.

Why then create them? The Texas researchers want to learn how genes determine embryo development. But you don't have to be a genius to see the true utility of manufacturing headless creatures: for their organs—fully formed, perfectly useful, ripe for plundering.

Why should you be panicked? Because humans are next. "It would almost certainly be possible to produce human bodies without a fore-brain," Princeton biologist Lee Silver told the London *Sunday Times*. "These human bodies without any semblance of consciousness would not be considered persons, and thus it would be perfectly legal to keep them 'alive' as a future source of organs."

"Alive." Never have a pair of quotation marks loomed so ominously. Take the mouse-frog technology, apply it to humans, combine it with cloning, and you are become a god: With a single cell taken from, say, your finger, you produce a headless replica of yourself, a mutant twin, arguably lifeless, that becomes your own personal, precisely tissue-matched organ farm.

There are, of course, technical hurdles along the way. Suppressing the equivalent "head" gene in man. Incubating tiny infant organs to grow into larger ones that adults could use. And creating artificial wombs (as per Aldous Huxley), given that it might be difficult to recruit sane women to carry headless fetuses to their birth/death.

It won't be long, however, before these technical barriers are breached. The ethical barriers are already cracking. Lewis Wolpert, professor of biology at University College, London, finds producing headless humans "personally distasteful" but, given the shortage of organs, does not think distaste is sufficient reason not to go ahead with something that would save lives. And Professor Silver not only sees "nothing wrong, philosophically or rationally," with producing headless humans for organ harvesting; he wants to convince a skeptical public that it is perfectly O.K.

When prominent scientists are prepared to acquiesce in—or indeed encourage—the deliberate creation of deformed and dying quasi-human life, you know we are facing a bioethical abyss. Human beings are ends, not means. There is no grosser corruption of biotechnology than creating a human mutant and disemboweling it at our pleasure for spare parts.

The prospect of headless human clones should put the whole debate about "normal" cloning in a new light. Normal cloning is less a treatment for infertility than a treatment for vanity. It is a way to produce an exact genetic replica of yourself that will walk the earth years after you're gone.

But there is a problem with a clone. It is not really you. It is but a twin, a perfect John Doe, Jr., but still a junior. With its own independent consciousness, it is, alas, just a facsimile of you.

The headless clone solves the facsimile problem. It is a gateway to the ultimate vanity: immortality. If you create a real clone, you cannot transfer your consciousness into it to truly live on. But if you create a headless clone of just your body, you have created a ready source of replacement parts to keep you—your consciousness—going indefinitely.

Which is why one form of cloning will inevitably lead to the other. Cloning is the technology of narcissism, and nothing satisfies narcissism like immortality. Headlessness will be cloning's crowning achievement.

The time to put a stop to this is now. Dolly moved President Clinton to create a commission that recommended a temporary ban on human cloning. But with physicist Richard Seed threatening to clone humans, and with headless animals already here, we are past the time for toothless commissions and meaningless bans.

Clinton banned federal funding of human-cloning research, of which there is none anyway. He then proposed a five-year ban on cloning. This is not enough. Congress should ban human cloning now. Totally. And regarding one particular form, it should be draconian: The deliberate creation of headless humans must be made a crime, indeed a capital crime. If we flinch in the face of this high-tech barbarity, we'll deserve to live in the hell it heralds.

From Where I Stand... (Journal Responses)

1. I think the creation of headless mice is _____
   _____ because
   _____.

2. To create a replica of myself would be _____
   _____ because
   _____.

3. Advances in science should/should not (choose either "should" or "should not")
   be regulated by the government because _____
   _____.

JUST THE FACTS

1. The main idea of this selection is that a) many scientific advances have been made having to do with cloning; b) Congress needs to enact laws about cloning; c) human cloning should not be allowed; d) human cloning is the mark of the future and will lead to great medical advances.

2. Labs at the University of Texas and the University of Bath created a) human clones; b) headless sheep and goats; c) headless mice and tadpoles; d) clones of sheep.
3. The author says "the true utility of manufacturing headless creatures" is a) for scientific advancement; b) for their organs; c) to save money; d) still to be determined.
4. Technical hurdles to human cloning include all of the following *except* a) determining where to find financial backing; b) suppressing the equivalent "head" gene in man; c) incubating tiny infant organs to grow into larger ones; d) creating artificial wombs.
5. The author's opinion is that human cloning a) should be banned; b) needs money from the government if it is to succeed; c) is an idea that needs to be investigated by various religious leaders; d) will never be possible.

Expanding Horizons

1. This selection contains several allusions (indirect or brief references to well-known persons, places, or things). For instance, Krauthammer states that the announcement about an attempt at human cloning brought about "another wave of Brave New World anxiety." This is an allusion to the plot of Aldous Huxley's novel *Brave New World*. A later reference, "artificial wombs (as per Aldous Huxley)," creates another allusion to the plot of Huxley's book. A third allusion in this selection is "For sheer Frankenstein wattage," referring to the Mary Shelley book. Still another allusion comes in the word "draconian" ("it [banning human cloning] should be draconian"). Draco was a magistrate in ancient Greece who transcribed particularly harsh laws. Even the title of the selection is an allusion to John Steinbeck's novel *Of Mice and Men*.
   Read the following allusions and see whether you can determine their reference:
   • When I gave in to the temptation, I was Eve eating the apple.
   • Parting from my last boyfriend was anything but sweet sorrow.
   • It's rained so long I think I'll have to build an ark.
   • I asked my date when he'd call me again, but he replied, "Nevermore!"
2. A suffix is a group of letters added to the end of a word to form a new word. Learning the meaning of various suffixes can help you figure out the definition of certain words.
   For instance, the suffix *-ment* means *action* or *process*. Looking at words in the selection, an *announcement* is the process of announcing, *development* is the action of developing, *treatment* is the process of treating, *replacement* is the process of replacing, and *achievement* is the action of achieving.
   Another common suffix, *-less*, means *without*. You've just read about *headless* mice, a *lifeless* clone, *toothless* commissions, and *meaningless* bans. Knowing the definition of the suffix easily helps you know the meaning of the word.
   Listed below are some common suffixes; look in the selection for words that use them" should be formatted like this (the space should be under "Examples from the selection"):

Suffix	Meaning	Examples from the selection
-ty, *-ity*	condition of, quality of	_____
-ly	like, having characteristics of	_____
-ness	state of	_____
-al	relating to	_____
-ic	nature of, like	_____

Look at Internet sites to learn more common suffixes and their meanings. Online sites to consult include these:

www.msu.edu/~defores1/gre/sufx/gre_suffx.htm

oaks.nvg.org/lg5ra16.html

www.dummies.com/WileyCDA/DummiesArticle/id-1186.html

3. Read "The Benefits of Human Cloning" at www.humancloning.org/benefits.php and write a summary of the points of that article.

4. At library.thinkquest.org/24355/data/reactions/cloningviews.html, read the opinions that various organizations have about cloning. With which of these do you agree, and why?

5. Read another article by Charles Krauthammer at www.washingtonpost.com/wp-dyn/content/linkset/2005/03/24/LI2005032401690.html and write a summary of that article.

WRITE ON!

1. Take the opposite view of that presented by the author and write arguments in support of human cloning.

2. Suppose your college or university announced that it was going to attempt human cloning. Write an editorial for your school newspaper giving your opinion about this.

3. Suppose that the year is 2106, and human cloning has been around for several years. Write about your first encounter with your clone.

Business Ethics' 100 Best Corporate Citizens for 2004

from www.business-ethics.com/ 100best.htm #Article

Below is a table of the top 20 companies in Business Ethics' list of "100 Best Corporate Citizens for 2004." If you're familiar with the name of a company, put a check mark beside it; if you can identify what the company's product or service is, put a star beside it.

A company's ticker is its unique combination of letters used to identify it on the various stock exchanges. The tickers of The New York Stock Exchange (NYSE) and the American Stock Exchange (AMEX) have three or fewer characters; tickers on the National Association of Securities Dealers Automated Quotation (NASDAQ) use four or five letters. Using the ticker as your guide, consult today's newspaper and find the closing price of one of the companies listed in 100 Best Corporate Citizens for 2004.

TABLE 9.1					
Rank	**Overall Score**	**Company**	**Ticker**	**City**	**State**
1	1.57706	Fannie Mae	FNM	Washington	D.C.
2	1.49654	Procter & Gamble	PG	Cincinnati	OH
3	1.27976	Intel Corporation	INTC	Santa Clara	CA
4	1.24255	St. Paul Companies	SPC	St. Paul	MN
5	1.2126	Green Mountain Coffee Roasters Inc.	GMCR	Waterbury	VT
6	1.17381	Deere & Company	DE	Moline	IL
7	1.17051	Avon Products, Inc.	AVP	New York	NY
8	1.16223	Hewlett-Packard Company	HPQ	Palo Alto	CA
9	1.15216	Agilent Technologies Inc.	A	Palo Alto	CA
10	1.08014	Ecolab Inc.	ECL	St. Paul	MN
11	1.06408	Imation Corporation	IMN	Oakdale	MN

continued on next page

TABLE 9.1 (cont.)

Rank	Overall Score	Company	Ticker	City	State
12	1.04102	IBM	IBM	Armonk	NY
13	1.03204	Nuveen Investments	JNC	Chicago	IL
14	1.02257	Herman Miller, Inc.	MLHR	Zeeland	MN
15	0.99185	J. M. Smucker Company	SJM	Orrville	OH
16	0.96783	Safeco Corporation	SAFC	Seattle	WA
17	0.95133	The Timberland Company	TBL	Stratham	NH
18	0.92048	Zimmer Holdings, Inc.	ZMH	Warsaw	IN
19	0.89266	Cisco Systems, Inc.	CSCO	San Jose	CA
20	0.88254	3M Company	MMM	St. Paul	MN

Source: www.business-ethics.com/chart_100_best_corporate_citizens_for_2004.htm

"Yes, I like that shirt," you reply after your friend asks your opinion about a new purchase. Inwardly, you wonder why in the world someone would buy something so gaudy. Just a little white lie—no harm done? Maybe, maybe not. **Sissela Bok** *discusses the ethics of telling white lies in this excerpt from* Lying: Moral Choice in Public and Private Life.

Starting Out…
Circle A if you agree with the statement or D if you disagree.

A   D   A white lie isn't meant to injure anyone, so it has little moral significance.

A   D   Saying that you "can't" go to a party when you really just don't want to go is not unethical.

A   D   Recommending a friend for a job that you think he or she is unqualified for is unethical.

Words to Watch
abomination: disgrace, atrocity
concocted: created, invented
duplicity: deceit, dishonesty
equilibrium: stability, balance
formulations: concepts, ideas
indiscriminate: not based on careful distinctions, unselective
indisposition: illness, sickness
innocuous: harmless, innocent
melancholy: sadness, sorrow
minute: miniature, tiny
momentous: meaningful, significant
pervasive: present everywhere
placebos: substances containing no medication but given to reinforce a patient's expectation to get well
subterfuges: deceptive tricks or devices
utilitarians: those who believe that the value of a thing or an action is determined by its usefulness

---

White Lies
by Sissela Bok

> Never have I lied in my own interest; but often I have lied through shame in order to draw myself from embarrassment in indifferent matters…when, having to sustain discussion, the slowness of my ideas and the dryness of my conversation forced me to have recourse to fictions in order to say something.
> —Jean Jacques Rousseau, *Reveries of a Solitary*

> When a man declares that he "has great pleasure in
> accepting" a vexatious invitation or is the "obedient
> servant" of one whom he regards as an inferior, he uses
> phrases which were probably once deceptive. If they are
> so no longer, Common Sense condemns as over-
> scrupulous the refusal to use them where it is customary
> to do so. But Common Sense seems doubtful and
> perplexed where the process of degradation is incomplete
> and there are still persons who may be deceived: as in the
> use of the reply that one is "not at home" to an
> inconvenient visitor from the country.
> —Henry Sidgwick, *Methods of Ethics*

Harmless Lying

White lies are at the other end of the spectrum of deception from lies in a serious crisis. They are the most common and the most trivial forms that duplicity can take. The fact that they are so common provides their protective
coloring. And their very triviality, when compared to more threatening lies,
makes it seem unnecessary or even absurd to condemn them. Some consider
all well-intentioned lies, however momentous, to be white; in this book, I shall
adhere to the narrower usage: a white lie, in this sense, is a falsehood not
meant to injure anyone, and of little moral import. I want to ask whether there
are such lies; and if there are, whether their cumulative consequences are still
without harm; and, finally, whether many lies are not defended as "white"
which are in fact harmful in their won right.

Many small subterfuges may not even be intended to mislead. They are
only "white lies" in the most marginal sense. Take, for example, the many
social exchanges: "How nice to see you!" or "Cordially Yours." These and a
thousand other polite expressions are so much taken for granted that if someone decided, in the name of total honesty, not to employ them, he might
well give the impression of an indifference he did not possess. The justifica-
tion for continuing to use such accepted formulations is that they deceive
no one, except possibly those unfamiliar with the language.

A social practice more clearly deceptive is that of giving a false excuse
so as not to hurt the feelings of someone making an invitation or request: to say
one "can't" do what in reality one may not *want* to do. Once again, the false
excuse may prevent unwarranted inferences of greater hostility to the under-
taking than one may well feel. Merely to say that one can't do something, moreover, is not deceptive in the sense that an elaborately concocted story can be.

Still other white lies are told in an effort to flatter, to throw a cheerful interpretation on depressing circumstances, or to show gratitude for
unwanted gifts. In the eyes of many, such white lies do no harm, provide
needed support and cheer, and help dispel gloom and boredom. They pre-

serve the equilibrium and often the humaneness of social relationships, and are usually accepted as excusable so long as they do not become excessive. Many argue, moreover, that such deception is so helpful and at times so necessary that it must be tolerated as an exception to a general policy against lying. Thus Bacon observed:

> Doth any man doubt, that if there were taken out of men's minds vain opinions, flattering hopes, false valuations, imaginations as one would, and the like, but it would leave the minds of a number of men poor shrunken things, full of melancholy and indisposition, and unpleasing to themselves? [1]

Another kind of lie may actually be advocated as bringing a more substantial benefit, or avoiding a real harm, while seeming quite innocuous to those who tell the lies. Such are the placebos given for innumerable common ailments, and the pervasive use of inflated grades and recommendations for employment and promotion.

A large number of lies without such redeeming features are nevertheless often regarded as so trivial that they should be grouped with white lies. They are the lies told on the spur of the moment, for want of reflections, or to get out of a scrape, or even simply to pass the time. Such are the lies told to boast or exaggerate, or on the contrary to deprecate and understate;[2] the many lies told or repeated in gossip; Rousseau's lies told simply "in order to say something"; the embroidering on facts that seem too tedious in their own right; and the substitution of a quick lie for the lengthy explanations one might otherwise have to provide for something not worth spending time on.

Utilitarians often cite white lies as the *kind* of deception where their theory shows the benefits of common sense and clear thinking. A white lie, they hold, is trivial; it is either completely harmless, or so marginally harmful that the cost of detecting and evaluating the harm is much greater than the minute harm itself. In addition, the white lie can actually be beneficial, thus further tipping the scales of utility. In a world with so many difficult problems, utilitarians might ask, 'Why take the time to weigh the minute pros and cons in telling someone that his tie is attractive when it is an abomination, or of saying to a guest that a broken vase was worthless? Why bother even to define such insignificant distortions or make mountains out of molehills by seeking to justify them?'

---

[1] From Francis Bacon, "Of Truth," in *Essays Civil and Moral* (London: Ward, Lock & Co., 1910).

[2] Aristotle, in *Nicomachean Ethics* (pp. 239–45), contrasts these as "boasting" and "irony." He sees them as extremes between which the preferable mean of truthfulness is located.

Triviality surely does set limits to when moral inquiry is reasonable. But when we look more closely at practices such as placebo-giving, it becomes clear that all lies defended as "white" cannot be so easily dismissed. In the first place, the harmlessness of lies is notoriously disputable. What the liar perceives as harmless or even beneficial may not be so in the eyes of the deceived. Second, the failure to look at an entire practice rather than at their own isolated case often blinds liars to cumulative harm and expanding deceptive activities. Those who begin with white lies can come to resort to more frequent and more serious ones. Where some tell a few white lies, others may tell more. Because lines are so hard to draw, the indiscriminate use of such lies can lead to other deceptive practices. The aggregate harm from a large number of marginally harmful instances may, therefore, be highly undesirable in the end—for liars, those deceived, and honesty and trust more generally....

Placebos

The common practice of prescribing placebos to unwitting patients illustrates the two miscalculations so common to minor forms of deceit: ignoring possible harm and failing to see how gestures assumed to be trivial build up into collectively undesirable practices....[3]

Truthfulness at What Price?

These examples [of harmless lying, using placebos, and stretching the truth on letters of recommendation] show that one cannot dismiss lies merely by claiming that they don't matter. More often than not, they do matter, even where looked at in simple terms of harm and benefit. Any awareness of how lies spread must generate a real sensitivity to the fact that most lies believed to be "white" are unnecessary if not downright undesirable. Many are not as harmless as liars take them to be. And even those lies which would generally be accepted as harmless are not needed whenever their goals can be achieved through completely honest means. Why tell a flattering lie about someone's hat rather than a flattering truth about their flowers? Why tell a general white lie about a gift, a kind act, a newborn baby, rather than a more specific truthful statement? If the purpose is understood by both the speaker and listener to be one of civility and support, the full truth in such cases is not called for....*

[3]This discussion draws on my two articles, "Paternalistic Deception in Medicine, and Rational Choice: The Use of Placebos," in Max Black, ed., *Problems of Choice and Decision* (Ithaca, NY: Cornell University Program on Science, Technology and Society, 1975), pp. 73–107; and "The Ethics of Giving Placebos," *Scientific American* 231 (1974):17–23.

*If, on the other hand, one is asked for one's honest opinion, such partial answers no longer suffice. A flattering truth that conceals one's opinion is then as deceitful as a flattering lie. To avoid deception, one must then choose either to refuse to answer or to answer honestly....

From Where I Stand... (Journal Responses)

1. The most common white lie I've told is _____
   _____. I've told it because _____
   _____.

2. If I were ill, I would/would not (choose either "would" or "would not") want to
   know if I were given a placebo because _____
   _____.

3. White lies are/are not (choose either "are" or "are not") trivial because _____
   _____.

JUST THE FACTS

1. The main point of this selection is a) it is dangerous to give patients placebos;
   b) saying that you are glad to see someone can be a white lie; c) white lies can be
   unethical; d) a person must sometimes tell a white lie in order not to hurt another's
   feelings.
2. According to Bok, white lies are a) the most common forms of dishonesty; b) acceptable if told in emergency situations; c) forms of dishonesty that rank the highest in
   being unethical; d) commonly told on television.
3. Bok writes that white lies told in an effort to flatter, to throw a cheerful interpretation on depressing circumstances, or to show gratitude for unwanted fits a) are never
   to be accepted; b) are always justified because of their intention; c) are cause for great
   alarm; d) do no harm in the eyes of many people.
4. Utilitarians say that white lies a) should be taken back immediately; b) can be harmless; c) are "a part of the moral fiber of our society"; d) are the reason for continuing moral decay in today's society.
5. According to Bok, many white lies a) are eventually discovered as being untruths;
   b) "come back to haunt the liar"; c) are not as harmless as liars think they are;
   d) eventually turn into larger, more immoral lies.

EXPANDING HORIZONS

1. Read part of another chapter of Sissela Bok's *Lying: Moral Choice in Public and Private Life*. Then write a summary of what you learn.
2. At www.moralmoments.com/chapter.html, read the essay "Off the Hook," which looks
   at whether or not using an electronic device that simulates the clicking sound of
   "Call Waiting" is ethical or not. Then write your opinion about the subject.
3. A polygraph, often used as a lie detector, is an instrument that records changes in a
   person's physiological processes, such as heartbeat, blood pressure, and respiration.
   Research current data about the reliability of a polygraph and write a summary of
   what you learn. Online sites to consult include these:
   www.apa.org/monitor/jun98/lie.html
   www.polygraph.org/betasite/apa5rev.htm
   www.epic.org/privacy/polygraph/

4. Compulsive (or pathological) lying is a far more serious type of lying than telling white lies. Often, compulsive liars are practiced in lying so often that their action seems natural. Research more about this disorder and write a summary of what you learn. Online sites to consult include these:

 www.healthdiaries.com/compulsive-lying.htm
 www.healthdiaries.com/mentalhealth/truth/
 www.mental-health-matters.com/articles/article.php?artID=153
 www.psychologytoday.com/articles/pto-20031023-000012.html

5. Read "The Battle of the Ethics!" at www.usethics.net/battle.html. Summarize at least three main points in the article and tell whether or not you agree with them. Defend your answer.

WRITE ON!

1. For the next 24 hours, keep a list of the white lies that you tell others. Then without revealing any names or circumstances, pick one of the white lies and tell whether or not you think you were ethical in saying it. Defend your position.
2. Defend or refute this statement: Telling a white lie is unethical.
3. You're the advice columnist for your school newspaper. Write your reply to this letter: I overheard two people in my class discussing the way I was dressed for the day, both of them saying they were surprised how sloppy I looked and how my hair looked uncombed. What should I do?

READ ON!

Alford, C. Fred. *Whistleblowers: Broken Lives and Organizational Power*. Ithaca, NY: Cornell University Press, 2001.

Bird, Frederick B. *The Muted Conscience: Moral Silence and the Practice of Ethics in Business*. Westport, CT: Quorum Books, 1996.

Brannigan, Michael C., ed. *Ethical Issues in Human Cloning: Cross-Disciplinary Perspectives*. New York: Seven Bridges Press, 2001.

"Case Studies: Ethics in Education." www.uvsc.edu/ethics/curriculum/education/.

Davey, Joseph Dillon, and DuBois Davey, Linda. *The Conscience of the Campus: Case Studies in Moral Reasoning among Today's College Students*. Westport, CT: Praeger, 2001.

De George, Richard T. *The Ethics of Information Technology and Business*. Malden, MA: Blackwell Pub., 2003.

"The Ethics of Lying to a Dying Person." forum.objectivismonline.net/lofiversion/index.php/t3304.html.

Levine, Carol, ed. *Taking Sides: Clashing Views on Controversial Bioethical Issues*. Guilford, CT: McGraw Hill/Dushkin Pub. Group, 2001.

"Lying." www.scu.edu/ethics/publications/iie/v6n1/lying.html.

Mandell, Judy. 2002. "Sometimes Honesty Is the Worst Policy." *Newsweek* Oct. 21.

"Protecting Human Subjects in Internet Research." ejbo.jyu.fi/pdf/ejbo_vol10_
no1_pages_35-41.pdf.

Purtilo, Ruth B. *Ethical Dimensions in the Health Professions*. Philadelphia: Elsevier
Saunders, 2005.

"Reviving Ethics in Sports: Time for Physicians to Act." www.physsportsmed.com/
issues/1998/06jun/pipe.htm.

Snyder, Carrie. *Death and Dying, Who Decides?* Detroit: Gale Group, 2001.

"Three Reasons Why Students Cheat." privateschool.about.com/cs/forteachers/
a/cheating.htm.

In the photograph above, taken in 2001, members of a congregation in Butler, PA, are tossing books, CDs, videos, and other items into a fire. What do you think might be the reason behind their actions?

Did you think that book burning was a thing of the past? Do you agree or disagree with burning books or other material? Why? What books or other material, if any, do you think should be burned? Support your opinion.

CHAPTER TEN

CENSORSHIP
Say the Right Thing—or Don't

An idea that is not dangerous is unworthy of being called an idea at all. —*Oscar Wilde*

Books and ideas are the most effective weapons against intolerance
and ignorance. —*Lyndon Johnson*

Censorship is advertising paid by the government. —*Federico Fellini*

Free speech not only lives, it rocks! —*Oprah Winfrey*

I believe in censorship. After all, I made a fortune out of it. —*Mae West*

I cannot and will not cut my conscience to fit this year's fashions. —*Lillian Hellman*

Our whole constitutional heritage rebels at the thought of giving government the power to control
men's minds. —*Thurgood Marshall*

The dirtiest book of all is the expurgated book. —*Walt Whitman*

The only valid censorship of ideas is the right of people not to listen. —*Tommy Smothers*

There are worse crimes than burning books. One of them is not reading them. —*Joseph Brodsky*

There is no such thing as a moral book or an immoral book. Books are well written or badly
written. That is all. —*Oscar Wilde*

To forbid us anything is to make us have a mind for it. —*Michel de Montaigne*

What progress we are making. In the Middle Ages they would have burned me. Now they are
content with burning my books. —*Sigmund Freud*

You don't have to burn books to destroy a culture. Just get people to
stop reading them. —*Ray Bradbury*

You have not converted a man because you have silenced him. —*John Morley*

Censorship: Say the Right Thing—or Don't

> Congress shall make no law respecting an establishment of religion, or prohibiting the free exercise thereof; or abridging the freedom of speech, or of the press; or the right of the people peaceably to assemble, and to petition the government for a redress of grievances.

Sound familiar? It should; you've probably read it sometime during your schooling. It's the First Amendment to the United States Constitution.

During the debate over the Constitution in the late 1700s, several of the Founding Fathers refused to sign the document as it was originally written because it did not specify certain liberties to which they felt citizens should be entitled. These men did not want citizens' civil rights to be violated the way they had been under British rule, so they demanded that a "bill of rights" be added to the Constitution. After much debate, the Bill of Rights, which contains the first ten amendments (changes, improvements) to the Constitution, was ratified on December 15, 1791.

The First Amendment, as you read, covers several rights. It states that the government may not establish a religion and guarantees that people may freely practice any religion they choose. It also gives citizens the right to assemble in a peaceful manner and to ask the government to make corrections to any problems that citizens think should be addressed.

In this chapter, you'll look at two other parts of the First Amendment—freedom of speech and freedom of the press—and decide when, if ever, censorship of speech and the press might be appropriate.

For instance, does another person have the right to use your name in a commercial endeavor—that is, in a way that makes money from your name? What if the way your name is used contradicts ideals that you have and have fought for? "Move to the Front of the Bus, Ms. Parks" studies this issue in the lawsuit the late Rosa Parks brought against the popular hip-hop duo OutKast.

Another part of censorship is addressed every year, when a number of books are challenged as being inappropriate. Libraries are asked to remove certain works because of a variety of objections. Author Will Manley takes on the issue what to do about freedom of speech in relation to books that have offensive language or controversial subject matter. In his selection "In Defense of Book Burning," he wonders if the age-old image of fire as a sign of authority could be used to remedy the problem. (Hint: Do you recognize satire?)

In looking at censorship from a different angle, ask yourself whether freedom of speech can ever go too far. Are there times when people—the same people who are guaranteed freedom of speech in the U.S.—should censor themselves? Should citizens think about how standards of decency are changing, and consequently change their own reaction to certain words? If so, whose standards of decency are appropriate? "Foul Words Permeate Pop Culture, Eliciting a Backlash" looks at how American society is reacting to several aspects of freedom of speech.

Now choose one of the quotations on p. 225 to write about. Be sure to defend your opinion.

Can freedom of speech ever go too far? Does a person or group have a right to use your name, without your permission, in a song or anything else that is sold for a profit? What should you do—what can you do—if your name is used in a way that you think is wrong? The selection below examines some of these questions as it details the court case between civil rights leader Rosa Parks and hip-hop duo OutKast.

Starting Out...
Circle A if you agree with the statement or D if you disagree.

A   D   Because of freedom of speech, an author or artist has the right to use the name of a famous person in any work.

A   D   A company that made T-shirts and coffee mugs with the logo "Mutant of Omaha" had a right to do so, even though the insurance company Mutual of Omaha objected.

A   D   The owners of the Dairy Queen trademark were right when they prohibited a company from releasing a film on beauty pageants with the title "Dairy Queens."

Words to Watch

the Bard: a reference to William Shakespeare

commodian: a made-up word that is a blend of "commode" and "comedian"

copyright: a legal right granted to authors, composers, and others for exclusive publication, production, sale, or distribution of a literary, musical, or other work

Court of Appeals: a court to which appeals are made on points of law resulting from the judgment of a lower court

crunk: a slang word meaning "get excited"

dockets: calendars of the cases awaiting action in a court

enjoined: prohibited or forbade

explicitly: in a fully and clearly expressed way

icon: one who is the object of great attention and devotion

i.e.: Latin for "id est," meaning "that is"

netherworld: the part of society engaged in crime and vice

Sixth Circuit, Eighth Circuit, Ninth Circuit: three of the twelve national courts of appeals, each covers a specific geographic area and hears cases from that area

spoof: a gentle satirical imitation, a light parody

trademark: a name, symbol, or other device identifying a product, officially registered and legally restricted to the use of the owner or manufacturer

_v._: the abbreviation for "versus," meaning "against in a legal case"

Move to the Front of the Bus, Ms. Parks

by Michael A. Kahn

"What's in a name?" Romeo asks as he gazes up at his beloved's balcony from the garden below. "That which we call a rose, by any other name would smell as sweet." "Better yet," his lawyer would add today, "it'll keep you out of court."

How times have changed. Back in Shakespeare's era, an enterprising businessman could have brought out a new perfume under the name "Juliet." Or even "Juliet Capulet." Or just "Capulet." Or he could have published a love song with one of those titles. And even if Juliet had been a real person, neither she nor the Capulet family nor the Bard himself could have stopped the use of her name as the name of perfume or the title of a song.

Today, though, the trial dockets increasingly feature disputes over names—of books, songs, motion pictures and the like. Titles exist in a misty netherworld between copyright and trademark law. You can't copyright a title, no matter how clever it is.

Generally, you also can't claim trademark rights in a title. But there are exceptions. Trademarks—unlike copyrights—are designed to protect consumers from confusion over the source of a product. The name of a book or a movie occasionally can function in the same way as the name of a soft drink or a car. Courts extend trademark protection to the title of a book, play, movie or record where the owner can demonstrate that the title has acquired "secondary meaning," i.e., where the title is sufficiently well known that consumers associate it with a particular source and no one else. Easier said than proven, however. The U.S. Trademark Office refuses to register trademarks in the titles of single works—even such famous works as *Gone With the Wind*. A more liberal rule governs titles of series, whether it is the *[Blank] For Dummies* book series or the *Rocky* motion picture series or the *Cheers* TV series.

But what about using the name of a famous person in the title of a work in which that famous person does not appear? Believe it or not, one of the first big cases in this area involved a portable toilet named after, well, the caption of the case says it all: *Johnny Carson v. Here's Johnny Portable Toilets, Inc.*[1] The defendant's marketing slogan? "The World's Foremost Commodian." Honest. Johnny won. They say he was flushed with victory.

But what if the celebrity's name appears in the title of a work of *art* instead of the title of a portable toilet? What happens along that battle line between celebrities and the First Amendment?

[1]308 F.2d 831 (6th Cir. 1983).

The first big case involved "Ginger and Fred," which was the title of Frederico Fellini's bittersweet film about the reunion of two elderly Italian dancers who had once been nicknamed Ginger and Fred because they imitated America's most famous dancing couple, Ginger Rogers and Fred Astaire. The real Ginger Rogers sued, claiming the movie title gave the false impression that she endorsed or was somehow involved in the film. The court of appeals rebuffed Ms. Rogers, holding that a title that includes a real person's name will be protected unless the title "has no artistic relevance" to the underlying work or if the title "explicitly misleads as to the source or the content of the work."[2]

The latest case involves civil rights icon Rosa Parks, who was dismayed to learn that the rap group OutKast had released a hit single entitled "Rosa Parks." She sued, claiming that the use of her name as the title of the song deceived the public into believing the song was about her or that she was somehow affiliated with the defendants or had approved the song. The defendants invoked their First Amendment rights to artistic creativity and pointed to the song's refrain:

> Ah ha, hush that fuss,
> Everybody move to the back of the bus.
> Do you want to bump and slump with us?
> We the type of people make the club get crunk.

The trial court agreed and dismissed Ms. Parks' case.[3] She appealed to the Sixth Circuit, where her attorney, Johnnie Cochran, argued that if the meaning's not in the verse, you must reverse. Specifically, he provided the court of appeals with the following translation of the above-quoted refrain into standard English:

> Be quiet and stop the commotion.
> OutKast is coming out with new music so all other rappers step aside.
> Do you want to ride and hang out with us?
> OutKast is the type of group to make the clubs get excited.

Persuaded by the translation, the Court of Appeals reversed the trial court's decision and sent the case back down for trial on whether the title of the song "is or is not 'wholly unrelated' to the content of the song."[4] If OutKast can prove that there is artistic relevance to the use of Ms. Parks' name as the title of the song, they will win on First Amendment grounds. But if Ms. Parks can prove that the title of the song was "a disguised commercial advertisement" or adopted "solely to attract attention to

[2]*Rogers v. Grimaldi*, 875 F.2d 994 (2d Cir. 1989).

[3]*Parks v. LaFace Records*, 76 F.Supp.2d 775 (E.D.Mich. 1999).

[4]*Parks v. LaFace Records*, 2003 WL 21058571 (6th Cir. 2003).

the work," then the First Amendment will not protect the defendants. Stay tuned.

But nothing is simple in this area. The "artistic relevance" test adopted by the Sixth Circuit in the *Rosa Parks* case is not the only test out there. In the Eighth Circuit (which includes Arkansas, Iowa, Minnesota, Missouri and Nebraska), the applicable rule is the "alternative avenues" test, under which a title will not be protected from a false advertising claim if there are sufficient alternative means for an artist to convey his or her idea. Under that test, Mutual of Omaha successful sued a company that made T-shirts and coffee mugs with a "Mutant of Omaha" logo[5], and the owners of the Dairy Queen trademark enjoined New Line Productions from releasing a mock documentary film on beauty pageants in rural Minnesota under the title "Dairy Queens."[6] Both cases would likely have come out differently under the *Rosa Parks* test.

In the Ninth Circuit (which includes California, Hawaii, Oregon and Washington), the courts appear to apply the traditional "likelihood of confusion" test used in trademark cases. Under that test, the issue is whether the title of the work creates a likelihood of consumer confusion over the source, sponsorship, approval or affiliation of the work. For example, Dr. Seuss Enterprises enjoined Penguin Books USA from publishing a spoof on the O.J. Simpson trial featuring characters and rhyming patterns reminiscent of many Dr. Seuss books, such as:

> One knife,
> Two knife,
> Red knife,
> Dead wife.

The title? *The Cat NOT In the Hat.* The ruling: use of that title created a likelihood of consumer confusion over the affiliation of Dr. Seuss with the book.[7]

The law of titles is thus a bit muddled. Our advice to Romeo is to name the song "Juliet" *only* if it's about her. As for the perfume, he better talk to Billy Shakespeare's agent about doing a deal because the First Amendment doesn't cover commercial products. Although Billy's agent has already given the master toy license to Mattel and he's done a deal with Sony for the BATTLE OF THE CAPULETS & MONTAGUES videogame, the perfume rights are still out there.

---

[5]*Mutual of Omaha Ins. Co. v. Novak* (8th Cir. 1987).

[6]*Am. Dairy Queen Corp. v. New Line Prods., Inc.*, 35 F.Supp.2d 727 (D.Minn. 1998).

[7]*Dr. Seuss Enterprises, L.P. v. Penguin Books UDA, Inc.*, 109 F.3d 1394 (9th Cir. 1997).

From Where I Stand... (Journal Responses)

1. If someone used my name in the title of a song, I would feel _____ _____ because
_____.

2. The most interesting part of this selection was _____ _____. It was interesting because _____.

3. If I could ask Rosa Parks or OutKast two questions, I would ask _____
_____
and _____.
I would ask these questions because _____
_____.

JUST THE FACTS

1. The main point of this selection is a) OutKast had no right to use Rosa Parks' name in its song's title; b) Rosa Parks had no right to object to her name being used in the OutKast song title; c) many legal arguments have arisen over the use of famous names in titles or other works; d) Romeo and Juliet had a number of legal battles to overcome.

2. Trademarks are designed to a) help make extra money for the company; b) protect consumers from confusion over the source of a product; c) let company presidents and other high-ranking personnel get extra income from use; d) help the union employees of a company in their trade negotiations.

3. The author cites a case that involved a) Oprah Winfrey; b) Dr. Phil McGraw; c) David Letterman; d) Johnny Carson.

4. *Ginger and Fred* was the title of a) a made-for-TV movie that featured two cats belonging to a couple who were dancers; b) a book that revealed how the famous couple got along onstage and offstage; c) a film about the reunion of two elderly Italian dancers; d) a CD that OutKast released in early 1999.

5. Rosa Parks's attorney was a) Johnnie Cochran; b) Perry Mason; c) Bill Clinton; d) never named.

EXPANDING HORIZONS

1. In April 2005, new developments were announced in the *Rosa Parks v. OutKast* case. Research these developments and summarize what you find. Online sites to consult include these:

    playahata.com/hatablog/index.php?p=419

    www.cnn.com/2005/SHOWBIZ/Music/04/15/parks.settlement/

    www.detnews.com/2005/metro/0504/15/D01-151386.htm

2. In the fifth paragraph, you'll notice a footnote at the end of this sentence:

    Believe it or not, one of first big cases in this area involved a portable toilet...: *Johnny Carson v. Here's Johnny Portable Toilets, Inc.*[1]

The footnote is the little number (in this case, the numeral "1") that's put in an elevated position, called "superscript," at the end of the sentence. It tells you to look for a corresponding number to get more information. Depending on the book or article, this number may be at the bottom of the page, the end of the chapter or article, or the end of the book. At the end of this article, you saw

[1]308 F.2d 831 (6th Cir. 1983)

a citation about the case that tells you where to find the case in print if you want to read it. The numeral "1," written in superscript, which is higher than the other material, tells readers that this information corresponds with the footnote numbered "1" in the article. For this citation, the "F.2d" means *Federal Reporter, Second Series*. (The *Federal Reporters* contain cases decided by the U.S. Courts of Appeals.) This particular case is in Volume 308 of the *Federal Reporter, Second Series*, and appears on page 831 of that volume. The part in parentheses indicates the case was decided by the Sixth Circuit Court of Appeals in 1983.

Now take a look at other footnotes in the selection and then give the case name and decision date for each.

3. Civil rights activist Rosa Parks died in 2005 at age 92. Read a biography of her life and write a summary of it. Online sites to consult include these:
   www.achievement.org/autodoc/page/par0bio-1
   en.wikipedia.org/wiki/Rosa_Parks
   www.detnews.com/2005/obituaries/0510/24/A01-360012.htm
4. In addition to the *Rosa Parks v. OutKast* case, the selection mentioned cases involving two other famous people, Johnny Carson and Ginger Rogers. Another case involving a celebrity was (Bette) *Midler v. Ford Motor Co.*, 849 F.2d 460 (9th Cir. 1988). Research the background and outcome of this case and write a summary of what you discover.
5. Several of the cases mentioned in this selection made their way to federal circuit courts. Read about these courts at www.catea.org/grade/legal/circuits.html and then summarize your research.

WRITE ON!

1. Ms. Parks objected to the lyrics of the song "Rosa Parks" because the refrain said, "Ah ha, hush that fuss/ Everybody move to the back of the bus" and the idea of moving to the back of the bus was in opposition to her principles. Address this question: Was Rosa Parks right to oppose OutKast's using her name as the title of a song that had a line she objected to? Why or why not?
2. Ms. Parks also opposed the "Rosa Parks" title because she objected to OutKast's use of profanity and racial slurs. Address this question: Was Rosa Parks right to oppose OutKast using her name because she objected to the language that the duo used?
3. Rosa Parks was a civil rights icon because of how she handled herself during the Civil Rights Era. Think of someone in your life who has handled himself or herself in an admirable way and write a short biography of that person.

Author **Will Manley** *is a former librarian and current city manager in Tempe, Arizona. He maintains his connection to the book world through a regular column in* American Libraries *magazine. This article, from the March 2002 issue, notes that for centuries people have recognized the image of fire as a sign of power and awe, and that perhaps an argument can be made in favor of using that image in burning books.*

Starting Out...

Read the following and circle A if you agree with the statement or D if you disagree:

A   D   Children should not be allowed to read books about magic.

A   D   Negative publicity can have a positive effect on a product.

A   D   Instead of banning books, book burning should be banned.

Words to Watch

black arts: witchcraft

character flaws: faults, vulnerabilities, weak points

clueless: ignorant, naive

conjured: called forth, with or as if by magic

Diem regime: the rule of Ngo Dinh Diem in South Vietnam (1955–1963)

dissidents: protesters, rebels

Goody Two-shoes: a slang phrase meaning "someone who is upright and virtuous, perhaps to a fault"

menacingly: threateningly, in a sinister way

mesmerize: captivate, spellbind

perspective: viewpoint, standpoint

ruse: trick, hoax

sidekicks: pals, friends

sorcerers: a name for those who practice witchcraft

thugs: hoods, aggressive and violent young criminals

wizards: a name for men who practice magic

In Defense of Book Burning
by Will Manley

If you want to make a strong statement about something, it's hard to find a stronger image to use than fire. When God revealed himself to Moses, he did so as a burning bush. When Jesus attempted to describe the pain of hell, he conjured up a terrifying portrait of eternal flames. When the white-hooded thugs of the Ku Klux Klan rode menacingly through the rural South to stir up the hatred of racism, they burned crosses on people's front yards. When anti-war dissidents protested U.S. involvement in the Vietnam War, they burned the American flag. When Buddhist monks protested the corrupt Diem regime in South Vietnam, they burned themselves. When the Nazis wanted to rid Germany of dangerous and undesirable ideas, they burned piles and piles of books.

Unfortunately, book burning is back in business, but not in Germany. It's happening right here in the U.S., and, oddly, it has nothing to do with our worldwide war on terrorism. In fact, there's probably been a book burning at a church or school near you. The target is Harry Potter, hero of millions of children. Harry is a fictional young boy who can perform extraordinary feats of magic. The fact that he has captured the hearts and imaginations of children has driven some clerics and parents into fits of frustration and rage. It's the kind of rage that bursts into fire.

The whole book-burning phenomenon is actually quite difficult to understand. You would think that Harry would be a cause for celebration by anyone sincerely interested in young people. With a wave of a wizard's wand he has done the utterly impossible. He has turned kids away from television, videos, and computer games and back into books. I never thought I'd see the day when kids would line up outside of a bookstore just to buy a book! Miraculously, that is what happens whenever a new Potter title is released, and that is precisely why Harry is driving his enemies crazy.

He's so popular that they think that he might mesmerize young children, turning them away from God and toward the black arts. Never mind the fact that Harry is a force of goodness and courage in a world that is creeping with evildoers. It's actually hard to think of a character in all of children's literature that is more a Goody Two-shoes than young, innocent Harry. In fact from a literary perspective, the only thing that I don't like about Harry is that he seems too good to be true. His sidekicks, Ron and Hermione, are much more appealing because they do have some minor character flaws.

So, how do you deal with a wizard who is mesmerizing your children? If you're really clueless about the magical arts, you will do something stupid like trying to burn him in hopes that he will instantly vanish. Anyone who knows anything about wizards or sorcerers however, recognizes that this approach is probably the worst thing that you can do. Wizards have a way of miraculously reappearing stronger than ever, and in Harry's case that is exactly what is happening. It's actually quite magical—the more you burn Harry, the more he multiplies. As a result, his creator, J. K. Rowling, is laughing all the way to the bank. I wonder how the book burners feel about helping finance her new castle in Scotland.

Book burnings bring big publicity. Nothing provokes public interest more than a fire, and nothing helps to sell books more than public interest. Book burners, therefore, are playing right into Harry's wily hands. He's not a wizard for nothing.

Not only are they clueless about wizards, the book burners are equally clueless about kids. What's the old expression—"don't tell kids not to put beans up their nose because that's exactly what they will do as soon as you turn your back." The same thing holds true here. If you burn a book because you don't want your child to read it, don't you think the kid will make it his first order of business to seek the book out on his own? He might even go to the public library to read it.

From Where I Stand... (Journal Responses)

1. After reading this article, I doubt that _____
   _____.

2. One idea or opinion in this selection with which I strongly agree/disagree (choose either "agree" or "disagree") is _____.
   _____. I feel this way
   because _____.

3. Other ways that people who oppose material in books could address the issue include _____
   _____.

Just the Facts

1. The main idea of this selection is a) book burning serves a noble cause; b) people who burn books should be commended for standing up against those who try to get inside children's minds; c) one famous book burner was taken to court but had his case thrown out; d) book burning helps to sell books.

2. Will Manley, the author of this selection, is a) clearly against book burning; b) trying to decide his opinion about book burning; c) clearly in favor of book burning; d) hiding his opinion about book burning and asking the readers to decide.

3. When Manley writes "I wonder how the book burners feel about helping finance her new castle in Scotland," he is writing about a) Queen Elizabeth; b) Madonna; c) J. K. Rowling; d) Oprah Winfrey.

4. Manley writes that if a wizard is burned, a) the wizard's death will be instant and lasting; b) the wizard will reappear stronger than ever; c) the wizard's death can be called off by certain witches; d) more wizards will immediately appear to take his place.

5. Manley writes that book burnings a) have little effect in the long run; b) are effective for children's books but not for adult books; c) are often staged by publishing companies; d) bring big publicity to the books.

Expanding Horizons

1. While author J. K. Rowling has become wealthy due to her Harry Potter books, she came from humble beginnings. Read about her life and then write a short biography. Online sites to consult include these:

   gaga.essortment.com/jkrowlingbiogr_reak.htm
   www.kidzworld.com/site/p924.htm

singleparents.about.com/cs/booksandmovies/l/aajkrowlingbio1.htm

www2.scholastic.com/teachers/authorsandbooks/authorstudies/authorhome.jhtml
?authorID=821&collateralID=5276&displayName=Biography

2. The Online Books Page, at onlinebooks.library.upenn.edu/banned-books.html, has a site devoted to books that have been banned throughout history. Use the information on this page to create a timeline of books that have been banned. If your instructor directs, add a synopsis (a general overview of a story, detailing the beginning, middle, and end) of one or more of the books.

3. A number of classic films deal with censorship of books. View one of these and then write a film review of it:

> *Storm Center*, starring Bette Davis as a librarian who's branded as a communist after she refuses to remove a book (1965)
>
> *Fahrenheit 451*, from the Ray Bradbury book about a firefighter whose duty is to destroy all books (the title comes from the temperature at which paper will burn) (1966)
>
> *1984*, an adaptation of George Orwell's novel of a society that rewrites history (1954, 1956, 1984)
>
> *The Seven Minutes*, about a clerk indicted for selling obscene material (1971)
>
> *Inherit the Wind*, about the famous Scopes "monkey trial" of the 1920s (1960, 1965, 1988, 1998)

4. Find at least two examples of alliteration in this piece. What does alliteration add to the way the article reads?

WRITE ON!

1. Play the devil's advocate (that is, for the sake of fairness, argue a point of view that isn't necessarily your own) and write a letter to the editor of American Libraries taking the opposite view from what Manley wrote.

2. Compare the issue of book burning to an issue that you feel very passionate about. Compare and contrast the two issues.

3. Write a short review of a book that you found disturbing. Why did it disturb you? Did you finish the book? Would you recommend it to someone else? Why or why not?

Most Frequently Challenged Books of 1990–2000

compiled by the American Library Association

1. *Scary Stories* (series) by Alvin Schwartz
2. *Daddy's Roommate* by Michael Willhoite
3. *I Know Why the Caged Bird Sings* by Maya Angelou
4. *The Chocolate War* by Robert Cormier
5. *The Adventures of Huckleberry Finn* by Mark Twain
6. *Of Mice and Men* by John Steinbeck
7. *Harry Potter* (series) by J. K. Rowling
8. *Forever* by Judy Blume
9. *Bridge to Terabithia* by Katherine Paterson
10. *Alice* (series) by Phyllis Reynolds Naylor
11. *Heather Has Two Mommies* by Leslea Newman
12. *My Brother Sam Is Dead* by James Lincoln Collier and Christopher Collier
13. *The Catcher in the Rye* by J. D. Salinger
14. *The Giver* by Lois Lowry
15. *It's Perfectly Normal* by Robie Harris
16. *Goosebumps* (series) by R. L. Stine
17. *A Day No Pigs Would Die* by Robert Newton Peck
18. *The Color Purple* by Alice Walker
19. *Sex* by Madonna
20. *Earth's Children* (series) by Jean M. Auel
21. *The Great Gilly Hopkins* by Katherine Paterson
22. *A Wrinkle in Time* by Madeleine L'Engle
23. *Go Ask Alice* by Anonymous
24. *Fallen Angels* by Walter Dean Myers
25. *In the Night Kitchen* by Maurice Sendak

Question

Circle each title that you've read; then interview four other people and ask them which of these books they've read. For both yourself and the others, ask whether

the reader found anything objectionable about the book.

the reader could identify what some others might find objectionable about the book.

the reader thinks the book should be removed from public libraries, and why or why not.

In this April 2004 article from The Christian Century, *writer* **Mark O'Keefe** *examines how the use of foul words has become more commonplace in modern society. Is this a sign that society is changing its standards? Have some people gone too far? Should limits to acceptable language be imposed, and if so, by whom? This selection looks at these and other questions regarding the increased use of foul language.*

Starting Out...

Circle A if you agree with the statement or D if you disagree.

A   D   Words that were previously considered curse words are now frequently accepted on television and radio.

A   D   Television networks are right to edit out offensive words that are said by people at awards programs.

A   D   I'm more shocked by a racial slur than I am by a curse word.

Words to Watch

abound: flourish, are plentiful

anecdotes: short accounts of interesting or humorous incidents

backlash: criticism, reaction, counterattack

concede: admit, grant

expletive: curse word

fight the good fight: an idiom meaning "fight for a just cause"

imprecision: vagueness, indistinctness

lexicon: word list, dictionary

linguistics: the study of the structure and development of a language

potty-mouthed: an idiom meaning "using curse words"

shock jocks: hosts of radio programs designed to upset or alarm listeners

taboo: forbidden, unacceptable

Foul Language Enters Pop Culture Lexicon

by Mark O'Keefe

Rasheda Williams, 24, recently walked through the Detroit neighborhood where she grew up. She observed a girl about 12 calling to a friend across the street.

"Hey, b—ch," the pre-teen said.

Had Williams used such language at that age, she said, "I might have a bar of soap for lunch."

But today, foul language is common, and not just among potty-mouthed children or shock jocks like Howard Stern. Consider John Kerry using the f-word in describing President Bush's war effort in Iraq, rock singer Bono using similarly raw language at the Golden Globe Awards or Garrison Keillor singing a ditty that included "pissed" and "ass" on his "A Prairie Home Companion" radio show.

Any sailor will tell you that foul language is nothing new. Even in political settings, cussing has sometimes been part of the vocabulary, as Richard Nixon's Watergate tapes showed. And language experts concede that outside of studies of network television, it's difficult to document a societal increase in offensive words.

But what is clear, these language experts say, is that society's standards are changing, with previously taboo words finding their way into the public lexicon.

A backlash may be brewing. The Federal Communications Commission—which ruled that Bono's f-word wasn't punishable because it was used as a modifier and not a sexually charged verb—has indicated readiness to fine broadcasters for foul language. Congress has held hearings on broadcasting indecencies and is threatening new legislation if the networks don't clean up.

In response, Clear Channel recently dropped Stern's radio show from its stations. CBS aired the Grammy Awards with a five-minute delay and ABC used a five-second delay at the Academy Awards, just enough time to cut or bleep out something questionable.

Network executives have so far refrained from their usual argument that the shows merely reflect changing societal standards. But standards indeed have changed.

In the 1970s, comedian George Carlin did a routine about the Seven Dirty Words you couldn't say on TV, but two of those—"piss" and "tits"—are now frequently uttered.

In the 1950s, it was common for people to say "H-E-double-tooth-picks." Today, it's arguable whether words like "hell" even qualify as cussing.

"'Hell' and 'damn' have lost their power in our society, not through prohibition but through overuse," said Timothy Jay, a professor at Massachusetts College of Liberal Arts and author of five books on profanity. "We did an analysis, and 'hell' and 'damn' are in the newspapers all the time. They're even in the cartoons. What was impermissible on TV in the '50s is what we consider appropriate for kids every day."

Not everyone sees cause for concern. Donna Jo Napoli, professor of linguistics at Swarthmore College in Pennsylvania sees such change as a normal part of the evolution of language.

"We're still shocked by lots of things," Napoli said. "We've just changed what we're shocked by. A racial slur, for example, knocks us flat."

According to research by the Parents Television Council, foul language on television has clearly increased. At its Alexandria, Va., headquarters, the organization hires analysts to watch and listen to every hour of prime-time TV. The council compared similar four-week periods of 1989 and 1999. Among the results:

"Damn"—up 323 percent.

"Hell"—up 432 percent.

"Ass"—up 2,108 percent.

"We observed this same phenomenon for every profanity and expletive we tracked," said Melissa Caldwell, PTV's director of research.

PTV pays careful attention to the first hour of prime time, which used to be called "the family hour." Analyzing that period on ABC, CBS, NBC, Fox, UPN and WB, it found that foul language nearly doubled, from an average 2.91 bad words per hour in 1998 to 5.67 in 2002. The only network to improve was Fox, which had the highest foul-word incidence by far in 1998, at 7.44, and declined to 5.58 in 2002 — third highest after NBC (8.20) and CBS (7.37).

But televised vulgarity is hardly confined to entertainment. In September 2000, not realizing his microphone was on while talking to running mate Dick Cheney at a campaign stop, George W. Bush referred to a New York Times reporter as a "major league –hole."

Sen. Kerry of Massachusetts, front-runner for the Democratic presidential nod, may have one-upped Bush when, in an interview with *Rolling Stone*, he said of his vote for war with Iraq: "Did I expect George Bush to f– it up as badly as he did? I don't think anybody did."

One problem with such language is its imprecision, said James O'Connor, founder of the Illinois-based Cuss Control Academy and author of *Cuss Control: The Complete Book on How to Curb Your Cussing*.

"There are other words a presidential candidate could use," O'Connor said. "He could have said Bush bungled the war, botched the war, mishandled the war or messed up the war."

According to O'Connor's research, the most used and imprecise profanity is an expression of disgust that begins with "s."

"We use this word for everything," he said. "I feel like s–. I smell like s–. I see like s–. I hear like s–. That music sounds like s–.

"If you're having dinner and say, 'This meat tastes like s–,' what you really mean is the meat is undercooked or too salty. You're not specific at all. It's just a crass way of expressing your displeasure."

But aren't there times when the excremental exclamation is appropriate, as when the hammer misses the nail but hits the thumb?

O'Connor would substitute "oldies but not so baddies": "Nuts!" or "Criminey!" or "Nerts!"

Rasheda Williams, who works for an education company that tutors young people, said she guards her speech, even avoiding the word "hate" around children. She said it appalls her that previously unmentionable expressions are finding their way into public discourse.

"For people to be able to use the f-word in any form or fashion is incredibly ridiculous," she said. "Freedom of speech my you-know-what. This goes beyond freedom of speech."

From Where I Stand... (Journal Responses)

1. The aspect of this selection that I found the most interesting was _____
   _____.

   It was interesting because _____
   _____.

2. A part of this selection that I strongly agree/disagree (choose either "agree" or "disagree") is _____
   because _____.

3. I think that people in a (name a certain subject area or class) should read this because _____
   _____.

JUST THE FACTS

1. The main idea of this selection is a) even politicians sometimes use curse words; b) the words "damn" and "hell" are frequently used in newspapers today; c) the acceptance of foul language has increased dramatically; d) foul language is too imprecise.
2. Rasheda Williams was shocked when a girl who was 12 years old a) called her "a real bitch" when Williams asked her to turn down the volume on her radio; b) asked her how to break the habit of cursing; c) called "Hey, bitch" to a girl across the street; d) referred to her mother as "a bitch."
3. The article did *not* give an example of cursing by a) Jimmy Carter; b) Richard Nixon; c) George Bush; d) John Kerry.
4. In the 1970s, George Carlin's list of Seven Dirty Words that couldn't be said on TV became famous. Now audiences frequently hear a) all of the words; b) all but one of the words; c) four of the words; d) all but two of the words..
5. The selection quotes Rasheda Williams as saying that, when she's around children, she avoids the word or phrase a) *hate*; b) *cuss*; c) *shut up*; d) *hell.*

EXPANDING HORIZONS

1. The selection mentions the fact that Clear Channel dropped Howard Stern's radio show from its stations. Read about this situation and then write an editorial giving

your opinion as to whether or not this was a wise decision. Online articles about the incident include these:

www.foxnews.com/story/0,2933,116594,00.html

money.cnn.com/2004/04/08/news/fortune500/stern_fines/

www.hollywoodreporter.com/thr/article_display.jsp?vnu_content_id=1000444731

sfgate.com/cgi-bin/article.cgi?f=/news/a/2004/04/08/national-1640EDT0725.DTL

2. The selection quotes Donna Jo Napoli, a professor of linguistics. Research what the study of linguistics entails and write a summary of your findings. Online sites about this subject include these:

www.geocities.com/CollegePark/3920/

www.zompist.com/langfaq.html

www.msu.edu/~linglang/linguistics/whatis.htm

www.ericdigests.org/pre-925/what.htm

3. The Parents Television Council hires analysts to watch and listen to every hour of prime-time TV. On its Web site at www.parentstv.org/, PTC gives rankings for current TV shows. State and defend why you would or would not consult this ranking in order to know how programs are rated by this organization.

4. The Cuss Control Academy maintains a Web page titled "So What's Wrong with Swearing?" at www.cusscontrol.com/swearing.html. Read the lists on the page, then state and defend why you agree or disagree with the author.

5. Suppose you heard a young person, someone with whom you're close, using curse words. Write a letter to that person, telling him or her what, if anything, was offensive about the language you heard.

WRITE ON!

1. A few weeks after this article was written, Vice-President Dick Cheney reportedly cursed on the floor of the U.S. Senate. Read about the incident at the CNN site www.cnn.com/2004/ALLPOLITICS/06/24/cheney.leahy/index.html and then write your response to Cheney's actions.

2. Write your views on this statement: A racial slur is more offensive than the worst curse word.

3. Write a letter to the editor of your local or school newspaper, giving your views on hearing students using curse words around small children.

READ ON!

Abrams, Floyd. *Speaking Freely: Trials of the First Amendment.* New York: Viking Adult, 2005.

Bald, Margaret, et al. *100 Banned Books: Censorship Histories of World Literature.* New York: Checkmark Books, 1999.

Beito, David, et al. "Who's Undermining Freedom of Speech on Campus Now." History News Network. hnn.us/articles/11276.html.

Bennett, Brett. 2005. "Parent Files Complaint about 70 'Sexually Explicit' Books in School Libraries." *Northwest Arkansas Times* June 23. nwanews.com/story.php?paper=nwat&section=News&storyid=29416.

Bock, Amanda. "Censorship and Banned Books Bibliography." www.seemore.mi.org/booklists/Censorship.txt.

"Censorship." en.wikipedia.org/wiki/Censorship.

"The Censorship Pages." www.booksatoz.com/censorship/index.htm.

DelFattore, Joan. *What Johnny Shouldn't Read: Textbook Censorship in America.* New Haven: Yale University Press, 1994.

Durbin, Kathie. "Books Under Fire." www.tolerance.org/teach/magazine/features.jsp?p=0&is=36&ar=566.

Fan-atic. "Athletes & Freedom of Speech." www.askmen.com/sports/fanatic/fanatic7.html.

"Freedom of Speech." en.wikipedia.org/wiki/Freedom_of_speech.

Green, Jonathan, and Karolieds, Nicholas J. *Encyclopedia of Censorship.* New York: Facts on File, 2005.

Heins, Margoris. *Not In Front of the Children: "Indecency," Censorship, and the Innocence of Youth.* New York: Hill & Wang, 2002.

———. *Sex, Sin, and Blasphemy: A Guide to America's Censorship Wars.* New York: New Press, 1993.

Hudson, Jr., David L. "Free Speech on Public College Campuses." www.first-amendmentcenter.org/speech/pubcollege/topic.aspx?topic=free-speech_zones.

———. "Hate Speech and Campus Speech Codes." www.firstamendmentcenter.org/speech/pubcollege/topic.aspx?topic=campus_speech_codes.

Kalman, Izzy. "The Importance of Speech and Freedom." *A Revolutionary Manual for Handling Children's Aggressions.* www.bullies2buddies.com/manual/adult/chapter04.html.

O'Connor, James V. *Cuss Control: The Complete Book on How to Curb Your Cursing.* New York: Three Rivers Press, 2000.

Suriano, Gregory, ed. *Great American Speeches.* New York: Gramercy, 1993.

This photograph takes place at the Memorial Wall, the most famous of the three parts
of the Vietnam Veterans Memorial in Washington, D.C. Designed by US architect Maya
Lin, the memorial is comprised of two black granite walls, one pointing to the
Washington Monument and one pointing to the Lincoln Memorial. Inscribed in the wall
are the names of all the Americans who died in the war; currently 58, 249 names are
inscribed.

Write about a specific emotion that you see somewhere in the photograph above.
Then compare your description to one written by another person in your class. Do the
two of you mention the same emotion? If not, why do you think a single image
generated different responses? If it evoked the same emotion, do you describe that
feeling in the same way? Write a comparison of your two responses.

CHAPTER ELEVEN

AMERICA
Recovering and Remembering

It is up to us to rescue one another.   —*Nancy Mairs*

Be scared. You can't help that. But don't be afraid.   —*William Faulkner*

To place absolute trust on another human being is in itself a disaster, both ways, since each human being is a ship that must sail its own course, even if it go in company with another ship.   —*D. H. Lawrence*

Don't let yesterday use up too much of today.   —*Cherokee Indian proverb*

What are we to do since the calamity has swept our all away?
> —*from a letter to Eleanor Roosevelt, written by a man suffering through the Great Depression*

You may write me down in history
With your bitter, twisted lies,
You may trod me in the very dirt
But still, like dust, I'll rise.   —*Maya Angelou*

If you turn your back on these people [with AIDS], you yourself are an animal. You may be a well-dressed animal, but you are nevertheless an animal.   —*Edward Koch*

Fighting terrorism is like being a goalkeeper. You can make a hundred brilliant saves but the only shot that people remember is the one that gets past you.   —*Paul Wilkinson*

If the culprits are Muslim, they have twisted the teachings of Islam. Whoever performed, or is behind, the terrorist attacks in the United States of America does not represent Islam. God is not behind assassins.   —*Muhammad Ali*

The object of war is not to die for your country but to make the other bastard die for his.
> —*George Patton*

We have survived and in that survival is our life, our strength, our spirituality. And we are telling about it.   —*Linda Hogan*

Death is an endless night so awful to contemplate that it can make us love life and value it with such passion that it may be the ultimate cause of all joy and all art.   —*Paul Theroux*

Not to transmit an experience is to betray it.   —*Elie Wiesel*

In today already walks tomorrow.   —*Friedrich von Schiller*

Unless there is the most intimate association between those who look to the far horizons and those who deal with our daily problems, then...we shall not pass through these stormy times with success.   —*John F. Kennedy*

America: Recovering and Remembering

Think about these questions: How did you spend your day one week ago? one month ago? one year ago? If you're like most people, you might be able to remember what you were doing a week ago—if you thought hard enough—but recalling farther back than that would be a real stumper.

Now answer this question: What did you do on September 11, 2001, the day of the terrorist attacks? Almost all Americans can remember many details of that day—where they were when they heard the news, how they were glued to the television and other media, what different rumors they heard as the day progressed, and which loved ones they contacted.

Depending on people's ages, they can probably tell you exactly what they were doing on November 23, 1963 (the day President Kennedy was shot), or December 7, 1941 (the day the Japanese attacked Pearl Harbor), and on September 11, 2001. That's because these days were so traumatic, so frightening, so life-changing that they have become red-letter days in the lives of every American who lived through them.

Now think about the time you spent in front of the television in late August and early September of 2005. You, along with people around the globe, watched in shock and sadness as the horror of Hurricane Katrina unfolded: so many people helpless and homeless, and so little that the outside world could—or would—do to come to their aid.

The articles in this chapter deal with these two recent American tragedies and how people have reacted to what happened. "One Day, Now Broken in Two" relates how the writer handles the seeming contradiction of remembering the tragedy of the terrorist attacks while at the same time celebrating her son's September 11 birthday.

One year after the attacks, Congress assembled near Ground Zero. Former Poet Laureate Billy Collins, who was in attendance, read his elegy "The Names" to honor those who died. As you read this poem, note the symbolism of the way that Collins presented the names of some of those who lost their lives that day.

As part of the recovery from the attacks, officials are determined to rebuild on the site where the World Trade Center stood, thus revitalizing the area. Construction of the Freedom Tower, part of that design, is scheduled to begin in 2006 and the tower should be ready for occupancy in 2010.

As you probably remember, many questions arose on September 11 and afterward. Who was responsible for the attacks? Why would anyone want to hurt so many innocent people? Did U.S. policies lead to the hatred that brought on the atrocities? What could we as a nation do, or what should we do? College student Alison Hornstein looked at "The Question That We Should Be Asking."

Since 2001, Americans have faced other adversities, including, of course, the wars in Afghanistan and Iraq. Our country was again tested in 2005 by a number of weather-related disasters, although Hurricane Katrina caused the most death and destruction. The end of this chapter asks you to look at three Katrina-related online articles. After the storm, displaced New Orleanian Blake Bailey offered readers slices of his uprooted life in "Going Back to Work After Losing Everything." In "What It Smells Like," writer Josh Levin's imagery brings readers the harsh realities that confronted those in the hurricane-stricken areas after the storm. Besides the human toll, Katrina wiped out much of the area's cultural and artistic legacy, as Maria Puente explained in her *USA Today* article "Storm Extracts a Cultural Toll."

Now that you have read the introduction to this chapter, go back and reread the quotations on p. 245. Then choose one of the quotations and write about whether you agree or disagree with it. Be sure to defend your opinion.

Versatile writer **Anna Quindlen** *(the first author to have works on the* New York Times's *fiction, nonfiction, and self-help best-seller lists) is also an essayist, a writer of children's books—and a Pulitzer Prize winner. Currently she writes for* Newsweek *magazine, where her popular "Last Word" column appears every other week. This article appeared in the September 9, 2002, issue.*

Starting Out...

Read the following statements and circle A if you agree with the statement, D if you disagree.

A   D   Our nation's prosperity is proof that we must be conducting ourselves in a moral or virtuous way.

A   D   Our nation will probably never experience a day as horrible as was September 11, 2001.

A   D   At this date, everything seems to be back to normal following the terrorist attacks.

Words to Watch

bifurcated: divided into two parts

embodiment: representation, symbol

headlong: in a rash or impulsive way

hyperbole: exaggeration

in lieu of: in place of, instead of

legacy: something handed down to future generations

machinations: devious plots or schemes

modernity: the present, the recent times

monotonous: without variety, boring

optimists: people who look on the positive side of a situation

personified: given human qualities

pessimists: people who look on the negative side of a situation

probity: goodness, integrity, virtue

psyche: consciousness, awareness

realists: people who see both the positive and negative sides of a situation

---

One Day, Now Broken in Two
by Anna Quindlen

We looked at our lives a little harder, called our friends a little more often. And then we complained about the long lines at the airport.

September 11 is my eldest child's birthday. When he drove cross-country this spring and got pulled over for pushing the pedal on a couple of stretches of monotonous highway, two cops in two different states said more or less the same thing as they looked down at his license: aw, man, you were really born on 9-11? Maybe it was coincidence, but in both cases he got a warning instead of a ticket.

Who are we now? A people who manage to get by with the help of the everyday, the ordinary, the mundane, the old familiar life muting the terror of the new reality. The day approaching will always be bifurcated for me: part September 11, the anniversary of one of the happiest days of my life, and part 9-11, the day America's mind reeled, its spine stiffened and its heart broke.

That is how the country is now, split in two. The American people used their own simple routines to muffle the horror they felt looking at that indelible loop of tape—the plane, the flames, the plane, the fire, the falling bodies, the falling buildings. Amid the fear and the shock there were babies to be fed, dogs to be walked, jobs to be done. After the first months almost no one bought gas masks anymore; fewer people than expected in New York City asked for the counseling that had been provided as part of the official response. Slowly the planes filled up again. A kind of self-hypnosis prevailed, and these were the words used to induce the happy trance: life goes on.

Who are we now? We are better people than we were before. That's what the optimists say, soothed by the vision of those standing in line to give blood and money and time at the outset, vowing to stop and smell the flowers as the weeks ticked by. We are people living in a world of unimaginable cruelty and savagery. So say the pessimists. The realists insist that both are right, and, as always, they are correct.

We are people whose powers of imagination have been challenged by the revelations of the careful planning, the hidden leaders, the machinations from within a country of rubble and caves and desperate want, the willingness to slam headlong into one great technological achievement while piloting another as a way of despising modernity. Why do they hate us, some asked afterward, and many Americans were outraged at the question, confusing the search for motivation with mitigation. But quietly, as routine returned, a new routine based on a new bedrock of loss of innocence and loss of life, a new question crept almost undetected into the national psyche: did we like ourselves? Had we become a people who confused prosperity with probity, whose culture had become personified by oversize sneakers and KFC? Our own individual transformations made each of us wonder what our legacy would be if we left the world on a sunny September day with a "to do" list floating down 80 stories to the street below.

So we looked at our lives a little harder, called our friends a little more often, hugged our kids a little tighter. And then we complained about the long lines at the airport and obsessed about the stock market in lieu of soul-searching. Time passed. The blade dulled. The edges softened. Except, of course, for those who lived through birthdays, anniversaries, holidays, without someone lost in the cloud of silvery dust, those families the living embodiment of what the whole nation had first felt and then learned not to feel.

We are people of two minds now, the one that looks forward and the one that unwillingly and unexpectedly flashes back. Flying over lower Manhattan, the passengers reflexively lean toward the skyline below, looking for ghost buildings. "Is everything back to normal?" someone asked me in another country not long ago, and I said yes. And no. The closest I could come to describing what I felt was to describe a bowl I had broken in two and beautifully mended. It holds everything it once did; the crack is scarcely visible. But I always know it's there. My eye worries it without even meaning to.

On Sept. 10 of last year my daughter and I went to the funeral of a neighbor we both loved greatly. We rushed home so I could go to the hospital, where my closest friend had just had serious surgery. Someone else took the cat to the vet after we discovered that he was poisoned and was near death. That night, as my daughter got ready for bed I said to her, without the slightest hint of hyperbole, "Don't worry, honey. We'll never again have a day as bad as this one."

Who are we now? We are people who know that we never understood what "bad day" meant until that morning that cracked our world cleanly in two, that day that made two days, September 11 and 9-11. The mundane and the monstrous. "Tell me how do you live brokenhearted?" Bruce Springsteen sings on his new album about the aftermath. September 11 is my boy's birthday; 9-11 is something else. That is the way we have to live, or we cannot really go on living at all.

From Where I Stand... (Journal Responses)

1. If a tragedy occurred on a day that you usually celebrated, how would you handle the day in the future?

2. The most interesting part of "One Day, Now Broken in Two" is _____

   _____

   because _____

3. Quindlen says that "[t]he American people used their own simple routines to muffle the horror they felt looking at that indelible loop of tape...." What simple routines do you go through when you are troubled?

JUST THE FACTS

1. The main idea of this selection is a) so they wouldn't cry, Quindlen and her son had to celebrate his birthday on a different day; b) Quindlen and her son have decided not to mention the terrorist attacks on his birthday; c) Quindlen says that she will differentiate between September 11 and 9-11; d) Quindlen's son objected to the way his birthday was to be celebrated.

2. To address the question of "Who are we now?" Quindlen writes that the optimists say a) we are better people than we were before; b) we have fully recovered from the effects of the September 11 attacks; c) that Americans have now "adjusted admirably" to the new America; d) our country is now safe again.

3. To address the question of "Who are we now?" Quindlen writes that the pessimists say a) we "are people living in a world of unimaginable cruelty and savagery"; b) our country is still under attack; c) "America is on its last leg"; d) the televised news media "does not tell the whole story."

4. Quindlen relates that, on a day in the previous year, all of the following happened *except* a) she and her daughter had gone to a funeral; b) Quindlen's closest friend had had surgery; c) the family cat had been poisoned; d) Quindlen warned that there might be a worse day to come.

5. Quindlen cites a song by a) Usher; b) Kenney Chesney; c) Bruce Springsteen; d) Ricky Martin.

EXPANDING HORIZONS

1. Quindlen writes, "Why do they hate us, some asked afterward...." Many articles give some insight into this subject. Read one and then summarize what you read. If you use online articles (a few are listed below), see if you can determine from what country they originated—and be aware that you may have your eyes opened by what is written by people from non-U.S. countries.

    www.mwarrior.com/WhyhateAmerica.htm
    www.the-idler.com/IDLER-02/2-19.html
    www.islamonline.net/english/Politics/2001/05/article8.shtml
    www.amerikabrev.nu/index.asp?page=artiklar&read=3

2. An anecdote is a short account of an incident. Quindlen begins this article with an anecdote about a trip her son took and the results of his being stopped for speeding. Why do you think that Quindlen began with that incident? What point did the anecdote serve?

3. In the seventh paragraph, Quindlen uses a metaphor, a comparison between two unlike things without using the words *like* or *as*. Reread this paragraph and determine what Quindlen is comparing. Do you agree that her comparison is accurate?

4. Quindlen also uses anaphora (deliberate repetition of a word or phrase at the beginning of several successive sentences, clauses, or paragraphs) in her piece when she begins three paragraphs with the question, "Who are we now?" Summarize the answers that Quindlen gives each time she asks this question.

WRITE ON!

1. Write about a time that you were sad but had to hide your sadness. What were the circumstances? Why did you have to hide your feelings? What did you do to mask your sadness? When could you finally deal with it?

2. Write a letter to a loved one, recalling what you were doing on September 11, 2001, both before and after you heard of the attacks.

3. Quindlen says, "We are better people than we were before." Do you agree or disagree with this statement? Cite your reasons.

To observe the first anniversary of the terrorist attacks, Congress held a special session in New York City's Federal Hall, near Ground Zero. **Billy Collins,** *U.S. poet laureate from 2001 to 2003, wrote this elegy for the ceremony and read it to the assembled audience.*

Starting Out...
Read the following sentences and circle A if you agree, D if you disagree.

A   D   The attacks on September 11, 2001, affected people of many national backgrounds.

A   D   The people who were killed in the New York City attacks had all been reared in the New York metropolitan area.

A   D   Someone can tell a great deal about another person just by knowing that person's name.

Words to Watch
amid: among, in the middle of
boughs: branches, limbs
concocted: made up, invented
etched: engraved, carved
monogram: a person's initials
peer: stare
spanning: crossing, reaching over
stole: entered silently or inconspicuously
unfurled: unfolded, opened out
updraft: a current of air with vertical movement

The Names
by Billy Collins

Yesterday, I lay awake in the palm of the night.
A fine rain stole in, unhelped by any breeze,
And when I saw the silver glaze on the windows,
I started with A, with Ackerman, as it happened,
Then Baxter and Calabro,
Davis and Eberling, names falling into place
As droplets fell through the dark.

Names printed on the ceiling of the night.
Names slipping around a watery bend.
Twenty-six willows on the banks of a stream.

In the morning, I walked out barefoot
Among thousands of flowers
Heavy with dew like the eyes of tears,
And each had a name—
Fiori inscribed on a yellow petal
Then Gonzalez and Han, Ishikawa and Jenkins.

Names written in the air
And stitched into the cloth of the day.
A name under a photograph taped to a mailbox.
Monogram on a torn shirt,
I see you spelled out on storefront windows
And on the bright unfurled awnings of this city.
I say the syllables as I turn a corner—
Kelly and Lee,
Medina, Nardella, and O'Connor.

When I peer into the woods,
I see a thick tangle where letters are hidden
As in a puzzle concocted for children.
Parker and Quigley in the twigs of an ash,
Rizzo, Schubert, Torres, and Upton,
Secrets in the boughs of an ancient maple.
Names written in the pale sky.
Names rising in the updraft amid buildings.
Names silent in stone
Or cried out behind a door.
Names blown over the earth and out to sea.

In the evening—weakening light, the last swallows.
A boy on a lake lifts his oars.
A woman by a window puts a match to a candle,
And the names are outlined on the rose clouds—
Vanacore and Wallace,
(let X stand, if it can, for the ones unfound)
Then Young and Ziminsky, the final jolt of Z.

Names etched on the head of a pin.
One name spanning a bridge, another undergoing a tunnel.
A blue name needled into the skin.
Names of citizens, workers, mothers and fathers,
The bright-eyed daughter, the quick son.
Alphabet of names in green rows in a field.
Names in the small tracks of birds.
Names lifted from a hat
Or balanced on the tip of the tongue.
Names wheeled into the dim warehouse of memory.
So many names, there is barely room on the walls of the heart.

From Where I Stand... (Journal Responses)

1. When I am awake in the middle of the night, to try to get back to sleep I _____
   _____.

2. To memorialize friends or family who died, I would _____
   _____.

3. "The Names" is particularly effective/ineffective (choose either "effective" or
   "ineffective") because _____
   _____.

JUST THE FACTS

1. The main idea of this selection is a) the victims spanned many cultures and backgrounds; b) insomnia can be a reason behind thinking about the attacks; c) the narrator lost almost 30 friends in the attacks; d) no one can know when he or she will die.

2. The poem began when a) the narrator walked to Ground Zero; b) a friend called the narrator to tell about the attacks; c) the narrator was awake and listening to the rain; d) the narrator turned on the television and heard about the attacks.

3. The names a) were listed by the states where the victims lived; b) were listed by the number of children they left behind; c) were written in a haphazard manner; d) were listed alphabetically.

4. The narrator said that X stood for a) both Xavier and Xalandra, who died together; b) for the ones unfound; c) the spot where the attacks occurred; d) the "shadow cast by the victims."

5. The narrator says that there are so many names a) "I cannot begin to elaborate"; b) "my mind boggles with the memory"; c) "the inscriptions will be cast for miles"; d) "there is barely room on the walls of the heart."

EXPANDING HORIZONS

1. Billy Collins is one of the foremost poets in the United States. Read several of these online biographies of him and summarize his life and works:

   "Billy Collins." The Academy of American Poets. www.poets.org/poets/poets. cfm?45442B7C000C040D0D

   "Poet Laureate Billy Collins." Lehman College. www.educationupdate.com/archives/ 2002/jan_02/htmls/college_billycollins.html

   "Billy Collins." Contemporary Poetry. www.contemporarypoetry.com/dialect/biographies/collins.html

   "Billy Collins." Big Snap. www.bigsnap.com/poet.html

   "Billy Collins." The Steven Barclay Agency. www.barclayagency.com/collins.html

   "Silent Stampede Leads Us to Pleasurable Side Streets." www.bigsnap.com/g-nyt01.html

   "Undressing Billy Collins." www.hermes-press.com/collins1.htm

2. Collins has said, "In times of crisis…people don't turn to the novel…. It's always poetry." Think about a time of crisis in your life. To what or whom did you turn for comfort? In a personal narrative, describe the situation and how you dealt with it. Alternately, compose a poem about a personal experience.

3. While almost 2,800 people were killed in the New York attacks, Collins used names of just 25 specific victims. He presented the names in alphabetical order, but he had another reason for choosing the particular names that he used. Take a look back at the names and see if you can determine why he chose those last names. (Hint: Look at the diversity of the names.)

4. The Internet site www.september11victims.com/september11victims/victims_list.htm lists the victims of all of the attacks on September 11, 2001, including those who died in Washington and Pennsylvania. The person's name and residence is cited, and a link is provided to see a picture of the person and learn more about him or her. Visit the site and read the biographies of some of the people. Then compose your own list of names, citing the reasons why particular people struck a chord with you. Alternately, visit the above site or www.cnn.com/SPECIALS/2001/trade.center/victims/rescue.victims.html and create a chart or graph depicting the nationalities of the victims.

5. Billy Collins was poet laureate of the United States from 2001 to 2003. Research the post of poet laureate and give an oral or written presentation of your findings. Be sure to include the following:

> Who is the current poet laureate, and who are the past poets laureate?
>
> What body appoints the poet laureate, how long does a poet laureate serve, and what is a poet laureate's annual stipend?
>
> What is the complete proper title of the poet laureate?

WRITE ON!

1. Write your interpretation of what this poem is saying. If you quote from it, be sure to use quotation marks in the appropriate places.

2. If I were to write a sequel to "The Names," I would write about _____ _____.

3. With imagery, a poet uses words to grab one of the reader's senses (sight, hearing, taste, smell, touch). In which lines in "The Names" did you find the most imagery? To which of your senses did these lines appeal?

The Freedom Tower
from Lower Manhattan Info.com

In June of 2005, officials released the revised design for the Freedom Tower to be constructed on the site of the World Trade Center and, it is hoped, to serve as an inspiration to all who view it. Read about some of the particulars of this new building.

Words to Watch
  spire: a steeple, a tall tower that tapers to a point at the top
  evoking: suggesting, calling to mind
  impermeable: impossible to pass through the openings of
  isosceles: having two equal sides
  parapet: a protective wall or railing along the edge of a raised structure

On June 29, 2005, a redesigned Freedom Tower plan was released, addressing security concerns raised about the original design. The new design retains essential elements of the original—soaring 1,776 feet into the sky, its illuminated spire evoking the Statue of Liberty's torch—but features a larger, cubic base set back further from West Street to protect the building against any future terrorist attempts.

Rising from its square base—constructed of impermeable concrete and steel—the redesigned Freedom Tower will taper into eight tall isosceles triangles, forming octagonal upper floors, 69 of which will contain office space, others of which will house mechanics, restaurants, and observation decks. An uppermost observation deck will be located 1,362 feet above ground, and there will be a square glass parapet at 1,368 feet—the heights of the original Twin Towers. From these, an illuminated spire containing a television antenna will rise to a final height of 1,776 feet.

Questions
1. What is symbolic about the height of the glass parapet?
2. What is symbolic about the final height of the building and its spire?
3. The selection says that a cubic base will "protect the building against any future terrorist attempts." Do you think this is true? Why or why not?
4. More information about the Freedom Tower is available at www.lowermanhattan.info/rebuild/timeline/rebuild_timeline.asp. Report on the latest progress.

*Two months after the terrorist attacks, Yale University student **Alison Horn-stein** used the "My Turn" section of* Newsweek *to address how her classmates were tackling the moral issue of judging others—even if those "others" were responsible for murder.*

Starting Out...

Read the following and circle A if you agree with the statement, D if you disagree.

A   D   Because we haven't "walked in another's shoes," it's difficult to judge the morality of another person's actions.

A   D   If I disagree with political statements that an instructor makes, I have every right to voice my opinion and not be penalized for doing so.

A   D   The refusal to take a stand on what is wrong results in its victory.

Words to Watch

circumcised: while this word generally refers to males, in this article it means having removed all or part of the female genitalia

curriculum: set of courses in a school

deficiency: insufficiency, shortage

ethnic: cultural, national

Hamas: an Islamic political group that opposes peace with Israel

Inuit: people inhabiting the Arctic (northern Canada, Greenland, Alaska or eastern Siberia)

perpetrators: people who are behind a wrongdoing, evildoers

plainclothes: ordinary, everyday clothing, as opposed to a uniform

potentially: possibly

problematic: difficult, challenging, tricky

provocations: acts that lead to some further action

relativity: being dependent for existence on relation to something else

seminar: a small group of students studying under the guidance of a professor who meets regularly with them

socioeconomic: having to do with both social upbringing and financial history

traumatically: with serious emotional wounds or shock

The Question That We Should Be Asking

by Alison Hornstein

Is terrorism wrong? My generation may be culturally sensitive, but we hesitate to make moral judgments.

On the morning of September 11, my entire college campus huddled around television sets, our eyes riveted in horror to images of the burning, then falling, Twin Towers. By evening there were candlelight vigils where people sought to comfort and be comforted. But by Sept. 12, as our shock began to fade, so did our sense of being wronged. Student reactions expressed in the daily newspaper and in class pointed to the differences between our life circumstances and those of the perpetrators, suggesting that these differences had caused the previous day's events. Noticeably absent was a general outcry of indignation at what had been the most successful terrorist attack of our lifetimes. These reactions and similar ones on other campuses have made it apparent that my generation is uncomfortable assessing, or even asking, whether a moral wrong has taken place.

I spent 14 years at a public school in Manhattan with students who came from a variety of ethnic and socioeconomic backgrounds. I benefited immensely from the open-minded curriculum. In second grade we learned about the Inuit (who don't like to be called Eskimos, our teacher taught us), and how, though they sometimes ate caribou hoofs and other foods that we generally did not find on our own dinner tables, they were essentially like us.

When my third-grade class read a story about one boy kicking another at a school-bus stop, our teacher talked about why the boy might have done what he did—maybe he was having a bad day or had had a fight with his mother that morning. The teacher stressed that the little boy had feelings that sometimes led him to do mean things. That these feelings did not necessarily justify his actions got lost in the discussion.

Later, in high school, my classmates and I learned about how women in some countries are circumcised and how, even though this seemed abhorrent to us, it was part of their culture. We discussed the pros and cons of imposing our standards on other cultures. And, overwhelmingly, we decided we should not.

We gained an important degree of emotional and psychological sophistication from looking at these issues. But being taught to think within a framework of moral and cultural relativity without learning its boundaries has seemingly created a deficiency in my generation's ability to make moral judgments.

In a college seminar on Sept. 12 a professor said he did not see much difference between Hamas suicide bombers (who, he pointed out, saw themselves as "martyrs") and American soldiers who died fighting in World War II. When I saw one or two students nodding in agreement, I raised my hand. I wanted to say that although both groups may have believed that they were fighting for their ways of life in declared "wars," there is a considerable distinction. American soldiers, in uniform, did not have a policy of specifically targeting civilians; suicide bombers, who wear plainclothes, do. The professor didn't call on me. The people who did get a chance to speak cited various provocations for terrorism; not one of them questioned its morality.

I had to drop the class.

The explanations students and professors give for the September 11 attacks—extreme poverty in the Middle East, America's foreign policy in that region and religious motivation—are insightful, but they cannot provide absolution for wrongdoing. Even if a woman wears a very short, tight skirt, she should not be raped. Even if the rapist was abused as a child. Even if his wife just cheated on him. Even if the woman looked really, really good in that skirt. The rapist is still accountable. And he still did wrong.

Just as we should pass absolute moral judgment in the case of rape, we should recognize that some actions are objectively bad, despite differences in cultural standards and values. To me, hijacking planes and killing thousands of civilians falls into this category. Others may disagree. It is less important to me where people choose to draw the line than it is that they are willing to draw it at all.

Continuing to neglect the place of moral evaluations in discussing current events is not only philosophically problematic; it is also potentially suicidal. There comes a point where the refusal to take a stand on what is wrong results in its victory.

I am so glad that I learned early on not to judge people who eat things that might make me gag, like caribou hoofs or cow brains (which I traumatically encountered years later in France). I am a little less enthusiastic about the conclusions my high-school class drew over the issue of female circumcision. I do know that much of the discussion on this campus since September 11 has failed to address the question of whether an absolute wrong has been committed.

I think it should.

From Where I Stand... (Journal Responses)

1. Hornstein says that her generation hesitates to make moral judgments. I think this is true/untrue (choose either "true" or "untrue") of my generation because _____

_____.

2. Hornstein says that in high school, she and her classmates "discussed the pros and cons of imposing our standards on other cultures" and then "decided we should not." I think that these students were right/wrong (choose either "right" or "wrong") about this because _____.

3. Hornstein dropped a class that she felt uncomfortable in. I think she was right or wrong (choose either "right" or "wrong") to do this because _____

_____.

JUST THE FACTS

1. The main idea of this selection is a) refusing to take a stand on a wrong results in a victory for the wrongdoer; b) no one can tell for certain who was behind the terrorist attacks; c) classrooms should be places where all opinions are welcomed; d) colleges should learn to be more tolerant of the diversity of their students.

2. Hornstein said that, by September 12, a) her friends had decided that they needed to do something to help their fellow man; b) no one was more terrified by the attacks than she was; c) a general outcry of indignation was noticeably absent; d) her professors had forced their classes to take a stand on several issues.

3. When one of Hornstein's professors said that he did not see a great deal of difference between Hamas suicide bombers and American soldiers who died in World War II, Hornstein a) dropped the class; b) wrote an editorial in the school paper to show how he was wrong; c) eventually came around to understand his logic; d) said that the professor had insulted her grandfather, who had fought in WWII.

4. Explanations given by students and professors for the September 11 attacks included all of the following *except* a) extreme poverty in the Middle East; b) foreign money from America's past enemies; c) America's foreign policy in the Middle East; d) religious motivation.

5. Since the September 11 attacks, Hornstein says her campus has failed to adequately address the question of a) why no one had taken responsibility; b) who would ultimately pay for the clean-up of the destruction; c) how the next attack would be handled; d) whether an absolute wrong has been committed.

EXPANDING HORIZONS

1. In *Newsweek*'s "My Turn" column, various writers react to something in the news. Read the online article about female circumcision at en.wikipedia.org/wiki/Female_circumcision and write a reaction to it in the form of a "My Turn" article similar to Hornstein's article.

2. Hornstein says that one of her professors thought that there was little difference between Hamas suicide bombers and American WWII soldiers. Read about the history of Hamas and then create a timeline of your research.

3. Hornstein says that two of the explanations for the attacks students and professors gave were extreme poverty in the Middle East and America's foreign policy in the Middle East. Use current data to research either of these topics and to determine if any change has occurred in the time since the attacks.

4. Hornstein writes about "being taught to think within a framework of moral and cultural relativity." Research either moral relativity or cultural relativity, and then write a summary of your findings. Include a short explanation of the term and your reaction to what you have read. Remember to use quotes around any material that you use verbatim and to paraphrase other material from your research.

WRITE ON!

1. I think that my generation is/is not (choose either "is" or "is not") deficient in its ability to make moral judgments because _____.

2. If I could write a response to "The Question That We Should Be Asking," my main points would be (identify at least three main points) _____
_____.

3. I agree/disagree (choose either "agree" or "disagree") with the quote "There comes a point where the refusal to take a stand on what is wrong results in its victory" because _____
_____.

*When Hurricane Katrina struck New Orleans in late August 2005, many people were killed and many more were suddenly homeless. Author **Blake Bailey** was one of those New Orleanians who lost everything. In the aftermath of the storm, he wrote a series of articles on Slate.com. This, the first of those pieces, was posted September 8, 2005.*

Starting Out...

Read the following and circle A if you agree with the statement, D if you disagree.

A   D   When I'm in a stressful situation, I can find comfort in working.

A   D   I have had to deal with trying to get satisfaction from an insurance company.

A   D   I have had stressful times when I thought my life had gone down the tube.

Words to Watch

anodyne: source of soothing comfort

dappled: spotted, mottled

dregs: remains, small amounts

furtively: secretly, stealthily

imminent: about to happen, looming

incongruity: strangeness, inappropriateness

larky: in a high-spirited or zestful way, silly, zany

limbo: an undefined or undetermined state

multitasking: taking care of two or more chores or jobs at the same time

per se: as such, in that capacity

remonstrated: argued, protested, objected

reverie: daydream, trance

scenario: picture, setting

solicitude: concern, consideration

tipsily: unsteadily, slightly intoxicated

My Year of Hurricanes: Going Back to Work After Losing Everything

by Blake Bailey
Access this article online at
www.slate.com/id/2125573/

From Where I Stand... (Journal Responses)

1. If I had to suddenly leave my house and go to live somewhere else, I would go

   _____

   because _____.

2. One thing I often do when I'm under stress is _____ because

   _____.

3. I would describe my outer/inner (choose either "outer" or "inner") life today as

   because _____.

Just the Facts

1. The main idea of this selection is a) the author was unsure about his insurance coverage; b) many people were forced to evacuate to other places; c) friends in Oxford, Mississippi, opened their hearts and homes to the author and his family; d) the hurricane created quite a disturbance in the author's life.
2. In times of trouble, the author finds relief in a) comfort food; b) his family; c) his church; d) work.
3. The author put in a call to a) amazon.com; b) Travelocity; c) eBay; d) Google.
4. The author is writing a) a biography of John Cheever; b) a travelogue about Cleveland; c) his family's genealogy; d) a book of poetry.
5. The author and his former student talked about a) why he had given her a failing grade on a paper; b) what had happened to several of the members of her class; c) the looting in New Orleans; d) when they could schedule the class reunion.

Expanding Horizons

1. This selection was the second that Blake Bailey wrote about his life dealing with Hurricane Katrina and its aftermath. Read the first selection, aptly titled "I Lost Everything in Katrina," at www.slate.com/id/2125573/ and then write a summary of what you learn. Alternately, write a summary of a later selection in the series by clicking on a link at www.slate.com/id/2127127/.
2. Hurricanes Katrina, Rita, and Wilma were particularly devastating in 2005, the year that broke the record for most hurricanes in a season. Research how hurricanes are created and create a summary of what you learn. Online sites to consult include these:
   kids.earth.nasa.gov/archive/hurricane/creation.html
   www.earthinstitute.columbia.edu/news/2004/story10-01-04e.html
   www.ns.ec.gc.ca/weather/hurricane/kids1a.html
3. Using online or printed material, research the answers to these hurricane-related questions:
   What is a hurricane called in the western Pacific?
   What is a hurricane called in the Indian Ocean?
   When does a storm become classified as a hurricane?
   When is a hurricane warning issued?
   In the Northern Hemisphere, in which direction do hurricanes rotate?

On the Saffir-Simpson Hurricane Scale, what are the sustained wind speeds for the five categories of hurricanes?

Define these hurricane-related terms: the eye, the eye wall, and spiral rainbands.

4. The author quotes Nostradamus (his real name was Michel de Nostradame), a six-teenth-century writer whose book of predictions, *Centuries*, caused a sensation in his time. Today, some continue to quote the book's prophecies, saying that parts of the text refer to modern-day events such as the attacks on the Pentagon and the World Trade Center. Read more about Nostradamus and then summarize what you learn. Online sources include these:

www.crystalinks.com/nostradamusbio.html

www.activemind.com/Mysterious/Topics/Nostradamus/biography.html

www.angelfire.com/empire/nostradamus/biography.html

5. The selection mentions Snake Plissken, the hero of the movies *Escape from New York* and *Escape from LA*. View either of these movies and write a review of it. Include in your review an explanation of why Snake Plissken was mentioned in "Going Back to Work After Losing Everything."

WRITE ON!

1. Hurricanes, tornadoes, mud slides, earthquakes, floods—every area of the U.S. is subject to some kind of catastrophic conditions. Write about a time that you weathered the storm (pardon the pun) in a difficult weather situation. What led to the problem? Where were you when the catastrophe occurred? Did you make any preparations? What was the outcome for yourself and those whom you were with?

2. The author and his former student talked about the looting that had taken place. Defend or refute this statement, and give reasons for your opinion: Looting is always morally wrong.

3. Think, for a moment, about having to evacuate from your home and move at least one hundred miles away. Your loved ones have already evacuated and are safe, and you are left with a small car. If you could take only what would fit in your car, what valuables would you take? Why those items in particular? If you had to live elsewhere for, say, two months, what about your home or town would you miss the most? Why?

*In the days immediately following when Hurricane Katrina struck New Orleans, author **Josh Levin** filed several eyewitness reports for Slate.com. This article, filed on September 12, 2005, recounts some of the sights and smells that he encountered.*

Starting Out...
Discuss or write about these questions:

What is the worst smell you have ever encountered?

What caused the smell?

How was the smell corrected?

Words to Watch

ethnic tension: pressure or strain between people of different races

FEMA: the acronym for the Federal Emergency Management Agency, the organization responsible for coordinating emergency planning and preparedness

feral: wild, untamed

fetid: rotten, putrid

forensic dentists: those who use teeth to identify the dead

fraught: weighed down, filled

holdouts: people who do not agree to something that progress depends on

meals ready to eat: meals that are kept on hand when no cooking or water facilities are available

MREs: the acronym for meals ready-to-eat

mural: wall painting

NOPD: the acronym for New Orleans Police Department

rendition: performance, version

shelf life: the length of time that a product will stay fit enough for human consumption

tetanus: an often fatal disease that often comes from an infection through a deep wound

vile: disgusting, extremely unpleasant

What It Smells Like
by Josh Levin
Access this article online at
www.slate.com/id/2125926/

From Where I Stand... (Journal Responses)

1. "What It Smells Like" should be read by people in a (identify a college class) _____ because _____
_____.

2. The parts of "What It Smells Like" I found the most interesting were _____ because _____.

3. If I were writing a follow-up to "What It Smells Like," I would concentrate on _____

(identify a particular aspect of "What It Smells Like").

JUST THE FACTS

1. The main idea of this selection is the author a) wishes that he had brought a number of supplies with him; b) is "eternally grateful" when he finds that his home was not a target of destruction; c) is shocked by what he sees and smells; d) wonders if "the sweet smell of the South" will ever return.

2. The author pointed out that 99 percent of New Orleans a) has left town; b) is under water; c) will be rebuilt; d) has fled to the Superdome.

3. The army men whom the author traveled with said that the black garbage bag contained a) the food that a number of people had been waiting for; b) artillery that had been requested; c) a dead body; d) some of the garbage that was creating the "foul smell."

4. The site that "looks like the ruins of a lost civilization" is a) the deserted streets and houses; b) the famous French Quarter in downtown New Orleans; c) the abandoned museum the author visits; d) St. Louis Cemetery No. 1.

5. The shirtless man named Ben a) swam to the boat the author was traveling in; b) was scooped up by members of the 82nd Airborne; c) refused to leave his waterlogged house; d) apologized for taking a shot at the author.

EXPANDING HORIZONS

1. This article mentions New Orleans' famous St. Louis Cemetery No. 1, the oldest graveyard in the city. Visit www.graveaddiction.com/1stlouis.html and use the links to read about the famous features of this cemetery. Then summarize what you learn.

2. The Army's 82nd Airborne Division ("America's Guard of Honor"), out of Fort Bragg, North Carolina, was organized during World War I. Read about the history

of this brave group of soldiers and summarize your findings. Online sites to consult include these:

en.wikipedia.org/wiki/82nd_Airborne_Division

www.globalsecurity.org/military/agency/army/82abn.htm

www.bragg.army.mil/82dv/

3. Dr. Lance Hill "gained local fame for organizing the grassroots campaign against David Duke." Read more about this man and write a letter to the editor of your school newspaper, giving your reactions to what Dr. Hill has done. Online sites include these:

www.bestofneworleans.com/dispatch/2004-07-06/cover_story.html

www.southerninstitute.info/contact_us/lance_bio.html

www.splcenter.org/intel/intelreport/article.jsp?aid=27&printable=1

4. New Orleans is famous for its music, including Ernie K-Doe's Mother-In-Law Lounge that is mentioned in the selection. Research this or other famous clubs in New Orleans. Online sites include these:

Ernie K-Doe's Mother-In-Law Lounge: www.k-doe.com/

links to various clubs: neworleanswebsites.com/cat/en/bc/bc.html

links to various jazz clubs: www.usa.worldweb.com/FeaturesReviews/General-Interest/8-1169.html

5. Author Josh Levin filed other articles from New Orleans. Read one of them and either summarize what you read or compare-and-contrast that article to the one in the text. Other articles can be found at

"The People Who Won't Evacuate": www.slate.com/id/2125820/

"What the Rescue Workers Find": www.slate.com/id/2126063/

"Mayor on the Verge of a Nervous Breakdown": www.slate.com/id/2125587/

"Mourning My New Orleans": www.slate.com/id/2125352/

WRITE ON!

1. Write about a time that you helped people in need. What had happened to the people? How did you help? How did you feel afterward? Why?

2. New Orleans has long been popular for its nightlife. Write about what your ideal night on the town would be, if money were no object. Where would you go? What would you do? Whom would you invite to be with you?

3. In the article, a rescued man did not like where he was taken and asked to be returned to his home. Write about a time that you made a decision that you later regretted. Include the circumstances behind your decision and what ultimately happened.

While the human toll of death, displacement, and suffering inflicted by the hurricanes of 2005 was—and continues to be—horrifying, other problems have also arisen. USA Today *writer* **Maria Puente** *looks at the destruction sustained by various cultural and artistic works.*

Starting Out...
As a class, discuss these questions:

What are the names of some museums in your area? What kinds of exhibits or works do these museums feature?

Who are some artists or crafts persons who work in your area? What type of work does each create? Where is the person's work shown?

What are some of the oldest structures in your area? How old are they, and what material are they constructed of?

Words to Watch

displaced: relocated

in the locals' DNA: DNA is an acid that carries the genetic information; this reference means that people in New Orleans are born with a love of history and culture

patrimony: heritage, legacy

Greek Revival: an architectural style that imitates designs of ancient Greek temples

archival documents: original pieces of work, like letters, photographs, diaries, or paintings

inundating: flooding, swamping

conservation: preservation, protection

salvageable: able to be saved

looted: ransacked, plundered

artifacts: objects, especially of archaeological or historical interest, made by humans

trickling: slowly coming

joie de vivre: French for "a carefree enjoyment of life"

Big Easy: the nickname for New Orleans

visual artists: artists who work in painting, photography, or sculpture

resilient: tough, durable

Storm Exacts a Cultural Toll

by Maria Puente

Access this article online at www.usatoday.com/travel/news/ 2005-10-13-katrina-art_x.htm

---

From Where I Stand... (Journal Responses)
1. One beautiful building in my area is _____. I think it is beautiful because _____.
2. One type of art or craft work that I like is _____. I like it because _____.
3. A museum that I have visited is _____. Something that I remember about the museum is _____.

JUST THE FACTS
1. The main idea of this selection is a) the author is certain that a number of artists will leave the area; b) many of the looters have been apprehended and now face time in jail; c) much of the area's cultural and artistic heritage was destroyed; d) the music will survive, no matter what damage the storm brought.
2. In Biloxi, a wing of the unfinished Ohr-O'Keefe Museum of Art was damaged when a) a waterfront casino barge was blown into it; b) a fire began and raged out of control; c) the constant rain damaged many of the works; d) the fierce wind blew a number of the art works into areas "at least five miles away."
3. Tullis-Toledano and Pleasant Reed were a) two streets that sustained especially heavy damage; b) to historic houses that were damaged; c) the areas of Alabama that were, surprisingly, not harmed; d) the names of people who were heroes during the storms.
4. *Virlane Tower* is a) the movie that is currently being filmed in the aftermath of the storms; b) where a number of people sought refuge from the storm; c) the site that was destroyed by looters; d) a 45-foot metal sculpture.
5. Of the storm, portrait miniaturist Thomas Sully said a) "I have lost friends and my artwork as well"; b) "No one wants to return to the area yet"; c) "Katrina will be with us always"; d) "This is only an interruption."

EXPANDING HORIZONS
1. A number of museums, art galleries, homes, and artists were mentioned in the article. Research any of them and summarize what you learn. Online sites include these:

    Ohr-O'Keefe Museum of Art: www.georgeohr.org/

    Mobile Museum of Art: www.mobilemuseumofart.com/

    Walter Anderson Museum of Art: www.walterandersonmuseum.org/

    New Orleans Museum of Art: www.noma.org/home.html

    Degas House: www.degas.org/

    Ogden Museum of Southern Art: www.ogdenmuseum.org/

    New Orleans African American Museum: www.neworleansmuseums.com/multiculturalmuseums/afammuseum.html

    National D-Day Museum: www.ddaymuseum.org/

    Arthur Rogers Gallery: www.arthurrogergallery.com/index.html

    George Ohr: mshistory.k12.ms.us/features/feature27/ohr.html

    Tullis-Toledano Manor: www.biloxi.ms.us/museums/tullistoledano/

    Pleasant Reed House: www.georgeohr.org/reedcoll.htm

    Frank Gehry: www.pritzkerprize.com/gehry.htm

Beauvoir: www.beauvoir.org/
Shearwater Pottery: www.shearwaterpottery.org/
Walter Anderson: www.walterandersonmuseum.org/frameset3.htm
Kenneth Snelson: www.absoluteastronomy.com/ref/kenneth_snelson

2. In addition to the places mentioned in the article, many other arts-related institutions sustained damage from Katrina. Go to www.danceusa.org/pdf/Damage_ Responses.pdf and summarize the damage sustained by at least three other places that were not named in the article.

WRITE ON!

1. Go to www.walteringlisanderson.com/shearwater_essay.html and read the article about Katrina's destruction at Shearwater Pottery. Then write a summary of the article.

2. Go to www.usatoday.com/travel/news/2005-10-13-new-orleans-art-museum_x.htm and read "'Protect Whatever Can Be Protected,'" an article related to this one. After you finish, summarize the main points of the article.

3. The New Orleans Museum of Art has a link on its Web site that shows photographs of the museum after Katrina hit. Go to www.noma.org/index.html and choose one of the pictures. Write as many details as you see in the picture.

READ ON!

Braiker, Harriet B. *The September 11 Syndrome: Anxious Days and Sleepless Nights.* New York: McGraw-Hill, 2002.

Cramer, Kathryn. *Staying on Top When Your World Turns Upside Down: How to Triumph over Trauma and Adversity.* New York: Viking, 1990.

Fisher, David E. *The Scariest Place on Earth: Eye to Eye with Hurricanes.* New York: Random House, 1994.

Heyen, William, ed. *September 11, 2001: American Writers Respond.* Silver Springs, MD: Etruscan Press, 2002.

Higgs, Robert. *Resurgence of the Warfare State: The Crisis Since 9/11.* Oakland, CA: Independent Institute, 2005.

"Hurricane Donations in U.S. Exceed Fundraising After Sept. 11." www.bloomberg.com/ apps/news?pid=10000103&sid=apJRsG4MgDoU&refer=u.

"Hurricane Season 2005 Breaks All Records." www.nasa.gov/vision/earth/ lookingatearth/record_breaker.html.

Junger, Sebastian. *The Perfect Storm: A True Story of Men Against the Sea.* New York: Norton, 1997.

Lincoln, Bruce. *Holy Terrors: Thinking about Religion after September 11.* Chicago: University of Chicago Press, 2003.

"Mold: Prevention Strategies and Possible Health Effects in the Aftermath of Hurricanes Katrina and Rita." www.bt.cdc.gov/disasters/mold/report/.

Reed, Jim and Mike Theiss. *Hurricane Katrina: Through the Eyes of Storm Chasers.* Helena, MT. Farcountry Press, 2005.

"September 11: Chronology of Terror." archives.cnn.com/2001/US/09/11/chronology.attack/.

"September 11: A Nation Remembers." www.time.com/time/covers/1101020909/.

September 11 News. www.september11news.com/.

Smith, Dennis. *Report from Ground Zero.* New York: Viking, 2002.

Appendix A

Writing Models

This appendix provides explanations and examples of various modes of writing you'll encounter in this text and in other college classes, as well as definitions of writing-related vocabulary.

Writing a Paragraph

If your assignment is to write just one paragraph, you need to condense all of your information into that single unit. To do this, first think about your topic and jot down any thoughts that you have about it (this is called "brainstorming"; it's discussed more later). You don't have to write your brainstorming list in any order; you don't need to write it in complete sentences; you don't even need to worry about correct spelling or punctuation at this point.

After brainstorming, look over the list to help you take the next step: deciding what the main idea of your paragraph is going to be. (You probably won't use everything on your list.) Then use that idea to form a sentence; this is called the topic sentence or thesis statement; the other sentences in the paragraph develop or explain it by providing supporting details. Topic sentences usually come at the beginning of a paragraph, but they can be placed anywhere.

Information from the following Internet sites can help you develop a thesis statement:

members.tripod.com/~lklivingston/essay/thesis.html
www.indiana.edu/~wts/pamphlets/thesis_statement.shtml
webster.commnet.edu/grammar/composition/thesis.htm

After you've written your topic sentence, look at your brainstorming list to see which parts of it you can develop into sentences that explain or expand your topic sentence. These sentences are called the supporting details, and they defend what you stated in your topic sentence.

A paragraph about items that should be in a home office might read this way:

A home office should include a number of items that make working easy and convenient. First, the office should include a computer. Having a computer with the latest upgrades would be ideal, but all that is essential is that the computer be equipped with whatever software the homeowner needs. A printer is also necessary; the printer may be a model that has additional features, such as a scanner, depending on the office needs. In addition, a telephone is a critical part of a home office. Even if the phone is not used for business purposes, having it in the office will save the homeowner time and trouble. The type of work conducted in the home office may dictate that a fax machine is needed. If so, it should be located near the desk where the computer sits. This, too, will save time. Finally, a home office should have the usual supplies: stapler, paper clips, pens, pencils, and tape and dispenser. Having all of these items on hand will ensure a complete home office.

Writing a Descriptive Paragraph

To write a descriptive paragraph, use the same format as you use for any single paragraph but write the supporting details sentences to describe, rather than simply explain, what you've introduced in your topic sentence.

Sites that have additional information about how to write a paragraph include these:

www2.actden.com/writ_den/tips/paragrap/
www.efc.dcccd.edu/er/LAC/HParagraph.html
www.occc.edu/mschneberger/CWParagraph1.htm

Writing an Essay

College assignments often include writing an essay. Essays are (often short) pieces of prose with several paragraphs: an introductory paragraph that contains a thesis statement, several supporting paragraphs, and a concluding paragraph. In general, an essay

- contains the author's analysis, argument, explanation, or interpretation of some topic.
- has a thesis statement (sometimes called a thesis sentence), the sentence that reveals the main point of the essay.
- usually presents the opinion of the author.

The thesis statement almost always is placed in the first (introductory) paragraph. Your instructor may stipulate that he or she wants the thesis statement to be in a particular place in the paragraph (usually either the first or last sentence), or the choice may be left to you.

Regardless of where your thesis statement is located, your introductory paragraph should include sentences that develop or build up to the thesis statement. (If your thesis statement is the first sentence, the subsequent sentences will develop it; if it's the last sentence, the preceding sentences will build up to it.) Every other sentence in your essay must support or elaborate on the thesis statement in some way. A common mistake made by inexperienced writers is veering away from the idea in their thesis statement.

In a multiparagraph composition, the introductory paragraph (the one containing the thesis statement) is followed by the body paragraphs. Each of these paragraphs expands on or defends the thesis statement in some way. Each body paragraph develops one subtopic (that is, one point). Body paragraphs begin with a subtopic sentence, in other words, the focus of the information in that particular paragraph. Use subsequent sentences in the body paragraph to elaborate on your topic sentence. You may write body paragraphs in chronological (time) order or in order of emphasis (going from least important to most important).

The last (or concluding) paragraph is a summary of what you have stated previously in your essay (using different wording, of course). Your concluding paragraph can review what you've already said, or it can emphasize points that you've made.

Writing a Five-Paragraph Essay

One often-assigned type of essay is a five-paragraph essay, which consists of (you guessed it) five paragraphs. Here's an outline of a five-paragraph essay:

Introductory Paragraph
- Contains the thesis statement (if your instructor has specified that the thesis statement be in a certain place in the paragraph, make sure you have it there)
- Has additional sentences that follow or lead up to the thesis statement and support it or elaborate on it

Body Paragraph #1
- Sometimes has a transitional word or phrase connecting the preceding paragraph and this one
- Begins with a topic sentence that elaborates on, explains, or gives an example of what was written in the thesis statement
- Contains other sentences that support, elaborate on, or give specific evidence for the topic sentence
- Contains transitional words or phrases throughout the paragraph wherever they are needed

Body Paragraph #2
- Usually has a transitional word or phrase connecting the preceding paragraph and this one
- Begins with a topic sentence that elaborates on, explains, or gives an example of what was written in the thesis statement
- Contains other sentences that support, elaborate on, or give specific evidence for the topic sentence
- Contains transitional words or phrases throughout the paragraph wherever they are needed

Body Paragraph #3
- Usually has a transitional word or phrase connecting the preceding paragraph and this one
- Begins with a topic sentence that elaborates on explains, or gives an example of what was written in the thesis statement
- Contains other sentences that support, elaborate on, or give specific evidence for the topic sentence
- Contains transitional words or phrases throughout the paragraph wherever they are needed

Concluding Paragraph
- Is more than just one sentence
- Has transitional words or phrases wherever needed
- Summarizes or emphasizes information in previous paragraphs

Here's an example of a five-paragraph essay:

All my life, I have lived by the banks of the river and watched many pleasure and commercial boats go by. I have always longed to be a part of one of their voyages. I intend to save enough money to have my own boat because with a boat I can enjoy many days and nights out on the river.

The first way that I would enjoy the river is through leisurely trips out to Diamond Island, just downstream from the dock. I have been to the island for summer parties and have always enjoyed the volleyball games and the cookouts that seem to be going on constantly. Even people whom I do not know have invited me to join their party, and I have made several new friends that way.

Another way that I would enjoy the river is through fishing. I have recently taken up the sport and have become quite a fan. Nothing beats an early-morning outing with a friend or two and our fishing gear. The stillness of the river at dawn, the quiet camaraderie, and the anticipation of fresh fish for dinner combine to make for a day of fellowship and fun.

But perhaps the main reason that I want to buy my own boat is so I can go waterskiing. When I was seven, I was first introduced to skiing, and I have been enjoying it ever since. I am certainly not the most skillful skier on the river, but I am probably the most enthusiastic. There is nothing that quite compares to racing down the river atop two narrow slats, pulled by all that horsepower.

I am just a river rat at heart. The parties on the island, the tranquil fishing trips, and the wild skiing sprees all contribute to my great desire for a boat of my own. Now all I need is for someone to contribute the money for the boat. I will gladly name it after my benefactor. Any takers?

Once you've become familiar with writing short essays, you can begin to create longer pieces, such as papers, articles, and reviews.

Writing a Compare-and-Contrast Paper

Compare-and-contrast papers show how two or more people, places, or ideas are alike *and* how they're different. If, for instance, you compare and contrast two brands of televisions, your paragraph might read like this:

Brand X and Brand Y are both good 13-inch color televisions. The picture is quite clear on each, and both brands' remotes are easy to use. In addition, the models are the same height and depth, so either could fit in the same space. One difference between the two is their price; Brand X is almost $50 cheaper than Brand Y. Plus, Brand X sports more features than Brand Y. In addition to its lower price, Brand X can play both VHS tapes and DVDs, and it has special cables that allow for external hookups, if needed. It is easy to see that Brand X is a far better buy than Brand Y.

Sites that have additional information about compare-and-contrast papers include these:

web.princeton.edu/sites/writing/Writing_Center/Handouts/CandC.pdf
www.unc.edu/depts/wcweb/handouts/comparison_contrast.html
depts.washington.edu/pswrite/compare.html

Writing a Newspaper Article

To write a newspaper article, concentrate on making sure your paragraph or article answers the "5 Ws and an H" questions that reporters ask: Who? What? When? Where? Why? How? A newspaper article about a train wreck might read this way:

At least 15 people were injured yesterday when an XRD train derailed near the county line. The cause of the derailment is still under investigation, but police report that the train jumped the tracks for some unknown reason. The injured, who were not identified at press time, were all taken to County Hospital. Three were treated and released, and the rest were kept overnight.

Sites that have additional information about writing newspaper articles include these:

www.ypp.net/wg_newsarticle.asp
memory.loc.gov/learn/lessons/98/brady/article.html

Writing a Company Newsletter Article

To write a company newsletter article, follow the formula for a regular newspaper article (that is, use the "5 Ws and an H" questions) but make sure that your focus is on something or someone connected to your company. Here's an example:

> Uninickel, the metal division of Pellington Industries, announced on Friday that Jonathan Fowler has been promoted to team leader. Fowler, who will be relocating from Monroe to the company headquarters in Robards, was praised by company president Madison Abbott as being "one of the top scientists in the field, and a man who has a real business head on his shoulders." When asked about his promotion, Fowler said that he is "delighted to be chosen as a team leader" and hopes that he will "make the company proud."

Writing a Movie Review

Movie reviews should include your opinion about the movie, information about why you liked it or didn't like it, and details about the film. Reviews should *not* include vague sentences such as, "I really liked this movie" or "This movie was awful." You must discuss both the good and bad points of the movie and provide readers with specific reasons why you feel those elements worked or didn't work. You can use some or all of the questions below to compose a film review:

1. Who played the lead and the supporting roles? Was the casting accurate? (That is, were the actors believable in their roles?) Did anyone steal scenes from the major players?
2. What is a short summary of the plot? Don't give away (or "spoil") the ending.
3. Did the plot hold your attention? Was it believable (this is also described as allowing viewers to "suspend their disbelief"), or did it stretch your imagination too much? Was the plot easy to follow or were you confused? Was the movie too long? too short? If the time had been lengthened or shortened, would that have made a difference in your enjoyment or appreciation of the film?
4. In what genre would you classify this film—science fiction? romance? action? comedy? combat? detective? film noir? musical? suspense or thriller? something else, or a combination of some of the above?
5. Did the movie contain gratuitous sex or violence? Did you note any crude or vulgar scenes or language use that would make the film unsuitable for particular audiences?
6. Where was the movie filmed? Was the site of the filming true to the setting of the movie? Did you see any obvious discrepancies between the movie's setting and where it was filmed?
7. Was this movie a period (or historical) piece? If so, were the costumes true to the era? Did the dialect and the characters' actions hold true?
8. Did any of the characters use accents? If so, were the accents believable or were they difficult to understand?
9. If special effects were used, were any memorable? If so, what were they, and what made them memorable?
10. Was this film intended for a particular audience? Might it appeal to an audience for which it wasn't intended?

Additional ideas for writing a movie review can be found at these sites:

> www.millikin.edu/mr/Entertainment/howto2.html
> www.ucls.uchicago.edu/students/projects/1996-97/MovieMetropolis/howto.html

Synthesizing Information

To synthesize information is to combine findings from two or more sources to form something new (a report, a chart, an essay, etc.). For instance, you might be asked to write about advances in cellular phone technology. You would then read several printed sources and perhaps conduct interviews with some professionals in the field. Then you would synthesize all of the information you'd obtained—that is, you'd take what you learned in your research and create a new document (usually a written assignment of some kind).

Writing a Synopsis

A synopsis is a general overview of a work; it gives details about the work's beginning, middle, and end. Individual instructors may mandate certain length requirements for an assignment, but synopses usually are no longer than two (double-spaced) pages. When you're writing a synopsis, identify the key scenes or plot points in a work of fiction, or name the major points in a work of nonfiction. Like a summary (see below), a synopsis must be written in your own words.

Writing a Summary

A summary

1. is a condensed version of the main points of original piece.
2. must be written in your own words. (This is *most important*. If you use the author's words, you'll be accused of plagiarizing.)

When you're asked to write a summary, first read the passage and make sure that you understand what it's saying. As you read, keep in mind that you're looking for the overall theme—the big picture—not the details.

Then, without referring to the passage, answer this question: What are the main ideas the author is making? (At this point, don't worry about correct spelling or punctuation; you'll have a chance to correct any mistakes later.) Keep in mind that the longer the piece, the more points the author believed to be important.

If you're stuck, pretend you're a reporter and, for each paragraph, ask some of the "5 Ws and an H" questions: Who? What? When? Where? Why? How? You can lengthen questions in a number of ways to increase their helpfulness. Take, for instance, the opinion piece written below.

Give Stoplights the Green Light

My fellow residents of Zion Heights, the fact is that several additional stoplights are needed. This is not just my opinion; look at recent traffic mishaps in order to verify this.

In the course of the last five years, traffic accidents within the city limits have risen an amazing 200 percent. Looking more closely at those statistics, they reveal that more than half of the accidents (175, to be exact) occurred along the two-mile stretch of Sommers Avenue where McDonald's, Burger King, KFC, and a number of other fast-food restaurants and strip malls have recently sprung up. Fast or reckless driving was to blame in almost every accident that took place in that area. Motorists simply will not slow down while driving along "the strip," nor will they allow sufficient time to get back onto the highway from the restaurants or malls.

The best solution to this problem is to install more stoplights. Only one stoplight is present in the area where most of the accidents take place. Additional stoplights—perhaps placed the equivalent of a half-mile apart—would have the dual advantages of slowing Sommers Avenue motorists and giving ample opportunity and time to those drivers trying to get back onto Sommers.

The plan to install more stoplights will not be popular because every driver believes that his or her time is precious and—of course—that no accident will befall him or her. Admittedly, the addition of four stoplights along this stretch of Sommers Avenue may lengthen drive time. But new lights would add—at most—only two minutes to a driver's trip.

Really, isn't two minutes a short time to ensure a safe trip for drivers and their families?

You might ask the "5 Ws and an H" questions in several ways: Who is the writer trying to convince? What does the writer want to accomplish? When does the writer want the lights installed? Where does the writer want the lights installed? Why does the writer want the lights installed? How does the writer come to the conclusion that more stoplights are needed?

Take a look at your answers and ask yourself, given what the author said, which are the most important points?

Another way to analyze a piece of writing in order to summarize it is to reread each paragraph and write one sentence (again, in your own words) that states what the paragraph is about. For the example above, you might write:

(First paragraph) Zion Heights needs more traffic lights.
(Second paragraph) Many accidents have taken place along a short section of Sommers Avenue.
(Third paragraph) More stoplights will make drivers go more slowly and will help those who are trying to get onto Sommers Avenue.
(Fourth paragraph) More stoplights will cause only a brief delay.
(Fifth paragraph) A safe trip is worth a slightly longer driving time.

Some students find that the easiest way to approach a summary is to identify the thesis (one sentence that gives the central idea) of the piece. Then they proceed from that thesis to determine the piece's major supporting details. The thesis of "Give Stoplights the Green Light" might be stated this way: Because so many accidents take place along a two-mile stretch of Sommers Avenue, more traffic lights are needed. From there, it's easy to figure out some of the primary points supporting this thesis. For instance, one point is that the number of accidents along this stretch has increased significantly in recent years; another is that additional stoplights will slow traffic and make it easier for drivers to access Sommers Avenue from the many businesses that line the street.

After you've finished your summary, proofread it to check for correct spelling (is it Sommers Avenue or Summers Avenue?), punctuation, and grammar, and make sure that the facts you've included are accurate. Then edit: Delete details that are too minor or don't contribute to the story (for instance, you don't need to list the names of the restaurants that are along Sommers Avenue). On the other hand, insert transitional words or phrases (such as *first, then, as a result*) that help your summary read more easily.

Make sure that your summary doesn't include your opinion of the topic at hand or of the author's work. Don't write, "I think this writer was easy to understand" or "Taxpayers already spend too much for stoplights"; neither of these thoughts is part of the original article, so neither should be a part of its summary.

Some instructors require that a summary be a certain length (a specified number of words or paragraphs) or that it not be longer than a stated portion (say, one-fourth) of the original work. Be sure to follow these guidelines when working on your assignment.

As with any assignment, if you have permission for someone else to read it and look for errors before it's submitted, be sure to do that. Ask your reader whether he or she understands your summary or sees any obvious mistakes.

Writing a Summary-and-Response

In summary-and-response writing, follow the steps for creating a summary, but add your reaction to the ideas in the article or story. A summary-and-response paragraph about an article concerning weight reduction might read like this:

> "Taking It Off the Sensible Way" appeared in the October 2006 issue of *Happy Weight* magazine. The article stressed the importance of losing weight gradually; the recommendation was to lose no more than two pounds a week. Several tips were highlighted about how to lose the weight, including using a number of recipes that the article referred to, as well as incorporating both strength training and aerobic exercise into a daily routine. This article was a rehash of most of the weight-reduction pieces I have read in the past; it contained no new or especially informative data about weight reduction. In fact, I have found that rapid weight loss, such as I have experienced by following a low-carb diet, has helped me more than anything else. Because of that, I do not recommend this article.

Writing a Personal Narrative

A personal narrative is a prose work about something you experienced or witnessed (so it must be true, not fiction). In essence, composing a personal narrative is writing a short story about a real incident. You can turn nearly any event from your life into a personal narrative: talking with a strange character during an airplane trip, convincing your family to get a dog at the local pound, foolishly driving through water that was too deep, realizing that you were finally an adult, walking away from a dangerous situation—all of these could be topics for personal narratives.

Because a personal narrative is about your life, use a first-person point of view when writing; that is, use "I," "me," "my," "we," "us," "our," and "ours" rather than pronouns that are less personal.

Compared to other academic writing, a personal narrative is far more relaxed in style. It should read as if it's a story you tell to friends or family. But keep in mind that a personal narrative shouldn't simply recount something—it must make a point; otherwise, it will be boring. For instance, if your personal narrative is about the time you convinced your family to adopt a dog, your point might be that negotiating with family members can lead to consequences you never imagined.

Using imagery in personal narratives, as in many other types of writing, creates a fuller, more vivid picture for readers. Instead of writing, "It was a hot day," add details such as, "The August day was so humid that even breathing was a chore." Describe how the street you were driving along looked or how your grandmother's kitchen smelled or how the birds at the beach sounded. The more descriptive you can be (without going overboard, of course), the better your reader will be in touch with your experience. If dialogue is appropriate to your narrative, use it to show your reader something about the characters you're describing. Let characters' speech reveal something about themselves or the situation.

As with all writing, when you begin your personal narrative, you have decisions to make.

- What structure is best? Should you write your narrative chronologically (in the time order in which you experienced it) or through a flashback (a transition from the present to something that occurred earlier)?
- What's your intent for the narrative? Do you want to make your readers laugh or cry, be frightened or feel pleasure or embarrassment, have sympathy for you for some traumatic or dramatic event, or learn from something you've experienced?
- Should your tone to be humorous, matter-of-fact, thoughtful ("now-I'm-older-and-wiser"), or something else?

Here's a hint about composing your narrative: after you've finished it—after you've revised it several times and you think that it's perfect—have a friend or colleague read it aloud. See if there are places where the reader stumbles or seems confused by what you've written. If so, see whether you can rewrite those passages to make them clearer.

For more tips, see these sites:

www.pagewise.com/write-personal-narrative-paper.htm
ncnc.essortment.com/personalnarra_rucu.htm
leo.stcloudstate.edu/acadwrite/narrative.html
www.orangeusd.k12.ca.us/yorba/more_on_narrative_essays.htm
www.tengrrl.com/tens/006.shtml
"Example of Personal Narrative." webster.commnet.edu/grammar/composition/subj2.htm

Understanding Graphs and Charts

Graphs or charts are used to convey information in a condensed manner and, thus, communicate points quickly. Common graphs and charts are:

- pie charts, which consist of a circle divided into segments; each segment represents a certain part (usually a percentage) of the whole.
- line graphs, which consist of a horizontal line (called an x-axis) bearing numbers to indicate time period and a vertical line (called a y-axis) bearing numbers indicating amounts of whatever is being measured. Line graphs usually show how something changes over a period of time.
- bar graphs, which use rectangular shapes of various heights placed side by side; the heights of the rectangles proportionately measure what is being compared.

Note: You can get help creating graphs online at nces.ed.gov/nceskids/Graphing/.

Writing a Letter to the Editor

Letters to the editor express a personal opinion about a topic that is on a citizen's mind. These letters should clearly state the argument or controversy the writer is addressing and should thoroughly explain the writer's reasoning. If possible, the writer should point out errors in the opposing side's arguments by discrediting any printed or broadcast material that the writer believes to be incorrect. Also, the writer should keep his or her letter brief and to the point because space is always an issue for newspapers; short, tightly written letters stand a better chance of being printed. For instance:

Dear Editor:
    I was outraged to read about what took place at the meeting of the water board last Tuesday. According to an article in the Dec. 16 issue of *The Gleaner*, a 33 percent rate hike has been proposed and will be voted on in two weeks.

Why is such a drastic hike needed? Bud Crawford, the chair of the water board, stated that operating costs have risen considerably. However, nowhere does he state what these costs are or how the board is trying to contain them.

It is my understanding that three employees at the water district recently attended a week-long convention concerning water treatment. Was that cost necessary? Could just one person have attended (thereby drastically cutting the cost that taxpayers bore)?

People on a fixed income will find a large rate hike extremely difficult—if not impossible—to afford. Has the board taken this into consideration?

The public needs more answers before the water board demands more of our money.

—Ed Shuttleworth

Writing a Response Journal

Response journal questions are intended help you hone critical thinking skills by extending and deepening your ideas about concepts presented in an article. These questions may be worded in a number of ways, such as asking

- how you related to the article in some way.
- how the article affected or enlightened you.
- what part of the article you could relate to another event.

When you write journal responses, keep the following things in mind:

- Each entry is personal—you're free to express your ideas, positions, questions, and opinions (in fact, expressing your views is the point of a journal response). You may use *I, my, me, mine, our, ours, us,* and *we* when writing such responses.
- A journal response is not a summary of what an article said; rather, you should answer the question or prompt in a thorough and specific way.
- Journal responses have no right or wrong answers. The completeness and insightfulness of your response will determine how good it is.

Appendix B

Research and Documenting
Sources for College Papers

Research is necessary for many college assignments, and it can be conducted in a number of ways. Students often use library, Internet, and personal-interview sources when researching papers.

This appendix is a reference to help you hone your research skills. Use it for learning about how to research in the library, for definitions of unfamiliar library terms, for suggestions about how and where to research on the Internet, and for various strategies to use when conducting an interview.

Getting Started

If you have free reign to decide the topic of your paper, make sure that you select a topic that interests you. Then ask yourself the big questions: Is the topic too broad? Too narrow? Is enough information available about it?

Researching in the Library

You may find it helpful to begin by acquiring some basic information from an encyclopedia or other reference book. If you're uncertain about where to find the reference books in your college library, ask any of the library staff.

After you've gained this initial information, make a list of key words and phrases for the topic. These can be the jumping-off point for getting additional information.

Use the catalog in your library to find books related to your topic. To find books, enter your topic or the key words or phrases at the computer terminal. Write down the call numbers of the book titles the database generates and then go to the stacks to examine these books. Save time by putting each title and its call number on an index card, and create separate cards for every title. That way, you can sort the cards by call numbers that are near each other, which will simplify the search process, and you can add information to the cards if you need to. When you've found one of the target books, look for subject-related titles just before and just after that one. Because books are arranged by subject, you may find something else that will help you.

To find magazine or journal articles relevant to your topic, use the library indexes. When you've determined which magazine issues you need, find out whether they're available at your library (ask a staff person where the list of available magazines is located).

When conducting library research, you may find it beneficial to learn the specific vocabulary associated with library science and usage. To acquaint yourself with some of this terminology, or if you need to understand a particular word, consult the glossary of library terms below.

Glossary of Library Terms

> **abstract:** a short written summary of a book, article, or video, sometimes provided along with citation information
>
> **abstracting journal:** a periodical devoted to publishing abstracts, usually in one particular field of research

almanac: a reference book, usually printed annually, that contains lists, charts, tables, statistics, and other data on a single topic or a wide range of topics

annotated bibliography: a bibliography giving a brief description of each article or book listed, usually with notes about the works

annotation: a brief description of an information source; it may contain data about the author and the content of the source, including a summary of the source, a description of the kind of source, and an assessment of the source

annual: a publication that is published once every year

anthology: a collection of works (poems, stories, essays, etc.) by various authors and collected in one volume

archives: an organized storage area for holding noncurrent records, usually those of historical value

atlas: a book containing a number of maps

audio-visuals: materials such as slides, cassettes, filmstrips, films, CDs, DVDs, and videotapes that convey information through sight and/or sound

author search: used in an electronic catalog or index, this looks for work by a particular author

back issue: any issue of a periodical prior to the most recent issue

bibliographic citation (bibliographic reference): information that identifies a particular publication; for a book, the information includes the title, author or editor, place and year of publication; for an article, the information includes the title of the article and the magazine in which it appeared, the author, the volume number and page numbers of the article

bibliography: a list of citations of written works by an author or on a subject; bibliographies must be written in one of several particular styles and are generally found at the end of a work; they are used to give information so that a reader can easily locate a source cited

bound periodical: several back (noncurrent) issues of a magazine or journal (usually one year's worth) that have been joined together into a single volume

call number: the "address" of an item in a library; a unique combination of letters, and sometimes numbers, showing a patron where material can be found

carrel: a library study table for one reader

catalog: a listing of the materials in a library's collection

check out: the process of borrowing library materials

circulation: the department in the library that's in charge of lending and returning library materials

circulation desk: an area in the library where books are lent and returned, and where reserve materials are kept

citation: a written reference that gives all the necessary information needed to find a particular work; citations usually follow a specified format (generally APA or MLA)

copyright: a method for protecting the creative works of authors, artists, and musicians; copyrighted material may not be duplicated without the consent of the author and/or publisher

cross-reference: directions given in publications such as catalogs, indexes, and encyclopedias to refer readers to additional information within the publication

cumulative index: usually printed each year, this is a list of previously published indexes and includes all the information in individual indexes that was printed the previous year

currency: how up-to-date information is

current periodical (current journal): the most recent issue; it doesn't circulate (i.e., you must use it on site)

database: a continuously updated collection of information that is arranged on a particular subject and is accessed through a computer

Dewey Decimal System (DDS): one style of arranging books on library shelves

directory: a source that lists contact information (names, postal addresses, e-mail addresses, telephone numbers)

documentation: the references (citations) that identify resources used in a book or article

eBook (electronic book): a version of a printed book that is sent in electronic format over the Internet or through an eBook reader

edition: all of the copies of a publication that are printed from a single master reproduction

electronic journals (e-journals): electronic (online) copies of print journals

encyclopedia: a book or, more commonly, a set of books that contains articles (arranged alphabetically) on subjects in every field of knowledge; a **subject encyclopedia** has articles on a single subject field

entry: an item (book, article, pamphlet, audiovisual, etc.) that is listed in a catalog or index

errata: a list of errors discovered in a book after it was published; the corrections of the errors are printed on a separate sheet and then attached to the book

ERIC database: a database of education articles published in journals and reproduced in documents from ERIC (the Education Resources Information Center, sponsored by a branch of the U.S. Department of Education)

footnote: a citation in a certain place in a book or manuscript (usually at the bottom of the page or end of the manuscript); it comments on or cites a reference for a particular part of the text

format: the way in which information is arranged and presented

frequency: the particular interval at which a work is published; common frequencies are daily, weekly, biweekly (every two weeks), semimonthly (twice per month), monthly, bimonthly (every two months), quarterly (every three months), semiannually (twice per year), annually (every year), biennially (every two years), triennially (every three years), and irregularly (with no set schedule)

full text: a note given online when all of an article, book, or other material is available

gazetteer: a dictionary that lists geographical items (place names; features such as mountains, rivers, etc.) or other historical and statistical information about places

glossary: an alphabetical list of technical terms in some specialized field of knowledge; it's usually published as an appendix to a text on that field

government document: publication produced by any government agency or organization (international, federal, state, county, or municipal)

hard copy: data (usually a document) printed on paper rather than on a computer; **soft copy** is data that's read on a computer screen

hold: a request to borrow library materials currently on loan to someone else, are on order, or are being processed

holdings: a library's collection, including the call number, location, and availability

ibid.: abbreviation for Latin *ibidem*, meaning "in the same place"; used in footnotes and bibliographies to refer to the book, chapter, article, or page cited just before; example:
> 1. Fowler, Allison C. *Violins for Fun and Frivolity*. New York: Class Act Press, 2003. p.104.
> 2. *Ibid.*, p.87.

in print: still available from the publisher

index: a section located in the back of a book; it lists the names, places, and subjects within the book and gives the page numbers where they can be found

interlibrary loan (ILL): a cooperative service that allows patrons to request books and articles not available in their library; the library searches for the requested material at other libraries

ISBN: International Standard Book Number, a unique identification number given to a book identify it

ISSN: International Standard Serial Number, a unique identification number given to serial publications like magazines and journals

issues: paper copies of magazines and newspapers

issue number: a number used with a volume number to designate a specific magazine or journal issue

journal: a periodical that specializes in a specific subject area

keyword search: a word or phrase that best describes the subject to be studied; the word or phrase may be found in any of several fields (e.g., author, title, or subject)

library catalog: an online database that library patrons use to determine what materials are owned by a library

Library of Congress classification: used by most college and university libraries, this is a call number system that classifies materials; all resources on the same general topic are shelved together

media: a general term for nonprint materials (e.g., films, filmstrips, video recordings, audio compact disks, audiotapes, CDs, DVDs, and computer software); synonymous with audio-visual materials

microform: material (usually magazines and newspapers) that is photographed and then reduced to save library shelf space or to preserve items that may deteriorate quickly; **microfiche** is a type of microform that contains small text that is read through a machine called a microfichereader; **microfilm** is a photographic film stored on a reel; it shows small images of publications; the text is magnified and read with using a reader/printer machine

multimedia: material that mixes any combination of text, graphics, audio, and video

noncirculating material: anything that may not be checked out from a library (e.g., rare books, books on reserve, current periodicals, etc.)

OPAC: Online Public Access Catalogue, the computer catalog of materials owned by a library

out-of-print: a publication that is no longer available from the publisher

oversized books: books that are bound too large to fit in normal library bookshelves; the library catalog will indicate a separate location for them

periodical: any publication printed at regular intervals (e.g., daily, weekly, monthly); newspapers, magazines, and journals are all periodicals

periodical index: a list of articles from magazines, newspapers, and journals that are arranged alphabetically by subject; the most common index is the *Reader's Guide to Periodical Literature*, which lists magazines and journals covering topics of general interest

plagiarism: the act of copying the work of another person and not giving credit to that person; strict penalties are in place for students who plagiarize material

primary sources: places where original information is found, including autobiographical material such as diaries, letters, scientific or literary notes; public records; manuscripts; newspaper clippings; and transcripts of interviews

readers/printers: machines used to read microforms and to make copies of articles contained on the microforms

recto: the right-hand pages of a book, usually with odd-numbered pages (opposite of **verso**)

reference: a type of help provided by library staff; usually a reference librarian assists patrons who have complex questions about their research or about the library's collection

reference books (reference collection): books such as dictionaries, encyclopedias, indexes, almanacs, and handbooks that are kept in a special section of the library and may not be checked out

reference desk: a place in the library where a patron can speak to a librarian to gain assistance in finding research topics

reserves: material that a teacher has requested be loaned for only a short period of time for the duration of his or her course; sometimes the material may be used only in the library (not checked out)

scholarly journal: journals that focus on particular fields rather than on information with a broad scope

secondary sources: records that are written by those who have looked at the eyewitness accounts of others or the original material written by others (e.g., encyclopedia articles, literary criticism, biographies)

search strategy: the means by which a patron systematically locates relevant materials on a topic

"see": a term used in catalogs, indexes, and encyclopedias to direct readers from a subject heading that is not used to one that is used

"see also": a term used in catalogs, indexes, and encyclopedias to direct readers to related subject headings

source: any material that provides a patron with the information that he or she is looking for

special collections: areas in libraries that contain materials that may be rare, old, expensive, or of a specialized nature (e.g., written by local authors); these materials usually may be viewed only by making prior arrangements with the library

stacks: shelves in libraries where books and other materials are kept

subject heading: a word or group of words used in libraries to describe a specific subject

style manual: a publication that gives writers specific formats for writing articles, essays, footnotes, endnotes, and bibliographies; two commonly used are the *Publication Manual of the American Psychological Association* (informally called "APA"), and the *MLA Handbook for Writers of Research Papers* (informally called "MLA")

subject search: a search of information by its topic, rather than by the author or title

subtitle: a brief, usually explanatory, phrase that follows the main title of a written piece of work

thesaurus: 1. a list of words, their synonyms, and sometimes their antonyms; 2. a list of the subject headings with cross-references for vocabulary in a specialized field (e.g., medicine, education, business, etc.)

topographic map ("topo map"): a map showing physical or natural features of an area, generally including altitude curves

unbound: the current, single issues of a particular periodical; at the end of a specific time (usually a year) these issues will be bound together between hard covers

verso: the left-hand pages of a book (the opposite of **recto**)

volume number: 1. in periodicals, volume number refers to all issues of one periodical for a specific time (usually one year); 2. in books, volume number indicates the order of a particular book that comes in a series

Researching on the Internet

In addition to doing research at the library, you can use Internet search engines, metasearch engines, directories, and online databases to find information about your topic. On the home page of these, enter the name of your topic or a topic-related word or phrase, and then these tools will generate a list of connections (called "links") to related Internet sites. This process generally yields many links, enabling you to access a wealth of material.

How do you find information that you need? Try using the following search strategy:

- Think about your subject and then narrow the wording as much as possible, to either a word or short phrase.

- You may have several search options, so jot them down. This way, you can expand or change your search if you need to.
- Identify the key concepts of your topic and jot them down so that you can look them up later if you need extra material.
- Ask yourself whether there are other ways you can express your topic and key concepts. If there are, write down these words and phrases. Again, you can research these if you need more material.

Below is a list of popular search engines, metasearch engines, directories, and online databases:

AllTheWeb: www.alltheweb.com/
AltaVista: altavista.com/
Ask: ask.com
Dogpile: www.dogpile.com/
Excite: www.excite.com/
Google: www.google.com
HotBot: www.hotbot.com/
Infomine: infomine.ucr.edu/
Internet Public Library: www.ipl.org/
Ixquick: ixquick.com/eng/
Librarians' Index to the Internet: lii.org/
MetaCrawler: www.metacrawler.com/
Metaplus: metaplus.com/
Search.com: www.search.com/
Vivisimo: vivisimo.com/
Yahoo: www.yahoo.com/

A handy resource for additional information about these research tools is found at the Best Search Tools Chart at www.infopeople.org/search/chart.html.

A word of caution: Once you've located information about your topic, you need to evaluate it. Just as you can't trust everything in print form, neither can you trust everything that appears on the Internet. Generally, however, sites that are maintained by government agencies, legitimate nonprofit organizations, colleges and universities, and legitimate news organizations (newspapers, magazines, journals, and broadcast networks) are reliable.

To determine the legitimacy of information found on the Internet, look for the information's source on the pages you're consulting.

- Is the source identified? Can you find the name of a person or organization and a contact address?
- Is the source reliable? To decide this, see whether you can determine whether the author is qualified (has the credentials, education, or experience) to write the article, whether the author is affiliated with particular organizations, whether the facts presented compare favorably to printed sources, and whether sufficient evidence is presented to support material in the article.
- Does the site contain a bibliography or other kind of list for supporting data?
- When was the site posted or updated? Does this date make the information questionable?
- How balanced does the information seem?

Another way to find information on the Internet is through discussion lists, which allow you to write to people who have similar interests on specific topics. To do this, you send a message (called a "post") to the list; then your post is read by everyone who subscribes to that list. Anyone who chooses can respond to you. Some of these lists even contain archives (records of past discussions). Checking a list's archives may save you time because you may be able to find answers to questions more quickly by using the archives than by posting to the list and waiting for list members to reply. For a file of discussion lists, try these popular sites (many more are available):

TileNet: www.tile.net/lists/
L-Soft List Search: www.lsoft.com/lists/list_q.html
groups.google.com/

On the home pages of each list you will find instructions about how to join the list. You can learn about exploring archives at www.webliminal.com/search/search-web11.html#-Essential%20Information%20About%20Discussion%20Groups.

You may be told to give citations about where you have found information; this is especially true if you quote from a particular source. Each site on the Internet has a unique "address" called a URL (Universal Resource Locator). The URL is located at the top of the page and typically begins with http://.

Different instructors require particular styles of citations because certain disciplines use particular style guides. The most popular styles are APA (used widely in psychology and other social sciences), MLA (used mostly in the humanities), Turabian, and the *Chicago Manual of Style* (used mostly in history). The site at www.lib.berkeley.edu/TeachingLib/Guides/Internet/Style.html has links that provide information about the variations among these citation styles.

How to Conduct an Interview

Interviewing experts on the topic you're researching can supply you with invaluable material. To get the most out of such interviews, however, make sure that you've done your homework before the interview. Gain thorough background knowledge of the topic that you're researching and about your interviewee.

Then, make a list of interview questions and if possible, send the list to the interviewee. This has two advantages: First, it saves time during the interview because you'll know what you want to say and ask; second, more in-depth answers may occur to your interviewee than would have on the spur of the moment because he or she will have had time to think about the issues beforehand.

Go over your questions and make sure that you've composed them so that they can be answered with more than a simple "yes" or "no." Ask the who, what, when, where, how, why, and would-you-describe questions that elicit more detailed responses. Be alert to answers or new points that take the conversation in an unexpected direction; if this occurs, you need to be flexible, to temporarily turn away from your prepared questions, and to ask spontaneous questions.

If you're planning to tape your interview, make sure that you have permission to do so from the interviewee. When you set up the interview, ask whether it may be audio- or videotaped. If your interviewee is uncomfortable with being taped, you'll have to write down his or her replies.

If you have permission to tape the interview, begin each tape by noting the date and site of the interview; your name; the name of the interviewee; and the name of the interviewee's organization, business, or other affiliation.

If you're videotaping your interview, be sure to use a quiet, well-lit room. Focus the camera primarily on the interviewee's face and upper body. If you're making an audio recording, place the microphone as close to the interviewee as possible. Make sure that you test the tape recorder to see whether the interviewee's voice and your own are being recorded clearly. And have extra batteries on hand.

After your interview, check the correct spelling of any names, titles, or difficult words. Ask your interviewee to spell anything you aren't sure of, or ask him or her where you can look up the correct spelling.

If your interviewee says that something is off the record, respect his or her wishes. Turn off your tape or put down your pencil and don't include the information in your paper.

As a courtesy, send your interviewee a printed copy (a transcript) of your interview, along with a thank-you note.

When using material from the interview in your paper, use the proper citation format. Links to formats for citing interviews in MLA, APA, and *Chicago Manual of Style* formats can be found at http://www.library.arizona.edu/help/tutorials/citation/.

Credits

American Library Association. 2005. The 100 Most Frequently Challenged Books of 1990–2000. Permission for reprint granted by the Office for Intellectual Freedom.

Bear, Jennifer Marie. 2003. Why Students Cheat. *Oregon Daily Emerald* (Reprinted with permission).

Blum, Deborah. 1999. What's the Difference Between Boys and Girls. *Life Magazine*, July 1, 1999. Reprinted by permission of the author. Deborah Blum is the author of *Sex on the Brain*, 1997, published by Viking Press.

Bodett, Tom. 1987. Symptoms of Fatherhood. *Small Comforts*. Reprinted by permission of DA CAPO PRESS, a member of Perseus Books, L.L.C.

Bok, Sissela. 1978. White Lies. *Lying*. Used by permission of Pantheon Books, a division of Random House, Inc.

Brady, Judy. 1970. Why I Want a Wife. Copyright © 1970 by Judy Brady. Reprinted by permission of the author.

Business Ethics. 2004. Chart of *Business Ethics'* 100 Best Corporate Citizens for 2004. Reprinted with permission from Business Ethics, PO Box 8439, Minneapolis, MN 55408. www.business-ethics.com

Collins, Billy. 2002. The Names. Reprinted by permission of the poet. Billy Collins served as United States Poet Laureate 2001–2003. Originally printed in the *New York Times*, Sept. 6, 2002.

Colwin, Laurie. 1988. Repulsive Dinners: A Memoir. *Home Cooking: A Writer in the Kitchen*. Used by permission of Alfred A. Knopf, a division of Random House, Inc.

Corliss, Richard. 2001. Go Ahead, Make Her Day. TIME, Inc. Reprinted by permission.

Davis, Rich. 2006. Names Are Destiny? Tell That to 'Richie.' *Evansville Courier & Press*. Reprinted with permission.

Dorfman, Marjorie. 2001. Blue Jeans: An American Phenomenon. Reprinted by permission of author. Visit "Pop Goes the Culture" (www.cultureshockonline.com) for more fun articles by Marjorie Dorfman.

———. 2005. Food Icons: Immortal in the Eyes of the Television Beholder. Reprinted by permission of author. Visit "Eat, Drink, + Really Be Merry" (www.ingestandimbibe.com) for more fun articles by Marjorie Dorfman.

Ford, Paul. 2005. Followup/Distraction by Paul Ford. Reprinted by permission of the author. www.ftrain.com

Gary, William. 2006. Reactionary. Reprinted by permission of the author.

Gabler, Neal. 1995. How Urban Myths Reveal Society's Fears. Reprinted by permission of the author. Neal Gabler is an essayist and author whose books include *Life, The Movie: How Entertainment Conquered Reality*; and *Walt Disney: The Triumph of the American Imagination*.

The George S. May International Company. 2004. Ethics in Business. Reprinted by permission.

Goodman, Ellen. 1979. The Company Man. The Washington Post Company. Reprinted with the permission of Simon & Schuster Adult Publishing Group, from *Close to Home* by Ellen Goodman. All rights reserved.

Hayden, Thomas. 2002. Gotcha! *U.S. News & World Report*, L.P. Reprinted with permission.

Hornstein, Alison. 2001. The Question We Should Be Asking. *Newsweek*, Dec. 17, 2001. All rights reserved. Reprinted by permission.

Kahn, Michael A. 2000. Move to the Front of the Bus, Ms. Parks. Reprinted by permission of author.

Kariva, Scott. 2005. What I Did Last Summer. IEEE (Institute of Electrical and Electronics Engineers). Reprinted by permission.

Krauthammer, Charles. 1998. Of Headless Mice and Men. TIME, Inc. Reprinted by permission.

Lichtman, Wendy. 2000. Knock on Wood. Reprinted by permission of the author.

www.lowermanhattan.info. 2006. Redesign of Freedom Tower.

Manley, Will. 2005. In Defense of Book Burning. Permission for reprint granted by the Office for Intellectual Freedom, American Library Association.

Marr, John. 1999. Confessions of an eBay Addict by John Marr. Copyright Scott Owen. Reprinted by permission.

Martin, Ray. 2003. Beware of Student Credit Cards. Reprinted by permission of author.

Merriam, Eve. 1964, 1992. How to Eat a Poem. *It Doesn't Always Have to Rhyme*. Eve Merriam. Used by permission of Marian Reiner.

Merritt, Jennifer. 2006. Three Credits and a Baby. From "College Life Survival: Surviving College as a Single Parent." Reprinted by permission of the author.

Messmer, Harold M. "Max" Jr. 2002. Resumania. Reprinted with permission by Scripps Howard News Service.

Nellie Mae. 2006. Undergraduate Students and Credit Cards. Reprinted with permission.

O'Keefe, Mark. 2004. Foul Language Enters Pop Culture Lexicon. Newhouse News Service. Used by permission.

Online NewsHour Extra. 2006. History of Money. MacNeil-Lehrer Productions. Reprinted with permission.

Parachin, Victor. 1997. Simple Solutions: Suggestions for Simplifying Your Life. Reprinted by permission of the author.

Quindlen, Anna. 2002. One Day, Now Broken in Two. First appeared in *Newsweek*, Sept. 9, 2002. Reprinted by permission of International Creative Management, Inc.

Rosandich, Dan. Let's Talk About Who You Know. Reprinted with permission: www.Cartoon-Stock.com.

Schlosser, Eric. 2001. Throughput. *Fast Food Nation*. Reprinted by permission of Houghton Mifflin Company. All rights reserved.

Singletary, Michelle. 2005. On Spring Break, with Their Heads in the Sand. The Washington Post Writers Group. Reprinted with Permission.

Teti, John. 1999. Regis Makes Contestants Rich on ABC 'Millionaire.' Reprinted by permission of The Dartmouth, Inc.

Trout, J. 1999. Complex Language. It Can Cloud People's Minds. *The Power of Simplicity: A Management Guide to Cutting Through the Nonsense and Doing Things Right*. Reprinted with permission of The McGraw-Hill Companies.

United States Federal Trade Commission. 2005. Identity Theft.

Photo Credits

Index